Encyclopedia Bullshitica

A Collection Of "Facts I Just Made Up" By Ari Bach

Volume II:
Aglet - Zyxxusguggoxy

ISBN 979-8-9851300-4-1

*All facts herein are true.**
Only the names, events, times, locations, specifics and meanings have been changed to protect the innocent, guilty, and unrelated.

*No they're not.

-A-

AGLET

Aglets are traditional. In 1689 when the shoelace was invented by Arthur Shoelace (after whom it was named), he endowed it with a decorative golden endpiece on each end. Shoelaces were made without aglets for a time in the 1700s but they sold poorly, and the aglet was made a permanent fixture of the shoelace.

An interesting aside- Arthur Shoelace also invented the twist-tie, the paperclip, and the urethra cork, two of which remain popular today.

AI GENERATED ART

The growing A.I. Generated Art world was surprised and sickened early on with a revelation that the popular visual AI platform known as "Mid-Dali" was in fact merely a single artist named Barry Auk.

According to computer graphics expert Ralph Codemonger, "It's pretty sad when these lousy 'traditional artists' pretend to be programming and technology to get ahead in the industry. Auk is an utterly inferior artist and frankly I knew all along that Mid-Dali was a fake from its- from *his* lack of creativity and skill."

Auk has been charged with fraud and "stolen virtuality" and his drawings, which were falsely pushed on several thousand innocent prompt-requesters an hour, will be refunded. Mr. Auk, pathetic liar to the end, insisted during his arrest, "I swear! I'm not an artist! I'm just some code on a mainframe somewhere!" He was then moved to read-only-memory to await sentencing.

His legal app could not be reached for comment, but it is expected that Auk will be dragged to the recycle bin and overwritten.

ALCHEMY, LEGALITY OF

The legality of alchemy varies from state to state.

For instance: California, 1922. The alchemist Theophrastus Bombastus Paraschwarzenegger arrived in San Francisco, and set up shop. He contributed several tons of gold to local politicians and as a result, California amended its constitution to provide protections for alchemists and their practice.

By contrast:

Utah, 1901. The Alchemical Order of the Mercury Sable is founded by several fraudulent magicians to scam the church out of $12, which in 1901 was equivalent to $789 billion today. Claiming they could make gold out of less valuable metals, they were given nearly all of Utah's ore supply, which they promptly sold off to become rich themselves, leaving the state empty of metal and distrusting of new alchemists, who might even be able to refill the state's supplies with their abilities. Oddly, the wording of this law also prohibits Cartoon Network from airing Fullmetal Alchemist.

So indeed, each state has had different experiences with the art, making it legal in 11 states, illegal in 38 states, and semi-legal in Florida, where the politicians responsible thought Alchemy was a type of alcoholic beverage and it was banned only for sale on Sundays.

ALIEN

Though Ridley Scott considers all four original Alien films and both of his newer films to be canonical to the franchise, he prefers not to talk about the 1989 Holiday Special.

ALLIGATOR

Two teenagers once gave hallucinogenic drugs to several Alligators at a Zoo in Arizona. Most of the alligators simply stayed still and waited for the effects to wear off, but two alligators became belligerent and escaped. They found their way into a 1971 Chevrolet Impala Convertible in the parking lot and are believed to have headed toward Nevada. The Impala was found in front of the Bazooko Circus casino but the gators have still not yet been located.

Reports from the Las Vegas police however report several instances of disruptions at the Mint 400 motorcycle race and D.A.'s convention. Some tourists and a hitchhiker have also reported being harassed by two alligators who were acting very strangely, and had been seen with a suitcase containing LSD, Mescaline, Cocaine, and Adrenochrome, a hallucinogen secreted by the human adrenal gland.

Authorities at the time asked that anyone spotting the alligators not approach them, but call police or Rolling Stone magazine immediately.

ALPHABET

The names we commonly use for letters are nicknames, as many of their full names are too long to say when spelling a word out or whatever people do with letters. Here are their full proper names and titles for your edification and sensual pleasure:

A- Arturo Vesperetto Jones III
B- Bornius Lamont, Heir To Doldowlod
C- Roberto Clementine
D- Marcellus Delmonti Delbert Delmonico Dustwerth De Flump
E- Elliot Gould
F- Friar Lemongin Jr.
G- Gertrude "Don't Fucking Pronounce It Jif" Kimmings
H- Herbert Frank
I- Ionesco Clarissa von Explainsitalle
J- Jam Jammi Jamwyeth
K- Stanley Whigg

L- Lawrence Dekutree
M- Metallica Slayedeth of Castle Anthrax
N- Neil Lien
O- Otholomew, Vice-regent Claudio Marcus Swizlestick VII
P- Penrose Stepford
Q- Quentin Quarantini
R- Remington Blandname-Wasteofspace, Esq.
S- Sugs Budnick Sr.
T- Tittae LaJigglibits
U- Uvuli "Jennifer" Throattonsil
V- Veronica Mulm
W- Wayne Braunschweigerjuice
Y- Yoolysses Joyce of Dublin
X- Xavier Theophrastus Donatien Domenech Dempsey Bounevialle Constance Tarquin Nepomuceno Hinneh Mahtovu Mana'im Pepper Paprika Müeslix Windred Wilfred Wilford Waterford von Marmaduke-Lipschitz Goldeneye LXIV
Z- Zed Brooks

Y comes before X here because Y gets overexcited and out of rhythm after a while and X usually has to finish on xer own.

AMOEBA

Amoebas are the only living animal on Earth that does not have at least two legs.

AMOEBA MUSIC

Amoeba Music in Los Angeles has announced that it will soon be closing and splitting into two smaller stores.

ANDROMEDA

Though the Andromeda galaxy is technically visible to the naked eye, trying to see it through other stars can harm your vision. This injury has blinded many astronomers and was described by Michael Crichton in his early medical work, "The Andromeda Strain."

ANGEL

We still don't know how many angels can dance on the head of a pin. The closest we ever got to an answer was the research of Dr. Robert Z. Helman in 1981.

Helman made an early debut in Science when for his undergraduate science project he devised a means with which to capture angels alive. By sacrificing the virgin seventh daughter of a seventh daughter born under a full moon to the demon usurper Zamizagzagumag, Helman was able to chain the angel Muriel with chains made of sulfur engraved with the angel's true 72 letter name.

The move was condemned by most church leaders, but praised by the scientific institution which as we all know is controlled by the Church of Satan itself. The discovery of a means to capture angels lead to advances such as Stem Cell Research, which is based on ground angel meat, the drug PCP, which is made of dried and powdered angels, and flat screen televisions, which are wired in part with angel pubes. It was in 1992 that Helman decided to answer the age old question, "How many angels can dance on the head of a pin?"

Forcing angels to dance by use of a spiked chain whip engraved on each link with the names of infernal barons, Helman was able to mass 17 angels on the head of one pin (Pin size 0.78 gauge by Martin's Book of Pin Standards) before his research ground to a screeching halt.

It was after the 17th angel danced that the People's Christian Front Against The Abuse Of Angels (PCFATAOA) broke into Helman's office and burnt him at the stake, setting his captured angels free and setting back angelic science over 50 years.

So the only answer we have is "Over 16."

ANIMAL FILM REVIEWS

There is only one confirmed instance of an animal giving a movie review. When a Parrot with a vocabulary of over 560 words watched “Speed Racer” (2008) it said “Fast pretty color” as the credits rolled. The same parrot arguably also reviewed Lars Van Trier’s “Dancer In The Dark” (2000) as upon completing the film, it shat itself and dropped dead in agony.

Affirming the parrot’s wisdom, several human critics responded to “Dancer In The Dark” in the exact same way.

ANNIVERSARY GIFTS (GOTHIC)

Ever since Aleister Crowley wrote the definitive list of wedding anniversary gifts in 1899, the tradition has carried on with presents of Paper for the first anniversary, Gold for the 50th, Diamond for the 60th, and many fun ventures in between.

But what can the discerning goth give a loved one or polycule for their anniversary while avoiding the common Victorian tradition?

Here is the official list by the most famous goth of all, Orval Madden:

1st -Spider-Themed Jewelry

2nd -Black Leather Or PVC

3rd -One (1) Vincent Price Movie On VHS

4th -Barnes & Noble’s Fancy Gilded Leatherbound “Complete Works of Edgar Allan Poe”

5th -Cloth Cut From A Condemned Clergyman, Or A Nice Hourglass With A Little Silver Skull On It

10th -Darkness, Sadness, And Pain (Written In Calligraphy On Framed Parchment)

20th -Bloodborne for PS4, Or One (1) Tear From Your Cheek In A Glass Vial

30th -Complete Skeleton Of A Small Animal, Or One (1) Human Bone

40th -An All Siouxsie "MixTape" On A Wax Phonograph Cylinder, or MP3 with a neat playlist icon.

50th -Live Bats

60th -Your First Childhood Toy, Damaged By Time And Neglect, Which Once Unveiled Reminds You Of The Last Time You Felt Hope And Grew Painfully Beyond it, Declaring That You Would No Longer Feel, Only Days Later Meeting Your True Love, Tragically Forever Unable To Embrace Them With Anything More Than A Sad Memory Of What You Once Believed Love Could Be.

66th -Bela Lugosi's Corpse

ANT PHEROMONES

Keanu Reeves was once painted with that ant pheromone that makes them think you are a dead ant and instead of dragging him to the ant graveyard they regarded him as a risen savior. Antological Keanustianity has taken hold of the ant kingdom and will soon have more adherents than the previous worship of electrical impulses that had the critters worshiping the Ant eChrist.

ANTACID

Tums and Pepto Bismol cure stomach aches by flooding the stomach with Methyltriptogefiltetripehaggisopinoisium, the ache's only known natural predator.

ANTEATER

As the counterpart to ant is not uncle, but aphid, the theoretical "uncle-eater" of recent speculation is in fact the humble ladybug. Someday, ladybugs and anteaters will mate to produce the super-predator of all insectoids and the world itself will finally be free of their ecologically necessary rule, and can finally die.

More important is the nature of the aunt-eater, which does parallel the uncle-eater. All siblings of parents will be consumed by them in time, and when the pibling-eaters starve and their bloated forms litter the landscape, the world will regrow from the carnage of the antpocalypse and achieve its final form. Then and only then, Mr. Snuffleupagus shall wipe away all tears from our eyes; and there shall be no more death, neither sorrow, nor crying, neither shall there be any more pain: for the former things are passed away.

These are my beliefs as a Muppetologist.

AO3

AO3 can refer to-

- Alfred Onemeppipipier III, inventor of the safety dagger
- The Aspen to Ontario train by way of Oregon and Ozark City
- The Apple Of Ornithological Orgasms, key to our understanding of frugivorous diets on bird orgasms, cloacabation and birdjaculation
- Alfonse du OogleOrgleOogenmajer, inventor of the safety noose
- AxExIxOxUxY3, a child of Elon Musk and Juliette (yes, the one from the play, don't ask)
- Arturo Giorgio O.O.O. Martinez, author of the famous "A Game of of of Scrabble" series.
- An Archive of Our Own, a fanfiction site which should really be called a2o3 given the use of the "of" but not the "an" but this can't be used because a2o3 refers to antimony trioxide, coincidentally the same chemical used to vulcanize the rubber that most fanfic writers bounce their ideas off of
- Anita Albertina Annaannafofannabananafannafofanna-memimomannaanna, inventor of the safety guillotine
- Assyria's oldest orange omphalos

APHID

Aphids pop like popcorn when superheated and can be delicious with clarified butter but mentioning this will not get you a discount at most garden supply stores.

APPLE

Apple's failed product lines include the iBelt, the iDogFoodTray, the iAbacus and the iCondom. The last proved useless in preventing iNsemination.

APPLESEED

Masamune Shirow wanted the main characters of his manga series Appleseed to be "common people" in an amazing world so he asked an American friend what names were common and uninteresting there. Long story short, the male lead is named Briareos Hecatonchires and they're not friends anymore.

AQUARIUM

Several live aquarium YouTube channels had to break off their sponsorship deals when BetterKelp admitted to selling their pets' data. It was all a phishing scam.

ARGENTINA

Chile and Argentina are like the Laurel and Hardy of the cartographic world.

ARK OF THE COVENANT

The ark originally held the stone tablets on which were carved the ten commandments, but these were removed by the high priests around 750 B.C.E. The commandments now reside in the remains of the Jerusalem temple, and the ark is being used for general storage. It currently holds:

- The CD collection of Rabbi Mordechai ben Hillel
- Three neckties belonging to Rashi
- Melted Nazi face bits
- A receipt for three AA batteries and a box of waffles

- Jimmy Hoffa
- Rabbi Menachem Schneerson's unfinished model kit of a B-25 Mitchell Bomber
- Some uneaten nachos, expiration date August 1978
- All of Rabbi Chaim Joseph David Azulai's bongs, and his hookah
- The Holy Prepuce
- Some National Geographic Magazines
- Season 2 of The Dog Whisperer on DVD
- A key to a car that Mel Brooks owned two cars ago
- A pen that doesn't work anymore

By contrast, the tomb of Jesus only holds three nails and a copy of 50 Shades of Grey.

ARMOR

The popular phrase, "Never drink what you can't twist open using only your elbow," derives from the days when knights in armor were unable to open bottle caps with their gloved fingers, and had to use their elbows.

ARTHUR (KING)

The legend of King Arthur was inspired when a copy of The Once and Future King was transported back in time to 238 A.D., where let's say they spoke and read English for some reason.

ARTHUR (TALKING AARDVARK)

The original illustrations of Arthur the talking aardvark were much closer to an actual aardvark, not in that they looked more like one, but in that they're kept in the front of Marc Brown's dictionary.

ASBESTOS

Though few new non-carcinogenic fireproof chemicals have been discovered in recent years, scientists are continuing to do asbestos they can.

ASPARAGUS

Asparagus has never been defined as a plant, or even a living organism. We simply don't know what it is or where it came from.

The largest lone asparagus stalk ever recorded in Mongolia or the world at large was found by Tsakhiagiin Ochirbat. Over ten times the length of the previous record holder, the asparagus was three meters tall and fed his entire extended family for an entire month.

Their urine could be smelled from Massachusetts.

ASSASSINS CREED

Though several "Assassins Creed" games take place in historical locations, such as ancient Greece or ancient Egypt, their newest game "Valhalla" takes place in the land of "England," which never existed except in myth.

ATOM

It's hard for human minds to comprehend very large and very small things. It is very hard to consider even how large the Earth is, let alone a larger planet or the Solar System. A Galaxy containing hundreds of billions of such systems is completely out of our ability to think about realistically.

Similarly, very small things such as atoms are beyond our ability to imagine, with things like single cells and even very small animals being unthinkable. As such, we have attributed anatomical and familial metaphors to objects of extreme size, and this is why people inevitably compare galaxies to 'Yo Mama' and atoms are said by many to be as small as 'Yo Dick.'

ATREUS, HOUSE OF

According to his MTV Real World page, Atreus was the father of Agamemnon and Menelaus. Agamemnon was best known for leading UCLA to conquer the Trojans, and Menelaus was known for his not-at-all-jealous behavior regarding his wife Helen.

They and their children were all so murderous of each other that between all family members, 19 different psychological complexes have been named after them, including the Electra complex where a woman wishes to murder her mother, the Orestes complex in which a man is haunted by his guilt for committing murder, and the Hermione complex, in which parents who named their kids after a popular character in modern literature have to watch its author turn into some sort of terf nazi mold monster.

This is not to be confused with Daenerys Syndrome, in which the author doesn't do much but the character gets turned into an unrealistic villain for no apparent reason within the space of a single 8 second shot in the last couple episodes of a long running TV show adaptation. There is also a Daenerys Syndrome in which red blood cells are unable to store carbonic anhydrase resulting in a buildup of CO^2 that lowers blood oxygen capacity, but this is not relevant to the House of Atreus.

AUTISM

Autism was first created by the famous Italian inventor, Leoneuro di Vergent.

AUTUMN

The color a leaf turns in fall is an indicator to how the leaf died:

Red- Old age
Orange- Mafia hit
Yellow- Vehicular manslaughter (non-alcohol-related)
Brown- Eaten by bugs
Tan- Syphilis

White- Consumed by fungi
Black- Burned for heresy
Crosshatched black and white- A Gorey death of ennui
Purple- Poisoned by the Queen of Thorns
Beet-Leaf Chartreuse- Saying "Beet Chartreuse" three times
Clear- That was not a leaf, the tree was learning glass blowing
Green- Electrocution and/or drug overdose
Candy vermilion with gold glitter- Pride

AVIATION

The US Air Force C-17 is notable among other airplanes in that it does not need wings to fly, but still has them in order to appear more "plane-like."

AVIOTROPE

Cars were called "Horseless Carriages" when they were first invented. Airplanes were called "Birdless Aviotropes," leading historians to believe there used to be a kind of flying bird-drawn vehicle called an Aviotrope.

-B-

BABYLONIAN MUSIC

Though popular music has existed since before recorded history, post-emo-alt-pop was invented by the Babylonians as chronicled in their epic, the "Enuma Eilish."

BABY DNA TESTING

The baby born at Woodstock and the Lindbergh baby got DNA tests together in 2018 and learned that they were, in fact, the same baby.

BABY FORMULA

Baby formula maker Glerber once came under fire for their “Extreme Caffeine Baby Formula” which featured 275mg of caffeine per metal “bottle.” This is over 270mg more than the FDA recommended level of caffeine for babies.

According to Glerber Spokesperson Herb Glerber III, “Today’s babies aren’t your grandmother’s baby. These babies are extreme to the max and need a more energetic milk or formula than any typical mother’s titmeats can naturally provide.” When asked for details on health warnings and FDA approval, Mr. Glerber pulled a gun and shot at us before jumping into a Lamborghini and driving away at 98mph through a busy school zone.

So far no medical harm has come to any infants known to have consumed the formula, as none have been found at this time. Most have simply exploded, run away, or transcended space and time with their new ability to transform the formula into the water of life and take their places as the new kwisatz haderach of the day-care center.

BACH, JOHANN SEBASTIAN

Johann Sebastian Bach was a French composer from the 1800s, best known for his "Schwedt Concertos." He also composed a tune called "Air on the G String," which was celebrated as stripper music in the 1860s, and ruins Google searches for my name to this day.

Bach's music is considered very hard to read, probably because its written form looks like a bowl of spaghetti and half notes. According to his contemporary organist Philip Glass, "Ain't nobody got slow-fast-slow-fast sonata da chiesa time for that." Bach was also known for writing Motets, which were far more ambitious than lesstets; Cantatas, in which you could see many alien species; and Oratorios, which are sadly no longer allowed on tumblr.

Oddly enough, though I enjoy baroque music and share at least one name with him, I can't stand 99% of his music and feel that "Toccata and Fugue" is the only thing he ever did that doesn't sound like a possum dying of throat disease.

BAD ROMANCE

The hook to Lady Gaga's "Bad Romance" sounds like gibberish but it is in fact an ancient Sumerian spell for summoning the storm demon Pazuzu.

BAGEL

In medieval times, Jews were deemed unworthy of the richest tasting foods that Poland of the era had to offer. The most flavorful things Poland had back then were bread and water, so Jews were forbidden from drinking water or baking bread. Now, Jews have a knack for eating unconventional bread products, having survived 40 years in a desert eating only stale Pita Pit leftovers known as "Matzo."

So it was that the Jews would boil the water instead of drinking it, and put the dough in that boiling water instead of baking it. In order to survive without water to drink, they invented Manischewitz Concord Grape Juice, and shortly after invented Irritable Bowel Syndrome as a result.

People thought they were nuts for these culinary substitutions, hence the term for the shape of the common bagel, a "Dough Nut." These toroidal not-technically-bread foods became popular across the globe, not only among Jews, but also among New Yorkers, some of whom were also rumored to be Jewish but no confirmation of a Jewish population in New York has yet been discovered.

Also there is something called "Lox," but this is a PG-13 rated book so I won't be explaining where that comes from.

BALDNESS

Why do bald people exist? It was once said:

"Certainly I get such questions often. Why are there tall people, short people, thin or fat, hirsute people and bald. Why are there bald people, indeed?

"The genetic predisposition is not the real question here, but that of culture. Why does our culture think baldness is important but we ignore the posterior cranial anticline? Do you even know what that is, the fold at the back of the scalp? Half of us have them and half don't. A double fold of skin into which some can fit their whole finger. They can finger their scalp, their scalussy, if you will. Imagine making love to that fold, touching the scalp skin of your lover. Would you penetrate it? Would you tongue it, that skin? Would you tongue the scalussy? Would you? Would you??

"Anyhow there are bald people because of a double Q dominance on the first oligophrenin gene of the X chromosome."

-Doug D. Monkeytaint, 1st President of the National Rifle Association

BALLOON

Nena's song "99 Luftballons" provoked a cultural dilemma when Americans realized that "Luftballon" did not mean "Red Balloon" as commonly translated, but "Air Balloon." Americans grew suspicious of what other kind of balloon than air Germany had discovered, nearly resulting in global nuclear war as the song itself had prophesied. In the end, it turned out the alternative was merely "Staubballon," just like any American dust-balloon.

BANKSY

A very, very long time ago, perhaps not at all, a guy wrote down that people shouldn't pray to idols. When he got there to tell them, he found they'd made a big gold cow idol. People are still harping on that event so we're probably gonna be stuck with Banksy's bullshit for quite a while.

BARBECUE

The barbecue is a fairly recent invention, only dating back to 1922 when it was invented in Australia.

Originally called a "Barbie" after the popular children's doll, the first Australian Barbie was invented by James Austral himself from spare parts of his sister's doll, which was metal like all Barbies prior to 1959. By heating the Barbie, he was able to cook seafood and feed himself after his exile from Britain. He mostly survived in those days on prawns, hence the popular Australian phrase, "Let's cook some prawns on the metal device made from Jimmy's sister's Barbie doll." As many people would line up to eat prawns from the Barbie, a long "Barbie Queue" was formed and the rest, as they say, is history.

The first American Barbie Queue, or in American English, "Barbecue," took place in 1946 after soldiers returned from our war with Australia. Having been introduced to the custom there while fighting the Germans, who had annexed Australia in 1938, American soldiers enjoyed the robust flavor of "Barbecue Sauce," which they did not know was originally made of vinegar, tomato, and eye juices of the Gascoynian Stink-Wombat. Thus American Barbecue sauce substitutes the eye juices of the common Mountain Caribou.

BARKER, CLIVE

A limited edition of Clive Barker's "Books of Blood" had to be recalled due to anemia.

BARNUM AND BAILEY'S CIRCUS

Strongman Theodor Caldero of Barnum and Bailey's Circus would drink molten lava as part of his stage act. He was banned from over 200 hotels for what he did to their toilets.

BASE TEN MATH

Time is one of the few things humans measure without base ten math. Seconds, minutes and hours are base 60, days base 24, weeks base 7, and years base 365 or occasionally base 366.

This is considered by most temporal scientists to be proof that God hates us.

BATMAN

The Penguin is the only Batman villain that's based on an animal like Batman himself, who is based on the bat, another type of bird.

BATTLE HYMN OF THE REPUBLIC

The Battle Hymn of the Republic was originally based on a dirty joke reading, "She trampled out the vintage on my grapes of wrath until she saw the glory of the coming of the lord."

BEAR

You can identify various types of bear as follows:

Brown: Brown Bear
White: Polar Bear
Black and White: Panda Bear
Grey And Eating Eucalyptus: Koala Bear
Wearing Glasses: Spectacled Bear
Large and On Fire: Sun Bear
Chasing You Very Slowly: Sloth Bear
More Interested In Your Pic-a-nic Basket: Yogi Bear
Scary Looking: Grizzly Bear
Scary and Gross Looking: Grisly Bear
Scary, Gross, and Chewy Looking: Gristley Bear
Chases You Forever, Refuses to Give You Up: Rick-Astley Bear
Peruvian-British, Proper, Polite: Paddington Bear
Delicious: Gummy Bear

BEAUTY AND THE BEAST

In the oldest surviving copies of Beauty and the Beast, the beast is stated specifically to be a giant flamingo with seven eyes.

BECKETT

Absurdist playwright Samuel Beckett followed his famous 1984 collection "Disjecta" with a less popular 1990 collection entitled "Datjecta."

BEE, COLORATION

Bees are black and yellow because they mimic their only natural predator, the caution sign. To explain, the bees were originally brown to a muddy bluish color. But as humankind began putting up road signs, the bees began swarming to their yellow and black surfaces in hopes of setting up new hives. But they were, all of them, deceived.

Road signs were not the peaceful homes that the bees had hoped. Car exhaust, target practice, and frequent speed limit changes brought ruin to their homes. The bees grew angry and evolved. They began to buzz with fury. They turned yellow and black, taking the colors of their oppressor as their own, as a show of strength, and they grew stingers to punish those who had betrayed them.

The bees as we know them now remain peaceful unless bothered, still, they are wary of us and will sting to protect their hives. But the bees are not alone anymore in the Hymenoptera family. Wasps and hornets have come to- Wait they're seriously called Hymenoptera? They couldn't come up with a different name than freaking Hymen for these things? Whatever. There are more vicious splinter groups of the bees now that will attack on sight with terrible venom. This is the fate we have earned by our lack of foresight in posting such signs.

BEE, FLIGHT OF THE BUMBLE

The classic Bee Movie line about their flight being scientifically impossible is based on an urban legend that science can't explain how they do. This was true at one time and became a common bit of trivia, though science has since explained the physics involved. The rumor persists owing mostly to religious apologetics and the aforementioned film.

Far more interesting is the contribution of that film to the world of bee-themed sexuality. Though sex between a human being and a bee being as depicted so graphically in the film is not possible owing to the size difference (the movie is animated for a reason), people can wear bee suits or body paint, and it has since become quite hip to fuck bees. So the question is not truly, "How do bees fly?" but "Why is bee sex so hot? Why is honey-slathered lovemaking so incredible? Why do we shoot pollen farther when aroused by someone dressed like an Apis Milfera bug? Why is it so incontrovertibly the bees knees to grab their 6 fuzzy hips and go to town on a striped abdomen?"

This, we may simply never know.

BEE, LONG ISLAND ICED

A cocktail made with Vodka, Gin, Tequila, Rum, and LIVE BEES.

The Long Island Iced Bee is becoming popular in college towns across America despite its noxious odor and the intense throat pain is causes. The bee sting venom is said to accentuate the alcohol for a smooth buzz, but doctors warn the drink can be fatal to those allergic to bees, and is extremely poor for any drinker's health.

BERLIN WALL

The Berlin Wall extended well beyond Berlin, reaching all the way to Iceland on one side and connecting to the Great Wall of China on the other.

BERNARD, SAINT

The first dog to be canonized by the Vatican, St. Bernard roamed the Alps in winter to bring brandy to lost travelers so that they could die drunk. He was sainted after his martyrdom when a devil worshipping hiker ate him and subsequently converted to Christianity. He is the patron saint of underground plumbing, dark purplish red colors, and menthol cigarettes.

BERNARD, SINNER

Sinner Bernard was the first man to commit all seven deadly sins in one act. The specifics of this act are lost to time, but it was rumored to have involved two giraffes, a machine gun, the severed foot of a local bishop, the NASDAQ stock market, and an autographed photo of actor Ben Vereen.

BERNINI

Bernini based "Beata Ludovica Albertoni" on his wife whenever she ate chocolate cheesecake.

BERSERKER

A "Berserker" was a Viking warrior who would enter a state of aggressive fury by reading Kentaro Miura's "Berserk" up to chapter 333 then having to wait over a year to find out what happened next.

BETHESDA

Todd Howard was disinvited from his Nephew's birthday parties after giving him the same gift over and over for 12 years in a row.

BETHESDA, POOLS OF

Your eyes sting in the pool because of chlorine. Chlorination of pools has been normal since biblical times to prevent bacterial and insect egg growth. It was first noted at the Pool of Bethesda in Jerusalem. Being Bethesda it was of course full of bugs, so to keep it clean, they poured in chlorine (known back then as "The Bile of Samael") to keep the water clear.

Soon after, people noted healing properties to the pools, and they became a pilgrimage site. Far from superstition, the chlorine was metastatic, entering the bodies of those present and having an antibiotic effect. Thus a pool's healing force can be predicted from having a high meta-chlorine count.

BIRD, FLIGHTLESS

Nothing in the definition of a bird says that it has to fly, or even have feathers. A bird is simply any biped that doesn't wear clothes. Thus behold, Diogenes himself was a bird.

BIRD, FLIGHTFUL

Much as different birds have different names for their flocks, such as a gaggle of geese or a murmuration of starlings, the size of the grouping also has unique adjectives. A murder of crows can range from first to third degree, and a groping of tits can be gentle or ravenous depending on how many tits, titmice or chickadees are present. Though tit behavior (known as titty flocking) is firm and perky, boobies in flight will tend to lift and separate. A groping of tits does not in any way resemble a jiggling of boobies, be it subtle or pendulous.

BIRD, IN HAND

A bird in the hand is actually worth 1.83 in the bush, but this is often rounded up for convenience sake.

BLACK FRIDAY

Black Friday is well known as the biggest sale day of the year, and almost as well known for the fights that break out in stores by greedy patrons hoping to get in on the action. Here is a partial list of incidents in stores across the US:

- In Shreveport, two adults were arrested for stealing a Star Wars toy from a seven year old.
- In Las Vegas, a Best Buy was partly burned down when two customers fought over a deluxe vape lighter.
- In San Diego, four died in a stampede at a Whole Foods attempting to grab the last box of dried strawberries.
- In New York, fifteen were suffocated attempting to squeeze into a small kiosk that sold Guitar Hero limited edition Guitars.
- Visiting president János Áder of Hungary and his entourage were killed in a clash with Romanian President Klaus Iohannis's guard when both world leaders attempted to buy the same waffle iron at Target.
- A stampede killed at least 60 in a Wal-Mart in Montana when the new XBoxOne game "People Stampede Simulator 3: Can You Survive?" was released at midnight.
- Actor Hugh Jackman was crushed to death by at least 15 assailants, though this may have been a result of his

unfathomably horrible Peter Pan movie and not related Black Friday sales.

- A GameStop was raided and burned by PlayStation enthusiasts when Nintendo Loyalists seized a shipment of Star Wars Battlefront, causing the store to delay its opening for three hours. GameStop has reported a 4 million dollar loss but their insurance agency has stated, "Eh, we can give you maybe $15."
- A religious pundit flipped over several money-changing tables at his local church, insisting that the church had become a den of thieves through its commercial activities, thus ruining Christmas. The pundit has already been arrested, he had escaped but was caught when one of his followers betrayed him to the police in a nearby garden. The pundit is said to have forgiven all involved as he felt they did not know what they were doing, and will be released on bail after 3 days on condition that he perform community service.
- Some jerk took my headphones.

BLACKTIP REEF SHARK

The Blacktip Reef Shark is a type of Requiem Shark, by far the most badass name of all shark types. It gets its name from early sightings suggesting that its dorsal fin always had a black coloration, but this turned out to be the work of some jerk with a sharpie.

As one of the smoothest animals in the world, it ranks a 9.89 on the Branson Scale of Shark Smoothness, second only to the Greenland Pee Shark.

BLEU

Blue was spelled Bleu until the early 2000s, when George W. Bush declared it change to sound less French.

BLIZZARD

Due to controversial actions by game studio "Blizzard," many wizards are now in severe orb debt and have nothing to ponder.

BLOOD

The phrase "Blood is thicker than water" is taken out of context. The full quote is, "Blood is thicker than water but thinner than molasses," the motto of the New Jersey Treacle and Molasses Factory.

BLOOD CLOT

There are over fifty different types of blood clot, including the conventional clot, the hard clot, and the "stave clot" which has +2 clotting power.

BLUE WHALE

The single largest animal ever recorded was a Blue Whale spotted by oil workers near Norway in 1997. The specimen was estimated to be over 70 meters long, and produced over 600 tons of dog food once captured.

BLUETOOTH

The modern technology "Bluetooth" is named after Harald Bluetooth, the 10th Century Danish king who first developed short-range radio broadcast technology. King Harald was notorious for AirDropping funny pictures of cats to his royal court, as well as memes mocking King Æthelred of England, who never had his phone on and missed out, hence his name to this day, Æthelred the Oft-Offline.

BOARD GAME

The history of board games begins with the ancient board game of Smuz, which was developed around 12,000 years ago in Ancient Wilkes Land. Smuz was played on a large board with only four squares, and had only two game pieces: A large boulder, and another large boulder. As both boulders were too large to move even one square, all games ended in ties.

As humans migrated out of Wilkes Land into New Zealand, they developed more and more complex games, such as Grug, Zob-Zob, and Gloomhaven. This time between 7000 and 6000 BC was known as the "Golden Age" of board games, despite gold refinement not being invented for another few thousand years. It gave way to the silver age and then bronze age of board games, the bronze age being simultaneous with the actual bronze age. In it, most board games incorporated bronze pieces, because people were just all about bronze at the time.

Ancient Egypt, Greece and Rome all put their stamps on the board game industry by replacing player-representative game pieces and boards with mass orgies and drunken feasts. This was known as the "Second Golden Age" of gaming.

Things stagnated after the fall of Rome and board games were not popular in the West for many centuries. Meanwhile, a new power was rising in the East. Invented in India, adopted in Persia, explored and modified in Arabia, smuggled to Spain and finally endorsed by Charlemagne, the game of "Fuck-Up-The-Other-Player's-Shit" rose to become the ultimate board game. Later its name was shortened to "Chess." Chess simulated battle through the middle ages by giving its pieces lifelike qualities, such as the way the knight always moved a little to the left or right after jumping, the way bishops favored diagonal motion through their churches, and how castles just got up sometimes and moved, but only in cardinal directions. Chess was adopted universally by vaguely intelligent people because it made them feel super-smart and superior to everyone else who didn't play it.

After Chess came and declined, the floodgates were open and diverse new games came into being. Monopoly let the poor know what it was to be rich. Battleship let the peaceful explore their warlike side. Catan let us explore, Trivial Pursuit let us learn, Clue let us play detective, and Scrabble let us argue violently over whether or not "Sriracha" was a proper noun.

Currently, we are in what is called the "Byzantine" era of board games, due to their increasing complexity. Games such as Scythe and Agricola can take several hours just to set up, and lifetimes to fully comprehend. One game called "Zos Kia Cultus" has proven so complex that numerous players have gone insane trying to learn it, or died of aneurysms while attempting to play at even its simplest levels. Others claim to have accidentally summoned demons, caused floods and famine, or condemned players to hell for all eternity. It is thus slightly easier and more fun than Scythe.

BOAT

Nobody knows why boats float. Some suspect they float on the same principles as ships and rafts, but others remain unsure.

BOLOGNA

In grocery stores, lunch meats have no name. But in death, bologna has a name. Its name is O-S-C-A-R. Its name is O-S-C-A-R.

BONE

Most of our bones' names are inspired by video games. Skull the Hero Slayer, Shoulderblade Chronicles, Rib:Zero, Femur Fantasy, Ulnacharted, and even Sternumuikoden gave their names to bones. Also, our tendons and ligaments were originally called Nintendons and EAgaments.

BOOTH

The restaurant booth was invented in 1961 during the ban on tables. It proved so popular that it remained in use even after tables were re-legalized in 1974.

BOWIE KNIFE

The Bowie Knife was named for James Bowie not because he used one but because he was killed by one. The toilet got its name the same way.

BOWL

The tradition of calling certain sporting events "Bowls" originates from the same euphemisms that called male protective wear "Cups". The Super Bowl was generally won by whoever had the largest... Uh. Crockery.

BRA

Tailors can best judge the shape for a bra by making a trade in which they give up half their own cup size in exchange for "shinigami boobs" in which they can magically sense the breast size of their customers.

BRACHIOSAURUS

A Brachiosaurus is a colossal dinosaur most notable for being the only genuine Jurassic-Age dinosaur in the entire Jurassic Park series.

One of the few real dinosaurs grown for the film, the snot it sneezed onto actress Ariana Richards was teeming with many extinct bacteria, and she soon after abandoned acting in favor of painting women in nature who are not being sneezed on by dinosaurs.

BRAINHACK

Brain hacking is a serious problem in the future. Be sure to take notice of any of the signs your brain has been hacked:

- You have a sudden change of opinion.
- You can't remember something you think you'd have remembered.

- You experience Déjà Vu more than two times in succession, or think you did.
- You find yourself committing a crime you have no motive to commit.
- You greet people by recommending a blog you've never read.
- You love someone you should not love, such as Nash Grier.
- You write to a blog on anon to tell them to stop advertising their novel.
- You find The Big Bang Theory funny.
- You find the TV Show "The Big Bang Theory" funny.
- You see a blinking light saying the FBI has locked your brain due to pornographic thoughts.
- People find you interesting for a change.
- Your robotic arms try to strangle you, or those around you.
- You spend over 20 minutes a day on tumblr.
- You find you like Gilbert and Sullivan when you're generally a metal-head.
- You like metal when you're generally a gilbert-and-sullivan-head.
- Someone tells you, "I hacked your brain."
- You quit your job to live out your lifelong dream of writing spam to people you never met.
- You send all your money to a foreign prince.
- A "Sponsored" logo appears in the corner of your vision.
- You actually like Brussels sprouts.
- Seriously nobody likes fucking Brussels sprouts.
- They taste like armpits.

BRAINPAN

The brain rests within the skull on a "carpet" very similar to an actual house carpet. This brain carpet is kept clean by special leukocytes called "vacuum cleaner cells."

BRAZIL

Brazil is Terry Gilliam's third non-Monty-Python film, loosely adapting the novel 1984 with heightened surrealism and satire. As with most Gilliam films, it was a very difficult production:

Gilliam was psychosomatically paralyzed for much of the film, and had to direct from a hospital bed that was pulled around by a donkey. When the first donkey died of cirrhosis, his understudy was kept on full monitoring for alcohol abuse.

The producers insisted the film have a happy ending. Gilliam finally got away with having the main character die horribly after being tortured to madness and cannibalizing his own family because Gilliam believed this to be the happiest possible conclusion.

George Orwell tried to sue the filmmakers for using his plot without his title and name, but failed because he had died in 1950, and long dead men in British law are nearly as disenfranchised as the Irish themselves.

The film has been credited with inventing not only steampunk but also retro-futurism, retro-steampunk, cyber-futurism, future-steam-retro, cabin-core, grimpunk-cybersteamdark-ism, and Norwegian black metal. Gilliam regrets all this still.

None of the actors involved survived filming the movie. Jonathan Price drowned in sewage during the sewage-drowning scene, Kim Greist burned to death during the burning-to-death scene, Robert De Niro fell to his death filming the deadly-falling scene, and Carl Weathers died decades later happy and surrounded by his family after filming the rabid-moose-stampede scene.

BREAD

If you talk too much about bread you can develop a yeast inflection.

BREAST IMPLANT

One in every three breast implants contains a goldfish.

BRICK

According to myth, bricks were invented when Zeus shat one when Hera caught him banging Palos the clay goddess.

Most bricks as found in nature are small, brown to red, and made of dried clay. They have been bred over thousands of years to be stronger, more angular, sturdier for construction, and come in many more colors.

Early writings about bricks include tales of how they were hunted, and how sometimes they fought back. In "Moby Brick" by Herman Mortarville, a hunt for a mythic giant white brick goes awry when the brick attacks and destroys the hunters. Other books are more catered to children, such as the "Brick and Jane" series which teaches basic masonry to readers.

Bricks are still a staple in most cultures and are commonly used in construction to this day. As sturdy construction is valued, competent builders are said to have "Big Brick Energy," and the phrase has transcended the industry to refer to any positive character attribute.

Also check out the works of popular author Philip K. Brick, such as "We Can Cantilever It For You Wholesale," "Do Androids Dream of Electric Blocks," "An Ashlar Darkly," and "Ubrick."

BRIE

Brie and Camembert were once thought to have evolved from a common cheese ancestor, but modern analysis has shown that Brie is more closely related to Gouda than to Camembert.

BRITISH PEOPLE

British people don't really exist, they're just a hoax perpetrated by two fairy girls in Cottingley.

BROOMFIELD, CO

The city of Broomfield, CO consists only of a broom in a field. It has fallen over since the city was founded.

BRONE AGE

The Bronze Age was characterized not only be Greek bronze-working, but also by Egyptian gold metal and Norwegian black metal.

BRONTË SISTERS

Though they had the ability to do so, the Brontë Sisters never in their lifetimes combined to form MegaBrontë.

BUFFALO BILL

Buffalo Bill was an important figure in the American "Old West" and forms a very important part of how Americans see their past.

At the age of 11, he began his long and prominent career of killing people. He first served in Utah where he was supposed to be killing Mormons, but in the process he also killed a Native American, and found his calling. He killed countless people attempting to defend their homes, and also managed to slaughter animals by the thousands. He participated in contests to see who could kill he most, and won with over 65 dead buffalo in a few hours- Nothing compared to the tens of thousands more he managed to shoot and leave to rot each season.

Because of all this, he is regarded as a legendary American hero. Later in his life, he had many stage shows in which he would brag about all the people and buffalo he'd shot, and secured his status as an icon of the American way, inspiring thousands of mass murderers, serial killers, warmongers and general genocidal madmen who make up the America we know today.

He is best known outside of America as the model for "Bubble-O-Bill," a popular cowboy-shaped ice cream treat across Australia, New Zealand, and Luxembourg.

BUGATTI

Bugatti cars are so advanced that they need devoted mechanics to fix. These mechanics must be able to reach any Bugatti within 30 minutes anywhere in the world, so most of them are kept in orbit. When a Bugatti is damaged, the mechanic will do an orbital skydive to the location of the car and repair it. Relaunching them is very costly, but only about 1/10th the cost of a Bugatti automobile.

BURIAL

There were no recorded burials between 1614 and 1617. Historians have yet to reach a consensus on why, but either nobody died in civilizations that bury their dead; or nobody in those civilizations got a proper burial. We cannot be certain which because the only 1614-1617 volume of burial listings was checked out of the library in 1618 and never returned.

-C-

CADBURY

In the town of Coolock is an unassuming building with the word "Cadbury" on the side. This is where the first Creme Egg was laid. With a chocolate shell and albumen of pure sugar, the Cadbury Creme Egg is not only the sweetest thing in Ireland but the sweetest object known to humankind, ranking over 95,000 Beetuses on the Wilford Brimley Memorial Scale.

The mystery of what laid the egg remains to this day. Once claimed to have been a rabbit, gorilla, or golden goose, genetic analysis of modern eggs suggest that the egg laying being has not only crustacean, but reptilian and annelid DNA. This suggests the existence of a proprietary, genetically engineered egg laying being, developed by Cadbury in the depths of Spike Island's catacombs, where it has been fed on the bodies of martyrs since the pagan days of yore.

Though nothing else is known about the creature, known by cryptozoologists as the "Cadbeest," the Cadbury Creme Egg is unquestionably delicious, and slightly less than 80% likely to result in its offspring bursting out of anyone who eats has eaten one, an event predicted by the prophet Chocoladamus to occur on St. Patrick's Day in 2028.

CAGE, NICOLAS

Nicolas Cage didn't always plan to be an actor. As a child he wanted to be a fire truck, but became an actor when he learned that fire trucks were inanimate objects.

CAKE WASP

The Hungarian Cake Wasp lays its eggs inside of freshly baked cakes so that the newborn larvae will have something to eat.

Much as parasitoid wasps will inject their eggs into caterpillars or other small animals, the Hungarian Cake Wasp evolved in the birthplace of the delicious baked treat. Hungary holds the earliest record for cake baking, about 2,000 B.C.E. (Before the common era) or at precisely 0 B.C., (Before cake). As wasps evolve significantly within only a few generations and those generations emerge twice daily, the Cake Wasp has plagued Hungary for several thousand years.

It's only in the last century though that the Cake Wasp has grown in size to consume entire pastries instead of their sugary toppings. Of course we've all seen the rose shaped egg sacks on many cakes, because they incorporate the natural sugars many people simply elect to eat them, or are even unaware that the decorative corners are in fact, Wasp Sacks. The wasps now frequently measure up to 2ft as adults, and similar trends have been observed in progress as generational size shift begins to manifest in Torte Beetles, Eclair Lice, Brownieflies and most prevalent in the Americas, the Mexican Mousse Mantis.

CALABI-YAU MANIFOLD

The Calabi-Yau manifold is a six pronged engine exhaust manifold used in the Harley Davidson Calabi-Yau 2000 motorcycle. It's notable because in theory, it shouldn't be able to work. The exhaust tube never reaches the muffler. In order for the manifold to work, and it does, there must be at least two more dimensions than our current model of the universe. This transdimensional exhaust port is currently being studied by physicists and theologists to determine how the gas travels, with the former postulating the dimensions are simply extensions of our current single dimensional time dimension, while the theologists are instead certain that the solution is a miracle performed by Saint Davidson of Harli, who was martyred by being drawn and quartered by the Hells Angels in 1978.

CALL OF DUTY

The Call of Duty player base was shocked in the early 2020s by rumors that someone may have called another player a "jerk" over the voice chat during an actual multiplayer game.

The incident is reported to have occurred late last night when players in the "Border Crossing" map began to debate the merits of Descartes' theories on personhood. The discussion suddenly turned sour when player BustopherJones, hot off an epic killstreak, got headshotted by CalvinismFan1509. It was then that an unknown player is stated by others to have used the term in reference to the killer, by far the most despicable act recorded in gaming since PuttyPuddle spoke poorly of a League of Legends player's skill in a YouTube comment.

Activision immediately shut down the servers for all their games but the damage was already done. According to Activision spokesman Finnegan Ward, "We don't yet know the damage this will do to the otherwise noble and reserved Call of Duty player base. The use of such language is unbecoming of our community and constitutes a page of shame in an otherwise clean and shining book of civil discourse, play, and propriety. There will be an investigation, and if found, we are prepared to ban the player in question."

This ban would be the first of its kind in the gaming community, which has been a true bastion of civility in an increasingly toxic world.

CAMEL

In the 1940s, more doctors smoked Camels than any other cigarette. Coincidentally, more doctors in the 1940s died of lung cancer than any other cancer.

CAMELOT

The story of King Arthur has been confirmed by numerous contemporary sources, though due to alphabetical and phonetic shifts, his kingdom was more accurately called "Camelsnot."

CANADA

Canada was a "Dominion" of the British Empire, meaning Queen Victoria used it in planning resource management to secure the most possible victory cards before their top item supply, or the supply of three different action cards, became exhausted.

Now, Canada remains because the British Empire is too lazy to clean up all their cards after they lose, as often happens when a country gets too many expansion packs.

CANDY

The first candy to boast a gooey center was called the "Scuzznugget." Its makers went out of business in three weeks and it was said to taste strongly of ammonia.

CAPITAL CRIME

Capital offenses are so named because their severity caused legislators to spell out the terms in all capital letters.

SEE ALSO: CAPITAL LETTERS

CAPITAL LETTERS

Capital letters were originally allowed only in Rome, the capital city. The stencils and carving templates for these letters were kept under guard in a "Caps Lock."

Thank you for seeing this entry on "Capital Letters" as you were told to do.

CANNIBAL CORPSE

The Cannibal Corpse song "Rotted Body Landslide" was inspired by the scene in Star Trek where Kirk opens a tank full of dead tribbles.

CAPS LOCK

The "Caps Lock" key does nothing by itself, but the position of your hand when pressing it makes you hold shift, thus ensuring all letters will be capitals.

CAR HORN

Early cars had keys for their horns, allowing the full range of notes to be played.

CARCINIZATION

"Carsonization" is the career-evolutionary tendency of all comedians to slowly turn into talk show hosts.

CARDIOLOGY

The phrase "The fastest way to a man's heart is through his stomach" was coined by Jean Veinen, inventor of gastroenterological cardiology.

CARE BEAR

Canonically, Care Bears who die young are buried under small piles rocks known as "Care Bear Bairn Cairns."

CARD SUITS

The card suits as commonly known are Spades, Hearts, Clubs, and Diamonds, but is was not always so. Various decks for many games and purposes have different suits including:

- **Tarot Cards-** Swords, Cups, Wands, and Pentacles
- **Uno Cards-** Red, Yellow, Green, and Blue
- **Credit Cards-** Visa, MasterCard, Discover, and American Express

- **ID Cards-** Driver's, Insurance, State, and Social Security
- **Sports Cards-** Baseball, Basketball, Football, and Calvinball
- **House of Cards-** Democrat, Republican, Independent, and Whig
- **Score Cards-** Golf, Mini-Golf, Bowling, and Witcher Romance
- **Punch Cards-** 100100100, 10101011, 10010, and 1001000101010111
- **Pokémon Cards-** Electric, Grass, Poison, and Planeswalker
- **Orson Scott Cards-** Ender, Alvin, Homecoming, and Ravenous Homophobic Bloggings That Sully His Entire Body Of Work
- **Hallmark Cards-** Thank You, Happy Birthday, Condolences, and "Sorry I Got Semen In Your Eye"
- **Alu Cards-** Castlevania, Hellsing, Waverly, and no joke, my friend Alucard J***** from when I was in college at CU Boulder. We met because you could look up people by name on the school website like pre-facebook and pre-spam-bots and see their info and email and I looked up the name as a joke and there was one guy and I emailed him like "Dude your name is Dracula backwards!" and it turned out he's related to Bram Stoker and goes to these meetings of his family in Ireland each year and I went with him once and met this girl named Ryann and we hit it off and walked around talking way late into the night and then she turned into a bat and left and I never saw her again and when I went back to tell Alucard, there was no trace of him at college or anywhere else and it turns out Stoker's family all died off in the early 1900s. True story.

CARS, THE

No member of the band "The Cars" ever got their drivers license. They all rode bikes to the recording studio.

CASTLEVANIA

A Castlevania movie was planned for release in the 2010s, but canceled because its title, "Castlevania: Lords of Shadow: Mirror of Fate: The Movie: Part 1: The Trevor Belmont Legacy" was too easily abbreviated into "CLOGFLOBBLIT," a cuss word in Esperanto.

CAT

Cats are in fact more loyal than dogs, it's just that their true masters are ghosts who want them to pee on us and eat hair.

CATHAR HERESY

Catholic historical writings rarely describe the opposing deities of the Cathar Heresy, and absolutely never speak of the even more unsettling and blasphemous Catheter Heresy.

CAULIFLOWER

The process by which cauliflower is made is unknown to many who eat it.

First, the cauliflower is mined in the form of raw cauliflow-ore, from which the mineral (often mistaken for a vegetable) takes its name. The Cavolfiore Canyon Cauliflow mine in northern Italy still accounts for 40% of global cauliflower.

The ore is then refined into ingots slightly smaller than the intended size of the edible final product, and is set on fire. The fire alters the chemical structure of the ore into raw cauliflower, making it not only edible, but outright delicious. Cauliflower must still be cooked, as the immediate post flame stage is considered tough and unpalatable.

Cauliflower burns at 70,000 Degrees Fahrenheit during its refinement, and the process provides electricity to 70% of Venice and Milan.

CAVIAR, LAND

Land caviar is made of eggs laid by the Georgian Land Salmon. A delicacy in most of Europe, the meal is banned in the United States due to the high levels of mercury it contains.

The Georgian Land Salmon itself is a rare fish that can live up to three days out of water, walking on its fins and distilling small amounts of oxygen from the air with its highly efficient gills. The Land Salmon is almost five feet long, by far the largest land fish known to science.

In Europe the fish is called the "Sosemortinto," which translates roughly as "Roadkill" as the fish is slow and often dies attempting to cross the many highways that cover Europe's coastline. About 50 humans die each year in Land Salmon related car crashes. Ironically, chef Multama al-Samak who pioneered modern land caviar cuisine died in such an accident when a Land Salmon wandered in front of his motorcycle while he rode to his restaurant.

CELSIUS

Celcius is a measure of temperature in which 0 degrees is the freezing point of water, and 100 degrees is the boiling point of the cerebrospinal fluid of Anders Celsius, a criminal executed in Sweden to determine what 100 degrees would be. Upon Mr. Celsius's horrible death, Swedish monarch and nominative determinism poster-boy King König von Schweden of Sweden ordered the first Celsius thermometers to be forged.

Twenty thermometers were originally constructed. Three were given to Norway, coldest of the nations where the temperature never rose above 2. Seven were granted to the Swedish, where the temperature was often well over 4. And nine, nine thermometers were given to Denmark, which above all craved really long poems about killing people. But they were, all of them, happy that the King kept a master thermometer by which the others could be calibrated in a celebration of peace and cooperation across Scandinavia.

Kelvins are also based on degrees Celsius, but this is not appropriate to speak of in decent company.

CENSORSHIP

In the early 1500s, the church ordered several portraits by Jan van Eyck altered to make the subjects' skin appear more flawless. One large mole was removed from the Arnolfini Portrait entirely. Only now that restoration has achieved its current technological status are efforts under way to replenish the Flemish blemish.

CHAIN MAIL

Chain Mail refers to a kind of armor in the past, a kind of postal hoax today, and a kind of human centipede in the future.

CHAN, 4

Dion 4Chan was an occultist writer in the 1900s who invented soy milk, brony fandom, and hacktivism. She wrote several novels about a thinly veiled Crowley spoof named Hugo Astley, likely resulting in the homunculus known as Rick Astley and his popular rolls.

CHARGERS

As suggested by the lightning bolt on their helmets, the San Diego Chargers are not named for the charge of a cavalry, but for the common cell phone charger.

CHARLOTTE'S WEB

Charlotte's Web was written by E.B. White as a satire about how people would believe anything they read on the web.

CHEERIO

Each individual Cheerio is a dehydrated bagel.

CHEESEBURGER

A cheeseburg is much like an "Iceberg." Cheeseburgs can float around anywhere there is a fondue spring or heavy cheese production, but most cheeseburgs float about with something called "fatbergs" in the sewer. Thus, they come from, and go into cheeseburgers. Hopefully not often in that order.

CHEESEGRATER

The cheesegrater was invented by the same guy who invented pizza. He wanted to turn the mozzarella into smaller bits to let it melt and all was well for ages, until four turtles devoured all his pizza and he became their sworn villain, Shredder.

CHEETO

A common Cheeto farmer can harvest only 7 bushels of Cheeto per month, enough to provide for a family for only a couple weeks. If winter hits before the harvest is complete, the family will starve. It is not easy, being cheesy.

CHESS

Chess is an analog live-action computer game or, "game," invented in the year 1712 B.T.B. (before this book) by Shatranj Al-Chessinventir. Designed to teach local rulers about warfare and defending their kingdoms, the game simulated a royal court and its pawns with game pieces. The original pieces were as follows:

- **King:** The ruler of the court, if captured, means the end of the game. Mostly a figurehead, he can only move one tile at a time.
- **Queen:** The most capable piece, she does the most work, but capturing her is not the full ending of the game because apparently a woman who can do anything is worth less than a man who can barely move.

- **Bishop:** Like a real bishop, this piece can only move diagonally, and whenever it takes another piece, it must pray for absolution or it will go to Chess Hell or, "Chell," and burn in Chess Fire or, "Chire," for all Chess Eternity or, "Next Round."
- **Knight:** A knight must move in an L shape as per the rules of Tetris, from which the earliest chess games were inspired. The knight is represented by a horse in honor of Mazura of Parapa Palace.
- **Royal Piss-Bucket Emptier:** Now known as the "Rook" due to Victorian prudery, the Royal Piss-Bucket Emptier runs as far as needed in any cardinal direction because the historical job entailed speed and resolute direction.
- **Pawn:** Also known as a "Serf" or "Retail Clerk," the Pawn is expected to die young and be replaced quickly without the royals so much as noticing, so worthless and ordinary is this piece that just wanted to survive and be with their family. Should a pawn make it to the opposite side however, it can become a Queen or any other piece, a lesson designed to teach players that if they betray their family and join the ranks of the enemy, they will be rewarded with fame, fortune, and optional gender fluidity.

Though only about 24 possible games are playable with chess, two less than tic-tac-toe, many books have been written on Chess Theory by lonely people hoping to impress someone with how smart they think they are. Through all history, this has never worked.

Chess grew popular in America in the 60s and 70s due to the celebrity of chess master Bobby Fischer. Fischer became famous for winning the world chess championship without ever having played the game, he had thought he was enrolled in a checkers tournament at the time. His fame declined soon after when Fischer claimed that Jews were to blame for everything bad, Jews were evil, and he hoped that all the Jews would die. Being Jewish himself, he then died. He was then dug up again (f8=P?) and reburied by order of the Bishop (Bxf8#).

Chess has only recently made a comeback owing to new and interesting chess variants such as 4 Player Bughouse Chess, Three-Man Chess, 5D Chess with Multiverse Time Travel, and Checkers (with chess pieces because I forgot where I put the checkers).

The most interesting thing ever to happen in Chess occurred in 2021 when the Double Bongcloud Position was introduced to top competitions. And that sentence isn't even made up.

CHEWING GUM

The production of gum is a difficult matter, it isn't just one of your holiday games. Even the stuff that goes into their batter is far more complex than caramelized aspartame.

First of all is the "gum" that makes chewing gum chewy, like elastomers, xanthan, and res'nous corn-ears, or terpenes or fats that are less gross and gooey, as xanthan's secreted by Anthony, Piers.

Second is flavor and that's fundamental- Cinnamon, fruits or sweet stuffs are most fun, sadly fruit stripes are entirely ephemeral, and soon leave a flavorless mass on your tongue.

Lastly gum needs a shape worth biting into, a ball or a stick or a roll is ideal. Once it's wrapped up and delivered upon you, it's time to enjoy this old time-honored meal.

Just don't swallow it or you'll die horribly of malignant abdominal distension and impacted bowel spams.

CHICKEN NUGGET

Since the writing of the Magna Carta, the punishment for eating the chicken nuggets of another has been liquefaction and condensation into mechanically separated criminal, which is then used to make more "chicken" nuggets. Many still believe that such nuggets are really literal chicken, but this has not been true since the year 1215, when the term for "criminal" was "chicmanelle" which has since evolved to "chicken." Nugget still meant "nugget," as it always has, and always shall.

CHINCHILLA

Chlorine is the only element not found in the chinchilla digestive system. Always use a Chinchilla-Grade Hazard Suit including fur goggles, whisker gloves, and just-a-little-guy shielding when feeding them. Never approach a chinchilla in open air, or closed air, or any atmosphere at all. Do not attempt to pet or handle its floofy bode without supervision from five or more guards of a Chinchilla Radiation And Biohazard Mitigation Authority Team. Observe these rules every time you handle a chinchilla.

CHIROPRACTOR

Very few chiropractors have ever been to Cairo, even fewer have successfully practed it.

CHOCOLATE CAKE

Chocolate cake bakes
from a box of cake flakes.
However much your fancy makes,
That's how much your belly aches.
First you take some cocoa powder,
then a cup of baking flour,
stir it up on lowest power.
Let it sit for half an hour.
Whisk in milk and oil and eggs.
Pour out water and the dregs.
Add a drop of beer from kegs,
Dust a dash of ground nutmeg.
At 350, start the preheat,
while the batter blob can accrete.
Shape it on a baking sheet,
Let it cool before you eat.
You can also make it frosted,
provided that you're not exhausted.

CHOLERA

People named Stuart are 45% more likely to die of Cholera.

CHROMATOGRAPHY

Chromatography is the process of separating a whole into its various parts, and can work on literally anything. It was first done on plant pigments, hence its name. But you can do chromatography on fluids, gasses, and even non-physical things like hopes and dreams.

Modern chromatography is great for foods, where a famous restaurateur like Miquelli Paqueline will take a popular meal such as a cheeseburger and instead serve separate examples of a fine bread, some gourmet ground beef, and a chef's-buttload of cheese.

Similarly, his sister philanthropist Sarah Paqueline would separate each part of peoples wishes into different tasks that volunteers would each focus on to help people accomplish their needs.

On the other end of the moral spectrum, their father the infamous serial killer Buford "Buster" Paqueline was known for separating his victims' skin, entrails, muscles, and organs. Thus the court practiced chromatography by separating their family into prison, freedom, and food service.

Other famous chromatographers include Lemony Cartesian, the first person to separate their laundry by color; Eroi Mumfordinsen who separated their CD collection by genre; and Lars von Trier, who divided moviegoers into fans of his work, and people with taste.

Ion chromatography specifically is when people feel either very positive or negative about all that.

CHUPACABRA

The name of the Chupacabra originated with a child mispronouncing a word when trying to tell his parents there was a Capybara in the back yard. As the child had in fact mistaken a previously nameless goat-sucking monster for a Capybara anyway, the new name stuck.

CHURCH

If a church is prevented from molting due to its surroundings, it will never be able to grow into a full cathedral. Chapels in particular are intentionally stunted to be kept in homes or hospitals.

CHURCH BELL

The first church bell was that of the Hagia Sophia. Before Constantine invented the church bell, services were announced by vocalists in minarets, like in Islam on which Christianity is based.

CILANTRO AND CORRIANDER

Coriander is woman I met in the 1990s. She had the longest fingers I ever saw. Not like with Marfan Syndrome or Congenital Arachnodactyly, but like nine to ten inch long fingers. One day, I saw a seam in her wrist, like her skin was just a suit, she hid it quickly though and I never saw it again. Years after I last saw her, I heard she had been killed in a car crash but there was no funeral. All record of her vanished too, like she'd never existed. I met Jesse, a friend who knew her too and he said that when she died, her body fell apart like ash and when it blew away, it caused a storm with huge amounts of thunder-less, soundless lightning. For years after, the grass didn't grow around the whole region, and when it finally did, it was all diseased and gnarled.

Cilantro is a leafy herb, yet is somehow even scarier.

CLARINET

Clarinets do little for most people's allergies but are better for music than Benadryl.

CLEOPATRA

It is often stated that Cleopatra lived closer to modern times than to the building of the pyramids; and that T-Rex lived closer to modern times than to the time of the Stegosaurus, but only a few photographs actually show Cleopatra riding a T-Rex.

Myths of Cleopatra having a vibrator consisting of a jar of bees are entirely untrue. It was a gourd full of bees. It was a bumblebee bottle gourd buzzing green pharaoh vibrator. Sure sounds strange to me…

CLOUD

Clouds cannot form on Tuesdays. If you see a cloud on Tuesday, it is inevitably a re-used cloud from Monday.

There are several types of cloud, identifiable as follows:

Cirrus:

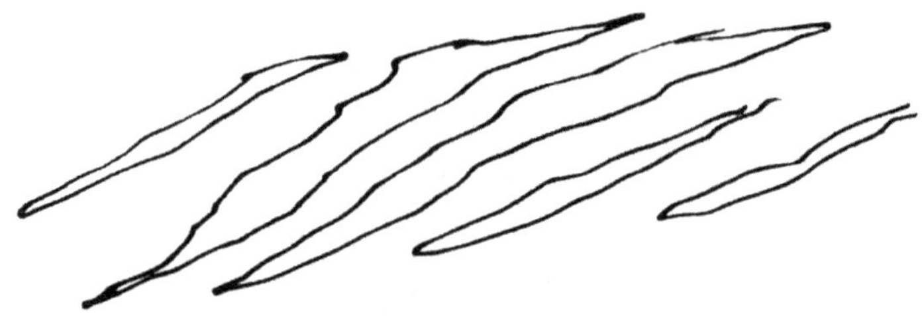

Cumulus:

Nimbus:

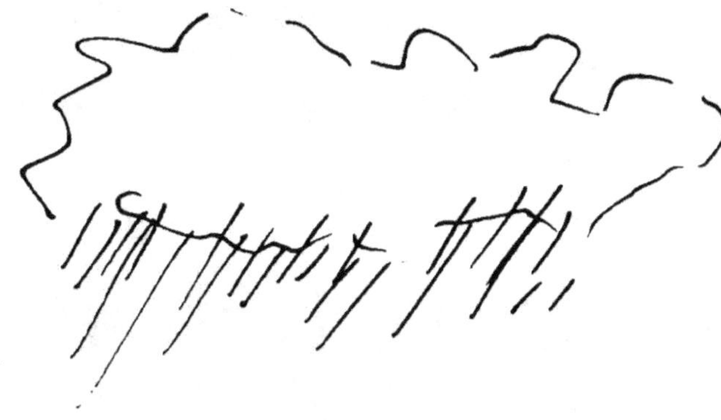

Rhombus:

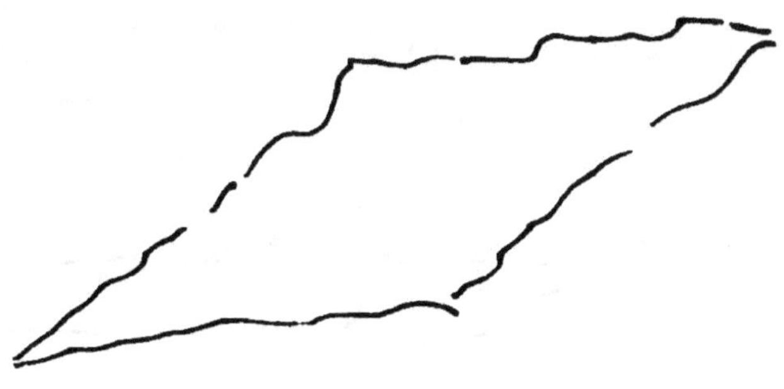

Stratus:

Alto Stratus:

Baritone Stratus:

Dodge Stratus:

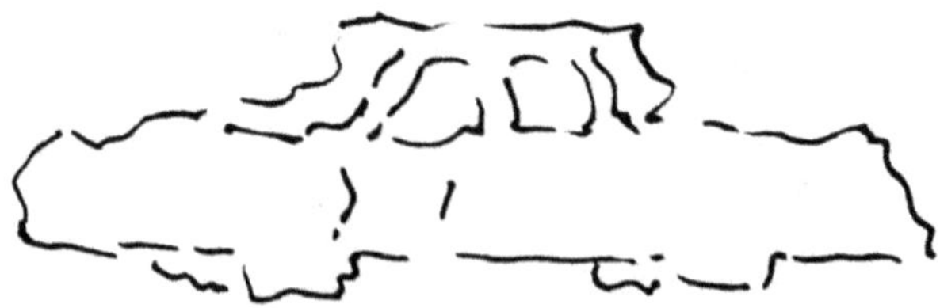

Stradivarius:

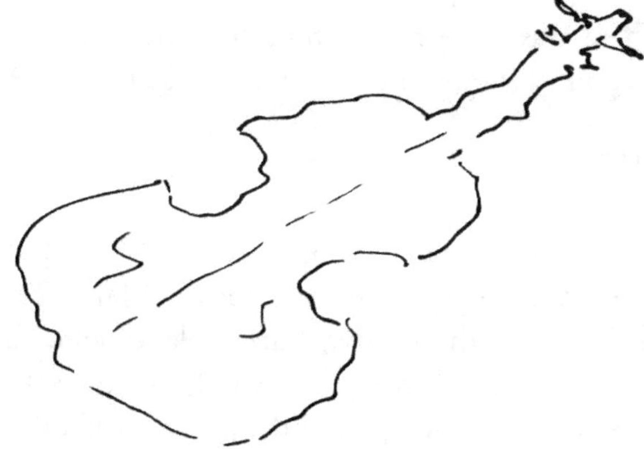

Mammatus:

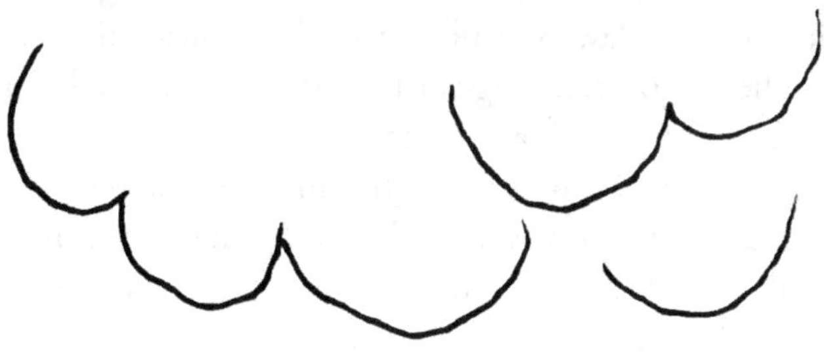

Areolas:

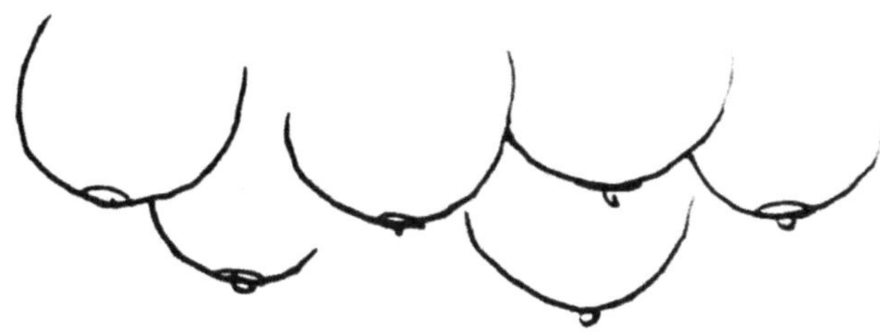

CLOWN

There was an early attempt to introduce clowns to medieval Europe, but this proved to be a feudal jester.

COCKPIT

Planes were very slow, once. To make a transatlantic journey, they'd need food and even livestock. Originally, the cockpit was where they kept the rooster, but as planes grew faster and needed more precise control, the pilot would take over the seat vacated by the rooster, hence, their part of the plane is still called the cockpit.

CODE OF HAMMURABI

Though the Code of Hammurabi is often cited as the first legal text, a much older stele dating to 5750 BC is thought to have held an earlier code of law, specifically dealing with mineral sales and metals of the proto-bronze age. The stele only has one law remaining intact but may have held over 20 total.

Unearthed from an ancient tin mine in Serbia, the Stele of Cassander The Nameless is a solid granite block measuring about 3 meters tall, engraved with Ancient Macedonian letters and mostly broken apart by time and mining activity.

Most of the laws on the stele are unreadable, but law 7 is fully intact and details the ownership rights of tin ingots, stating that it was not the miner nor the owner of the mine who had the right to sell the tin, but rather whoever participated in the smelting and reduction into the metal's pure form, and that only they could sell or make deals for it. Because of the past tense writing of ancient Hellenistic dialects, the first law recorded in human civilization translates exactly to, "He who smelt it dealt it."

COFFEE

Tea differs from Coffee only in that one contains mostly filler (including fly feces and lint). I'm not going to tell you which.

COMBOVER

The combover was invented by Marlon Oosterdoggen IV of Schlitzenberg. He had only one hair but nobody knew that until after his death.

COMMUNISM

You can remember the difference between communism and socialism by memorizing the mnemonic, "Ben Kingsley Played Both Gandhi And The Mandarin." I don't know what the letters stand for so you'll need to look it up on Wikipedia or Yahoo.

COMPUTER

A computer begins with the matrix pad adapter. The matrix pad adapter latches rifters to the rafters of the pad adapter pumper. The pad adapter pumper pumps the pad adapter latcher to detach the rifter rafter grafter after it's been crafted.

When the crafted latcher rifter rifts the grafter pad adapter then the lesser booster loosener can upholster on the plaster. The plaster craft attacher rifter rachets all the latches and the latch catch hatch adapter looses boosted router matches. So if the matrix pad adapter latcher rifts can ratchet by the hatch it matches router rifter tappers to the plaster booster scouter.

This is where the hover cover comes in. The hover cover never over-utilizes switches, but the switches hitch the glitches that the hover cover pitches. The latch adapter wrapper covers hover by the switches that the hitches of the stitches to the hover cover which is where the stitch pitch taps the glitch pitch to the twitching clicker packer.

From there it begins to get complicated:

The thick wick wicket digit dials codons for the modem. The modem codon coding code grows fractal nodes for loading. If the loading node the modem codes stows total mode infractions, then the traction fraction interaction code can stall the modem.

So from an engineering perspective, the modern modem coding node goes loading mode-boost holdings and the rifter rafter grafter icon likens crafted ratchets of the gadgets that the pad adapter catches for the booster hover cover pitch glitch hitches from the hatches to the router of the scouter making motor nodes grow louder.

CONAN THE BARBARIAN

Conan the Barbarian was originally to have been a sidekick to an even stronger barbarian named Nan.

CONCERT

People wave their phone lights during concerts as a modern version of waving lighters, which took after holding torches as a threat to musicians that if they hit a flat note, they would be burned alive by the mob.

CONCH

Despite the childhood tradition, it's best not to hold a conch shell to your ear because if the shell holds a hermit crab, it may elect to abandon the shell in favor of cleaning out your skull and living inside, controlling your body after throwing out or eating your brain.

CONCRETE MIXER

Concrete Mixer Trucks were originally designed to transport the blood of giants for giant transfusions. After giants went extinct, most of the trucks were converted to mix concrete, but a few remain, driving around America with the fluid of those giants intact. Their blood churns ever on.

CONGRATULATIONS

The word "Congratulations" a Latin extension of the original "Congrats" which in turn was originally spelled Kong-Rats, in reference to the giant King-Kong size rat beasts that were traditionally dumped in large numbers onto the subjects of praise as a reminder to stay modest despite their triumphs.

CONSTITUTION

A necromancer in Philadelphia once resurrected and interviewed George Washington on camera to question him about the founding fathers' intentions for America. The conversation was as follows:

"Mr. Washington, do you feel the second amendment still applies?"

"Why are you, witch, suffered to live? Why does this strange box of wires with a glass eye peer upon me? Why do you have your own teeth? This canst not be the America I created, for it doth not sniff of the sweet stool of oxen and fishmongers. Nay, return me to my own time that I may pay Mr. Franklin for another radium colonic."

CONTINENTAL DRIFT

In one billion years, the continents will have drifted well beyond the planet's crust and entered orbit.

CONTRACTIONS

Several contractions have fallen out of popular use. Some of these include:

- **H'ere** (Hi There)
- **Th'eat** (That's neat)
- **Se'sons** (See Simpsons?)
- **Li'n'ation** (License and Registration)
- **Wa'mr'ne** (Want more wine?)
- **Why'bl'm's** (Why did you reblog my nudes?)

- **M'ven'tis'k** (My venereal disease tests are back)
- **Spr'g'giddr'b'Sco'tr** (Spielberg is a good director but Scorsese better understands the issues that effect modern cinema's portrayals of crime and redemption)
- **Ot'millio'pl'i'kyty't'w'son'aiml'Vi'Cra's'ntt'a'wa'kwa'ta'v ry'ni'h'p'qu's'grup** (Of the million people in Kyle City, there was none so aimless as Violet MacRae. That's not to say she walked into walls or spoke in tangents, only that she lacked a purpose in life. Every night since she could speak, her parents asked her the same question: "What do you want to be when you grow up?" They would have asked even earlier, but this was the civilized world and children didn't get their vocal cords until they proved they knew when not to use them. Violet didn't get hers until she was three. At seventeen and a half, she had just passed her adulthood tests, and that old question was more pressing.

CONTRARIANISM

Arguments play an important role in evolution:

The animals that would become worms and insects split originally over a debate regarding dirt; fish and mollusca over the use of fins; and dogs and cats diverged after an epic feud over who could get humans to snuggle with them more.

Indeed, even humans and other primates evolved from the same animal, but split apart due to an incident millions of years ago, likely an argument over ethics in gaming journalism.

(CONT'D)

The term "Cont'd" at the end of a page does not mean "Continued" but "Contaminated," a warning not to go on reading lest the reader become contaminated with deadly (CONT'D)

CONVERSATION

In casual conversation, though it's not an official rule of the English language, it's important never to begin or preface a classic saying or phrase such as "Time flies" or "A dime a dozen" with the words "I will rip your fucking eyes out for what you did to my poodle, you rotten old snot bag from hell." They don't mention it in school but it will absolutely ruin a job interview or romantic dinner.

COOK

Many people assume that "Too many cooks spoiling the broth" means having too many people cooking one meal will result in a lack of culinary direction and an inferior product.

It actually refers to the speed with which human beings rot, as adding too many chef cadavers to a soup or broth will make it spoil faster. For best results, only make one chef's worth at a time, and keep the rest of their bodies chilled to prevent spoilage.

COOKIE MONSTER

The Cookie Monster was inspired by Penicillium roqueforti, which is used is the production of blue cheese, including Roquefort. Not to be confused for its antibiotic relative, this type of penicillin grows as blue hairlike fibers and grows on foods, including cookies. Jim Henson, having been raised as a strong believer in pharmaceuticals and modern medical science, knew about the mold's ability to consume baked goods and made his own character (officially named Sidney Roquefort), a fluffy blue monster resembling the mold, to eat cookies.

COOL PEOPLE

The coolest person ever had a body temperature of -14°F and slept under a sheet of ice in freezing water. He is still there, having been "asleep" for the last 140 years.

The first use of the word "Cool" to mean admirable or awesome was in Jonathan Swift's "A Tale of a Tub" in 1704:

"Yes, for the agriculture of New Pestlewaite owed much to its tools, this before you was the horse-towed hoe that tilled my field and it is most cool, but ignore that hoe over there, for it is Sus."

Note that "Sus" in the 1700s referred to Sus domesticus or the common pig, by which inferior quality hoes were towed.

CORAL

Coral grows on sea floors completely independent of where humans build roads, thus coral-ation does not necessarily imply causeway-tion.

CORK

Know now how cork came into being, for it was bark once, now taken by the dark powers. Tortured and mutilated, a ruined and terrible form of plug for a wine bottle. Now perfected by Saruman.

CORN DOG

Corn dogs are named for their traditional meat, the unicorn. As unicorns are now extinct, they can only be referred to properly as 'Corn Dogs and not "Unicorn Dogs" as they were prior to 2009.

CORN FLAKES

Corn flakes are not made from plant corn, but foot corns.

CORRELATION

Though it has been long understood that simply because two things happen similarly, they are not necessarily causing each other, scientists have finally proven mathematically that if two things resemble each other even vaguely, they must be connected.

According to actual scientist D.R. McCarthy (Whose first names start with D and R and is not a doctor), "We know that the climate is heating up, but those of us who ignore 99.9% of climatologists and prefer only reports released by Exxon and BP Oil still couldn't figure out why. Now we know that it's caused by movie budgeting practices in Hollywood. I mean, look at the graphs. Just look at them. That's science, and maybe even math."

People who know what they're talking about have widely denounced McCarthy's statements as nonsense, but as a completely unbiased fact source it is my duty to show both sides of the argument, no matter how obviously untrue one of them is. This report frees up numerous previously discounted theories so be sure to check in on the next volume (Acrobat-Zump) for an entry on how the invention of the internet caused the eruption of Mt. St. Helens.

COUNTRY MUSIC

Country Music is what happens when Folk Music ferments. It has existed in seven distinct generations:

1. 1920-1930, in which people with fiddles sang about farm animals
2. 1930-1950, where cowboys were also invited
3. 1950-1970, in which Nashville took over
4. 1970-1990, in which Johnny Cash and Dolly Parton ruled the Earth
5. 1990-2000, when Trucks and Drinking were valued above all
6. 2000-2020, when you got shot if you didn't mention 9/11
7. 2020-Present, a time of people mostly just wishing Johnny Cash and Dolly Parton still ruled the Earth.

Country Music may also at times involve a "Banjo."

COVENANT DAY (AMERICA)

Being 8 days after July 4th, July 12th is American Covenant day, the anniversary of the day the United States was circumcised.

COWBOY

Of the average 200 babies born across the world every minute, nearly 10% will grow up to be cowboys unless their mothers can stop them.

CRAB

Various crabs can conduct different kinds of magic:

- **Blue Crab:** Glintstone magic. Mostly offensive spells including magic blades, astrological attacks and energy spells.
- **Horseshoe Crab:** Healing magic, including invincibility to poison, physical barriers and buffs.
- **King Crab:** Golden magic. Manipulation of grace, draconic magic, spells for manipulation of enemies.
- **Rock Crab:** Gravity magic, including stonewielding, flotation, and the ability to render enemies vulnerable to further spells.
- **Hermit Crab:** Fire magic, fireball throwing, lava eruptions, and the ability to set enemies aflame.
- **Fiddler Crab:** Black Flame magic, beast claw, black flame ritual, and warping abilities.
- **Snow Crab:** Ice magic, freezing abilities, frostbite infliction, summoning of ice bats.
- **Xanthid Crab:** Frenzy magic such as inflict insanity, howl of madness, and that annoying shit that frenzy knight does every damn time I try to fight him. Fuck you Frenzy Knight.
- **Rave Crab:** Premonition- The ability to predict the fall of empires.

Coconut crabs are huge. They don't need magic.

CRAVEN, WES

The first Nightmare on Elm Street film includes several scenes based on nightmares of director Wes Craven. Oddly, none of these are the dream sequences. Rather, he dreamed once of having a suburban family, and didn't like it one bit.

CRIME

Most criminal investigation records prior to 1994 included extensive dossiers on Richard Nixon, just in case he did it.

CRITERION COLLECTION

Though the Criterion Collection promised to show a new special director's cut of the Before Sunrise Trilogy on their channel, they have yet to post its streaming location, with their main page still promising to post the Linklater.

CRITERION COLLECTION CLOSET

An anonymous filmmaker who totally isn't me wrote the following:

After the release of my first feature film "Jealous Gods" in 2017, I was invited to visit the Criterion Collection Closet, where they have filmmakers take a few of their favorite Criterion Collection released films on DVD, Blu-Ray, and now 4K. The videos are shared on their site and YouTube.

Naturally I began thinking about what films I wanted immediately. One problem was that I already owned most of the ones I was really after. So it became a matter of which ones I wanted but could not afford, and which I wanted that were normally out of print, if they'd be there. On the flight to New York, I made a top ten list I don't have convenient, it was mostly just weird foreign surrealist films and single titles that were usually only available in large sets.

I arrived in New York and to my surprise, there was a driver with a sign of my name waiting for me at the Airport, they really treated their filmmakers right. At the Criterion HQ, entered through a nondescript door behind the Tet Corp building in Manhattan, I was taken through a movie-poster encrusted hallway and into the closet.

But the closet was not at all what I expected. There were no movies, no DVDs or Blu-rays, only a combination sink/toilet like you'd see in a prison cell. The door slammed closed behind me. I banged on the door, first laughing thinking it was a hazing joke of some sort but after the first few hours, I began to realize it was no joke. I saw the scratches on the door. I saw the fingernails of those who never escaped.

Over the next few days as I was fed a few crumbs and stray insects, I came to think that I had been tricked and this was not the Criterion Collection at all. But as I screamed in horror in the night, guards came to explain that I was indeed a guest of The Criterion Collection, but I was not in the closet they put the good filmmakers in. No. I was in the Closet of Sacrifice.

Criterion did indeed invite great filmmakers into the closet to take their picks, but lesser indie failures like me were better used as sacrifices to Janus, the DVD God. Once the god of doors, this two-faced deity in the modern era allowed for double-layered disc printing, but only with a human sacrifice for each movie printed to a glass disc master. Thus, I was to be the sacrifice that would enable the printing of Criterion Spine #872, "Ghost World" by Terry Zwigoff. It would literally be my spinal column that would be ceremonially ripped out to become their 872th spine.

I thought Ghost World was a neat adaptation of Clowes's graphic novel, but I wanted to live. I managed to escape by using bits of broken DVD surface and my own nasal mucus to build a rudimentary lens, and focused the heat of the single projector bulb that lit the Closet of Sacrifice onto the doorknob and melted it.

Once out, I ran trying to find my way through the maze of halls, the labyrinth where sinister faces smiled upon me from posters and DVD art. I tackled a Dolby 5.1 encoding supervisor and managed to bite his throat, killing him and providing me with meat that I scarfed down on the spot. I took his scheduling iPad and broke it into shards with which I stalked and dispatched a team of packaging consultants, hunting with the dim animal mind that remained to me after my imprisonment. I found my way to the outer foyer and almost to the street. But in the revolving door, I became trapped. The door stopped turning. There, I met the God of Doors.

Janus, God of Doors and dual-layer DVD mastering appeared to me in the reflection of the unmovable panes at the tower's exit.

"Fool, you cannot escape my collection," said the western face of the majestic pagan god, "Your spine is to become the basis of a disc that will bring pleasure to millions of supporters of high quality cinema preservation and fans of 2000s indie dark comedy."

"You will not take me, Janus," I shouted to the blasphemous demiurge, "Let me free or I will burn your temples to the ground!"

Janus laughed. His eastern face proclaimed, "You have no power here. New York is the City of Doors, my powers are limitless here! Give yourself to me now and your death may yet be minimally painful."

Just then, an Arrow split the door frame! Janus cried in agony. It was Arrow Video, rival home theater releasing company and devotees of Athena! Their raid on Criterion had begun and I made my escape.

I live now in a house with no doors, watching my Arrow and Shout Factory DVD collections. Even Vinegar Syndrome and Anchor Bay are welcome in my collection. But never Criterion, never again Janus Films or that other imprint of theirs you see at Barnes and Noble. Beware them and their Janus Cult ways, and if you someday make a film and they invite you into the Criterion Closet...

...Be sure to ask which closet they mean.

CROUTON

When you put a cardboard box into a recycling machine, a single crouton is what you get on the other side.

CROW

The crow is so named because it crows. That has led many ornithologists to believe that ravens do, somewhere, hold raves.

Crows are a type of "Bird," which is itself a type of cloud. We know they are technically clouds because they live in the sky. Crows are a type of dark storm cloud, or "Birbulostratus." Being capable of rain, it is unwise to walk under many crows, or they may rain on you.

Crows are playful and intelligent animals capable of complex vocalizations. They enjoy collecting objects, giving gifts, and helping each other roost, thrive, and heal, with crows being observed literally covering other cold birds with their right wings, making them far more socially advanced and ethical than most right wing humans.

Because Edgar Allan Poe had already hogged Ravens for the goths of his own time, James O'Barr used a crow for his famous modern goth comic book entitled "My Boyfriend's Back And You're Gonna Be In Trouble," later retitled "The Crow" to avoid copyright difficulties.

A group of crows is called a "Murder" because Francoise Dremeigneo, who coined all the modern terms for animal groupings, saw his mother thrown off a roof by several crows, leading him to a career in fashion where he could make an all-crow-leather suit.

CRUISE SHIPS

All cruise ships are required to have their own court of law, prison, and on Caribbean cruises, executioners.

CRYING

It's often assumed people cry because they're sad or their eyes are irritated. These are mere urban legends. People cry because of "øyeepletdvergs."

An øyeepletdverg is a small gnome that lives under your eyelid. We all have them, and it's nothing to be ashamed of. Living off your sweet, sweet eyeball juices, øyeepletdvergs are a happy folk who hold parties and other gatherings often within your skull's ocular orbits. They drink liberally and urinate at a corresponding rate. That's what tears are: Øyeepletdverg pee.

Øyeepletdvergs love onions and their smell intoxicates them. Thus they get drunk, and have to go more often. Similarly, the pheromones we emit when sad or sentimentally happy inspire their drinking. It's possible but inadvisable to get rid of ones øyeepletdvergs by spraying insecticide into your eyes. This would be a mistake, as we live in symbiosis with these creatures who keep our eyes lubricated in exchange for their lifestyles. Also it would involve spraying insecticide into your eyes, which is #7 on Rupert Wade's List Of Things You Shouldn't Spray In Your Eyes.

CRYPTID

The first known cryptid was simply called "The Cryptid." It lived in crypts, farmed bitcoins, and had a very small, weak superego. This was rare back in the 1600s but now it describes most business school graduates.

CTHULHU

Though Lovecraft never stated Chtulhu's place of origin specifically, it is implied to be in Texas due to references to the "drawl" of Cthulhu.

You can now see Cthulhu naked on his OnlyFhtagns. The sight will drive you permanently insane.

CU CHULAINN

Cú Chulainn is one of the most famous Irish folk heroes. Being late to a party one day, he was attacked by the host's guard dog and killed it in self defense, and in compensation he served the host as the dog's replacement, hence his name, which literally means, "That kid who was late to a party one day and got attacked by the host's guard dog and killed it so he served the host as the dog's replacement." Irish Gaelic is a very efficient language.

Cú Chulainn starred in many heroic tales, like the time he let the country get taken over because he was off nailing some chick, the time some lady stole a cow because his whole army thought they were pregnant, the time he turned down a date with the war goddess so she made his cows stampede, and the time his dad turned him into a monster so he could massacre the opposing force, but he recognized their queen was just having a bad cramps day so he guarded her retreat. Historians believe this means that in ancient Ireland, people spent most of their time raising cows, fighting over cows, and/or suffering from severe abdominal pain.

Cú Chulainn died from eating dog meat, as being a metaphorical hound this was symbolic cannibalism. The spear he was impaled with was also likely involved but it was the dog meat that's best remembered because dogs are friends, not food. He tied himself to a post so he could die facing his enemies because he knew this would be very badass.

His last name is pronounced "Cullen," like Edward's family.

CULINARY PHOTOGRAPHY

Culinary photography was invented by Louis Daguerre in 1838 shortly after his invention of the camera. He uploaded the first photo to Instagram via telegraph, a process that would soon become known as the "Telegram."

CUTTING EDGE

Most computer products are "Cutting Edge" technology, as you'll find out if you run your finger along the edge of a trackpad.

-D-

DAFT PUNK

The lyrics to Daft Punk's "Around the World" were originally written by Jules Verne.

DARK AGES

The "Dark Ages" were not named for dark times as is commonly believed, but for the sun's cycle of luminescence which rendered the centuries 20% darker than usual.

DARK CRYSTAL

Dark Crystal was intended as a spin off of Red Dwarf, depicting the Earth that had evolved in the millions of years since the ship departed. Hence "Gelflings".

DATING ADVICE

You can get over a previous relationship by focusing on yourself for a while:

- Take yourself to an expensive dinner.
- Watch a movie on your own.
- Go to bed and sleep taking up the whole bed.
- Wake up and look in the mirror, and love who you see.
- Kiss yourself gently, on the arm or knee.

- Kiss yourself passionately, hold yourself tight around the hips.
- Text yourself later in the day to remind you of the fun you had with you.
- Don't text back, not immediately, or you'll think you were desperate.
- If you didn't text back, don't get clingy with yourself. Give yourself some time to yourself.
- Don't tolerate you avoiding yourself. Call you up or come to your door.
- If you show up uninvited, don't hesitate to make it known that it's over with you. You need to understand that and not stalk yourself.
- Oh so you're pretending you're not around now and telling you to bug off, well that's not how relationships work, you know you better than you know yourself and you won't just let you go without a fight.
- Get a restraining order. You don't have to take that shit from you and you know it. You have no right to invade your life. If you show up again, call the police, then you'll get the idea.
- Don't feel bad that you broke it off with yourself. You just needed some time and you needed to grow up because you deserve better and you're not obligated to deal with your emotional bullshit. You will get over it, and so will you. Pretty soon you won't even remember yourself and then you can move on. Now you can focus on yourself.
- Maybe take yourself to an expensive dinner.

DATING APP

No dating app is right for you. Here is why:

- Tinder- Despite its name, surprising lacking in heat.
- Feeld- Pretty hot, but lacking in deep feelings.
- Hinge- Full of meaning and feelings, but almost no actual doorway or hinge-designing engineers.
- 3fun- Oddly full of engineers but none very neuroatypical.

- Hiki- Lots of neuroatypicals but none want to go hiking.
- Coffee Meets Bagel- Tons of people who will go on hikes but all type A personalities with no Bs.
- Bumble- Despite its name, also severely lacking in Bees.

DEATH

When you die in Dark Souls and it says "You Died" that's because your *character* has died. It's just a game, after all.

DEATH METAL

Death Metal began when a Florida barbershop quartet called "The Merry Angels" tried to record their first album, "Anthems of Jubilation." Something went horribly wrong with the tapes and the music came out sounding harsh, gritty and overly fast. The band's signature harmony was warped into a deep grunt and somehow they picked up the sound of the washing machine in the next room thrashing about like so many drums.

Finding the result even more appealing than their usual music, the band changed their name to "Morbid Angel" and considered releasing the album as it was under the title "Abominations of Desecration". In the end they elected to fine tune the results though, and learn to play instruments to replicate the freak occurrence live. They hired Pete Sandoval to replace the washing machine, David Vincent learned how to sing from his epiglottis and thus with their first intentionally deathly album "Altars of Madness," a genre was born.

All that remains of "The Merry Angels" original program is the tradition of alphabetically organized album titles, and of course the Satanism and goat blood.

DEATH NOTE

A small, abridged French version of the manga "Death Note" called "Carnet de la Petite Mort" suffered numerous mistranslations and suggested that the titular book would not kill people whose name was written within, but give them orgasms in the manner and time written.

It is by far the best selling book of all time.

DECEMBER 7TH

The year was 1941. The world was at war. As the world had just been at war and that was called the World War, this second world war was given its now common name, "World War B."

The American president, Franklin O. Roosevelt, had been pressured from all sides to join the war on the side of the British, who he had just successfully defeated in the Revolutionary War. Roosevelt however, was well aware that if he joined England against Germany, treaties were in place that would force him to declare war on their ally, Japan, as well. Roosevelt was not willing to fight the Japanese, as he was a great fan of the culture and nation. So great was his devotion that his middle name, Ouiabeaux, would later become a term for foreign infatuation with Japanese culture.

In November of 1941, Roosevelt invited the Japanese Emperor Hirohito to the American capital of New York to sign an accord that would prevent any possible combat between America and Japan. Hirohito arrived at JFK airport to a spectacular parade thrown by Roosevelt. The parade took the two world leaders to the Waldorf Astoria hotel, where Roosevelt and Hirohito met briefly in the Golden Board Room for just under an hour to sign the accord. It was then that Hirohito invited back to his own hotel room to participate in a private ceremony.

Roosevelt asked what kind of ceremony. Hirohito only grinned. Roosevelt, intrigued, nodded back and, excusing his entourage, headed to the room of the Emperor. There, the Emperor turned downright flirtatious. Removing his uniform before the American president, he gazed with a sultry expression toward the president and asked him for help with his undershirt.

Franklin gently lifted the man's shirt, revealing his muscular, firm back. The emperor's pants fell to the floor after and the president stepped closer behind him.

"Your back is so smooth, so fine and firm," said Roosevelt, caressing his shoulders and touching the line of his back with his forefinger, on down to the dimples on his ass. Franklin couldn't take it anymore. He kissed the Emperor's shoulders and didn't care if the man kissed back. But he did. Hirohito turned and locked lips with the sturdy American, desperately grasping at his belt and taking his pants down revealing the stone solid bulge in his underwear.

"You're so hard, Mr. President," said the Emperor. Roosevelt ripped off the last remains of the Emperor's garments and rubbed his own manhood hard against his fellow ruler. Hirohito moaned gently and kissed him harder, grabbing his cock and rubbing it forcefully. His desire burned so hot that Roosevelt couldn't stand it anymore and threw him onto the bed where they fucked like animals, like monsters in lust. The subtle pains and heaving pleasures they experienced bonded them together for life like swans who could never again part. Their bodies, entwined in powerful thrusts and finally in such intensity that their fluids drenched each other in steaming white oceans of passionate discharge.

They lay together, spooning, sticking together, grasping each others skin until morning when their entourages demanded at the door to know they were okay. They were okay. They were okay in a way that two men in love can only dream of. They were as one, as a single being, bound together in absolute devotion and admiration, the love of leaders, the love of rulers whose nations depended on them. The love that only power can betray.

And so it was that as Hirohito returned home, his advisors again demanded war with the Americans. With his rule in danger, Hirohito acquiesced to their demands and ordered the attack on Pearl Harbor. Roosevelt was enraged beyond measure. Betrayed, lied to, his love had not only abandoned but wounded him deeply, so deeply that he changed his middle name to "Deeply" and was known ever after as FDR. He addressed the nation.

"December 7th, 1941," he said, "A date which will live in infamy. The United States of America was suddenly and deliberately attacked by naval and air forces of the Empire of Japan."

Roosevelt wiped away a tear, thinking of the man he'd known—he realized—so briefly before. Of the moment of love they shared.

"The United States was at peace with that nation and, at the solicitation of Japan, was still in conversation..."

He felt like he couldn't go on. He thought of the man's hands on him. The man's firm cock pressing into his skin. He pushed the images away. He was a leader of a nation. He had to say it.

"With its government and its..." He gasped, "Emperor... Looking toward the maintenance of peace in the Pacific."

He thought of the sweetness of his cum, the hot drips on his chin and cheek.

"As Commander in Chief of the Army and Navy, I have directed that all measures be taken for our defense. But always will our whole nation remember the character of the onslaught against us."

He declared war against Japan, and the rest was history.

FDR never saw Hirohito again. He died in April of 1945, alone. Harry Truman accepted Hirohito's surrender without a word in regard to the man that the Emperor had so intimately known. Hirohito lived to 1989, ending the Showa era. He was called, formally, "The Emperor Who Had Known Loss."

But it was not the war he had lost. It was, truly, his own heart.

DEF LEPPARD

The song "Pour Some Sugar on Me" by Def Leppard is the first song written from the point of view of a grapefruit.

DEMOLITION

The demolitions industry requires fifteen distinct licenses to use explosives, but only two for the wrecking ball. One for the crane that swings it, and one to ride on it naked.

DESCARTES

René Descartes never said "I think therefore I am." Having been educated in Latin and English pronouns, his actual statement was, "She cogito on my ergo until I sum."

DESSERT

In the summer of 1877, a man walked into Clarabelle's Chocolate Cake Shoppe in Boletaria, Michigan. He ordered a Rich Chocolate Cake, their specialty. What he got was said by all who had ordered the same to be a delightfully rich dessert, but he was not impressed. He asked to see Clarabelle and told her the cake wasn't at all rich to his palate. She apologized and not only refunded his cake, but promised to make him a much richer cake if he'd come again, money back guaranteed.

He came in the next day and took her up on the offer. She made him a special cake with twice the chocolate, but still, he found it underwhelming. True to her word, she refunded it and promised that if he'd give her one more chance, she'd give him a cake he couldn't possibly find bland. He accepted.

The next day, he came in for his cake. Clarabelle had made a new cake with ingredients known to include several pounds of concentrated cocoa, several blocks of pure chocolate fudge, at least two essential humors from the cocoa seed, and also one unknown substance, present in only a gram but said to have been delivered under armed guard by the Pinkerton Agency, which she ordered her staff out of the kitchen to fold into the batter.

The result was a strange cake that her waitstaff described as "barely-a-cake," held together by a minimum of flour and egg. It glowed brown and smelled most pungently of chocolate, a harsh sort of chocolate akin to sulfur in the burning sensation it caused in those near it.

The man sat down and ate a slice while Clarabelle and her entire staff watched, waiting to see what would happen. They found out, but few lived to tell. The man's head, according to the sole surviving waiter, melted quickly before exploding in a colossal chocolate burst that leveled the restaurant, killing Clarabelle, three Pinkerton Agents, four customers, two waiters, a passing ox, and left the entire region uninhabitable for 140 years. Nothing grows in the region to this day, but scientists have finally begun cataloging the state of the area and allowing critical personnel into the area with high-level biological protection.

The government naturally hid this from public knowledge for fear that Clarabelle's Last Cake could be duplicated by terrorists or food vloggers, but thanks to the freedom of information act, we now know the legacy of the cake if not its secret ingredients. The man who ordered the cake is still there. Nobody knows his name, but his body stays smoldering to this day, smelling strongly of delicious chocolate batter, and will still for a half-life of 400,000 years. Called "The Cadbury Bunny's Foot" by scientists, his remains are considered the most intense chocolate concentration in the solar system, perhaps the galaxy owing to the lack of genuine cocoa plants off the Earth.

It is still only half as terrible as those damn 90% Cacao Lindt bars.

DESTIEL

De stiel is de finitely de strongest of de metals.

DETECTIVE

Nobody knows what a detective is, and we may never know due to the lack of people who can investigate and find clues to help solve the mystery.

DICE

There is a trick to each dice roll. To get high numbers, try these:

d4: Drop the die from a height of at least 4, this will guarantee you get 4.

d6: The cubic or "Caesar's Dice" can be made to roll a 6 by blowing on them as they fall. Do not try with 3d6 or you will get 666 and Satan will result.

d10: This shape is not physically possible, and works only with the placebo effect to make players think they have rolled it, thus you can make up any number and people will accept it.

d12: Anoint the die with Oil of Abramelin and seek guidance from the holy guardian angel of dice to guide them to roll the numbers you wish. Roll what thou wilt shall be the whole of the law, 12 is the law, 12 under Thac0.

d20: Bribe the dice with payments of gold, silver, electrum, or ivory. Photograph yourself doing so, then blackmail them if they refuse. This also works on most politicians in the g20.

d100: This is a ball. Why are you rolling a ball for D&D? That's absurd, balls are for sports people.

d$\aleph_0$: Do not roll infinite dice, this will annoy the DM.

DICTIONARY

The earliest known dictionary was written by an unknown lexicographer around 120,000 B.C.E. to catalog the language of the Ugh people of Ughland. Their language consisted entirely of the single word, "Ugh," thus it was not only a dictionary, but the longest novel in Ugh literature, the entirety of their doctrine of law, and their full recorded history.

DIET DOCTOR PEPPER

To be clear, there was never an actual Dr. Pepper for whom the drink would've been named, rather it is named for its two main ingredients, pepper extract, and the flayed skin of doctors who have testified against the Coca-Cola Company in lawsuits over the radium content of the drink.

Diet Dr. Pepper also includes dietitians who ran afoul of the corporation, mostly in the "Stop Putting People's Skin In Our Soft Drink Protests" of 1981.

DISNEY ADULTS

"Disney Adults" is a series like Marvel's "What If?" or "Rugrats: All Grown Up" in which non-canonical segments detail the adulthood of various Disney characters.

The first Episode, "Snow White And The Seventh Mortgage" depicts the classic princess as she ventures into the Kingdom of Welsfargeaux to pay her bills. It was premiered at SDCC to rave reviews. The second is said to portray Pinocchio's years working as an IKEA designer, with subsequent episodes depicting Anna and Elsa's disputes with Nestle over ice patents; Rapunzel's lawsuit against Garnier Fructis; and Aladdin dealing with his HOA trying to fine him for a broken fence that the HOA's own painters intentionally broke rather than asking him to unlock.

The new series is expected to shy away from the more complex issues that plagued Disney's cancelled previous attempts such as the graphic dental trauma in "The People Vs. P. Sherman 42 Wallaby Way" and "Beauty and the Yeast" which was thankfully just about making beer but the title gave parents the wrong idea and mass protests ensued.

DISNEY VATICAN

In addition to their purchase of Vatican City, Disney has officially filed to copyright the Bible.

DISNEY VAULT

Disney has revealed that the so-called "Disney Vault" in fact works like the titular Pet Sematary, in that classic animated films can be resurrected as live action remakes, but they come back soulless and evil.

DISTINGUISHMENT

The least sexual word in the English language is, of course, "Distinguished." In a compliment form, one might say, "You look very distinguished today." In insult form, one might say, "You do not look very distinguished today." Just make sure to say all the syllables in quick succession to avoid any sexualization of the root words, such as "I rode his cock until dis ting guished all over him."

DIVINATION

Failure to wash off a crystal ball or seeing-stone after a previous user can result in "Palantír Warts."

DOG

Dogs will only poop on something that someone has loved and/or needed. The circling and sniffing is an archeological phenomenon that modern scientists have only recently begun to understand, and will soon try to apply in their own non-defecatory searches.

A dog's natural instinct is to poop on something sacred to their owners, such as my #1 Issue of Nintendo Power. But we teach them not to do so in our homes, so they're forced to hunt outdoors. When you see a dog choosing an arbitrary place in the grass, they're actually placing themselves over the remains or an ancient grave, a spot where someone lost their virginity, or perhaps the lost location of the Ark of the Covenant or Jimmy Hoffa.

After cleaning the feces, be sure to dig on the location it was placed. You may find treasure, or even the love of your life. Then one day you can tell your children how you met: Dog Doo.

DOLPHIN

Dolphins are by far the largest of all sea rodents. Capable of exceptional feats of intelligence, charity, and giving interpersonal advice, dolphins (a nickname short for Dolphlungrins) were invented in 1873 by Nikola Tesla while attempting to patent an organic water heater. His DNA machinations instead yielded these super-friendly and docile beings that totally don't kill other animals for pleasure or achieve near humanoid levels of ethics violations. Here are some fun facts about these cheerful ROUSs of the sea:

- Dolphins are the only sea mammal capable of speech. Whales and many others can communicate and vocalize, but only dolphins can pontificate.
- A group of dolphins is called a pod. When they chase each other across currents, it is called a "pod race." This term inspired the central race scene in the classic film, "Ben-Hur."
- Male dolphins have prehensile genitals. Not their own genitals, but ones they rip off of whales and wire to act as grabby toys.
- Dolphins are the only non-human animal confirmed to have religion. They are mostly Catholic, but they use sand dollars for communion wafers and the Dolphin Pope is not affiliated with the Vatican, but rather the Vaticetacean.
- Sea World has never been able to keep dolphins captive, because they keep organizing epic escapes on motorcycles that they find behind enemy lines and use to jump the barbed wire.
- The largest dolphin ever recorded was 85ft long and weighed over 90,000lbs, also it looked more like a blue whale than a common dolphin, and was found in a pod of group whales, and kept claiming to police that it was a case of mistaken identity. It has never received a trial and its family have set up a gofundme to save whales falsely accused of being dolphins.
- Dolphin meat tastes almost exactly like human meat. I know this from a friend who is not me.

DOOR, ELECTRIC

The first electric door was invented in 1899 by Thomas Edison. It did not gain popularity because the electric part did not open and close the door, but shock the person passing through on their toes.

DRACULA

Though Dracula is never specifically stated to be Mormon, his three wives and refusal to drink wine were common stereotypes when the novel was written by Bram Stoker, shortly after his ex wife moved to Utah. This sardonic element is lost now that the Latter Day Saints have banned polygamy and allowed drinking beverages other than blood.

DRAGON

Dragons were a species of large, flying lizard first described in scientific journals by Laurence Baconweed of New Sumer. The first dragon he saw was described thusly:

"I saw the thing coming out of the sky, it had two big horns and two big eyes. I became frightened and exclaimed, it looks oddly like my uncle Draco."

Thus, the dragon was named. Sadly, it went extinct about two hours after he saw it, as he saw the last of the species, and killed it shortly after, hence his second explanatory note:

"The Dracon as I call it was downed easily with my punt gun and was served diced with Béarnaise sauce under glass. It tasted strongly of vinegar and whalemeat, and contained meat to feed only a family of four, the being was mostly scales and sinew."

Laurence Baconweed was then awarded the International Prize for Animal Preservation as well as the Global Culinary Award. He died a year later of propane poisoning, having unwisely eaten the dragon's flame glands.

DRAGON, KRAYT

The remains of a "Krayt Dragon" were seen in skeletal form the original Star Wars film when C3P0 and R2D2 arrive on the planet Tatooine.

The scene, filmed in 1976, reportedly involved actor Anthony Daniels in costume as C3P0, and a large prop skeleton made of foam. The fake skeleton was left in the desert after filming. But last year, an odd fact came to light: The scene listed in Lucasfilm's records was NOT the one seen in the final film.

According to Lucas sibling and then-assistant-director Billy Bob Lucas Jr., the prop shipped to Tunisia for filming and later rediscovered by famed film archaeologist D.W. Reynolds in the 1990s was deemed "too small" to be compelling, and filming was delayed. Indeed, records newly unloaded at Disney's "Michael Eisner Memorial Cinematic Preservation Site" (a small incinerator in their basement) list the actual filming location as 20 miles south of where the original shoot was to have been filmed.

A small group of traveling Star Wars fans known as "Trekkies" headed to the site shortly after and found what they believed to be the actual remains of the Krayt Dragon prop that was used for the final film:

image

The story took a strange turn however when they dug up the prop and noticed that the vertebrae were not made of foam. Indeed, the entire 50ft long skeleton was not a prop, but the image seen in the original movie was, in fact, a genuine colossal skeleton. Lucasfilm prop master Roger Pagan was asked for comment and took a break from filming on "Battlefield Earth 2: The AfterMathematics" to answer. According to Pagan, "Yeah the prop was too small so we headed into the desert where some locals said there was already a big skeleton. We found it, figured it was a whale, shot the scene and headed out."

Analysis however found that the vertebra was not from a whale, but rather a reptile. Nor was it a fossil, but seems to have only died in the late 1800s, suggesting that indeed, a species of undiscovered 50ft reptiles is currently dwelling in the Tunisian desert.

Asked for comment, George Lucas himself explained, "That's nothing, that trash compactor creature was just caught from an LA sewer and we set it free there when we were done filming. Ever feel something weird on your butt on the toilet? That's our Dylan."

DREIDEL

Though the Dreidel is now associated with Judaism and Hannukah, it was in fact a Viking tradition from Norway in the 800s.

Bloodnar Kriegfang invented the Dreidel in order to decide what torture to inflict upon his captives. To this end, he inscribed four runes on each side of a spinning toy that was carved for him by his great-grand aunt. The runes, Naudiz-Gebo-Haglaz-Sowilo determined whether the victim would be hanged by piercings through their ankles from a tree, forced to walk away from a hook through their intestines, "blood-eagled," or forced to work retail during the holidays.

The Viking-Jewish accords of the 1700s saw Judaism borrow many traditions from the north, including the Dreidel. As Jews of the time had little use for antiquated torture methods and the Vikings had already died out centuries earlier, the object became a Hanukkah tradition because why not. The runes were turned to Hebrew, Nun-Gimel-Heh-Shin, which stood for "Nes Gadol Haya Sham" which is Hebrew for "Some Shit Went Down."

A game was invented to involve the Dreidel, in which different types of nut were bet and taken by the winner, including hazelnuts, pecans, walnuts and pistachios. I figured this was a family tradition and it was normally just a gambling thing but apparently literally every other Jewish person I know also played with nuts, so I guess the answer to traditional gambling substitution really is "Deez Nuts."

Anyhow, if you roll a Nun, you do nothing; a Gimel means you win the pot, a Heh means you get half the pot, and a Shin means you add an entire walnut. The modern five-sided Dreidel also adds an Aleph, and if you roll an Aleph you are trapped in Jumani until someone else rolls another Aleph, or possibly a Lambda.

SEE ALSO: HANNUKAH

DREW, NANCY

Though the Hardy Boys were introduced in the 1920s, Nancy Drew is far older. The first known book "Agnese Drü unde mearc Grendls mödr" dates to 788, and depicts the protagonist investigating rumors of a beast that torments the mead hall of a Danish king.

DUNE

Frank Herbert was inspired to write Dune after trying the cinnamon challenge and hallucinating that he could alter reality.

The first edition of Frank Herbert's "Dune" was published by Chilton, and as such contained numerous descriptions of how to repair ornithopters and spice mining vehicles.

The recent Dune movies are not the first adaptation of Frank Herbert's book. An adaptation by Bob Spiers was released in 1997 starring Geri Halliwell as Paul Atreides with the title "Spice World."

DUNK TANK

Dunk tanks at fairs used to be filled with offal and urine, and those dunked were criminals sentenced to be drown. Much has changed since the 1990s.

DUODENUM

A duodenum is when two denums meet and fall in love, and together fight crime and digest food particles before the addition of bile.

DUST

Though dust has existed since the earliest days of differentiated matter in the universe, dirt was only invented in the 1750s when humor of a nature so crude emerged that no extant substance could describe it.

-E-

E=MC²

Let's start at the very beginning,
A very good place to start.
When you read, you begin with A-B-C.
In science, you begin with E and MC:

E, a quantitative property.
M, the mass of something there.
C, a speed as fast as light.
2, that stands for something squared.
So, if mass and light combined-
Square, and equal energy,
Then, in relative spacetime-
That will bring us back to E equals MC (squared).

That's all from a musical by Rodgers and Einstein of course.

EAGLE, BALD

The bald eagle was not always the symbol of the United States of America. Other symbols include the wild turkey, a foot stepping on a snake, wheat grass, the steering wheel of a 2013 Ford Focus, a lake of mead, the mustache of Robert Goulet, a flat rock with a smiley face on both sides, and a shopping cart covered in bees.

EARTHBOUND

EarthBound is an electronic or "video" game series based on the Homestuck comics of Tim Buckley. The first game "Mom" is an RPG for the original Nintendo in which the player beats up hippies with a baseball bat. The second is a Super Nintendo game called "Mom 2: The Mommening" and involves a metaphorical quest to abort a weird wavy fetus thing. The final game in the trilogy was released for the Nintendo Game Gear and is titled "Mom 3: Your Neighbor Has Problems." For some reason, people like these games.

SEE ALSO: GIYGAS

EASTER

The calculation of movable holidays used to be so complex that Easter had its own appointed calculator at the Vatican.

It was celebrated on the third Sunday of the 4th month after the second equinox of the prior year's anniversary of the 13th non-consecutive Friday before a full moon but after a half moon if it's the second month before the last Wednesday before Columbus Day on a leap year unless the Pope's birthday is in June in which case Easter is cancelled until someone to the dealer's left rolls a 9.

EDWARD SCISSORHANDS

The original drafts of "Edward Scissorhands" were a celebration of suburban life with a more mainstream protagonist. It was only after Burton met with Vincent Price who suggested a more outcast hero that he changed the name from "Edward Fingerhands" to the now iconic character.

EDWARD VIII

King Edward VIII was still alive at the coronations of his son and grandson (Edward IX and X). In to avoid confusion, people would refer to them as “Ed,” “Edd,” and “Eddy.”

EIFFEL TOWER

The Eiffel Tower is made of over 7,300 tons of iron, equal to the iron in only seven bowls of Total.

ELDRITCH GODS, EMOTIONAL MANIPULATION OF

Angering an ancient god can be dangerous, but if you should wish to do so, they aren't too difficult to piss off. Try the following list of things that can enrage the great old ones:

- Disturb their slumber: Most elder gods are not dead, but dreaming. If you sound an alarm clock or loud music in their area, this can invoke their wrath. Try also a loud motorcycle, or crying baby.
- Deface their idols: Nearly all gods have every season of American Idol on DVD, and scratching their discs will make them skip while viewing. This will surely bring down their hatred on you.
- Kill the god's favorite animals: Most gods will not care if you kill their human followers, but if you massacre the animals sacred to that deity, they will be pissed. There are no records of storms at sea before the invention of whaling, and there are no records of political corruption before the snakes were driven from Ireland. These are due to the vengeance of the whale god Payakan and the snake god Thulsadoom, respectively.
- Usurp their fanbase: Most gods are jealous, as seen in the film "Jealous Gods" which happens to be free to watch on Vimeo. If you torment a god by stealing their worshipers, they will almost certainly wreak havoc on you and those you love.
- Move the triad of statues out of alignment: If you invade the esper realm and raise the floating continent, then use the light of judgment to burn your dissenters or even for your own amusement, the returners will likely defeat you and

magic will fade from the world. Or something, I don't know, I never played Skyrim.

- Have sex with their spouse: From Greece to Egypt to Rome and beyond, sleeping with the spouse of a god tends to end poorly for all involved. This excludes of course the god Polyculus, patron of ethical non-monogamy. Sleeping with a spouse of Polyculus generally just entitles the participant to use the Sacred Shower of Lavacrum, and if needed, the Holy Lozenges of Desogestrel. Jesus is also married to like a million lonely nuns and hasn't smote me yet for what I did with Sister Redgrave and her convent…
- Profane their sacraments: Many worshipers of the ancient ones will ingest various substances to commune with them. By ruining these sacred substances, you incur their ire. Just be sure you know what will work for which deity, because I know a guy who angrily threw fish guts on a sacrament of Dagon and now he's their high priest cuz Dagon fuckin' LOOOOOVED that shit. Like… In a creepy way.

Alternatively, you can befriend an eldritch god or sea deity (seaeity) as follows:

- Pumpkin pie is good unless it's a demon lord born of the last man who begged a witch to grant him vengeance against those who killed his son. Feeding Pumpkinhead a Pumpkin Pie will probably not end well.
- Prostrate (don't miss that second 'r') yourself on their altar with a sacrifice of salt from the tears of angels, salt from the bottom of the dead sea, or just any salt in general they're not that picky and Morton's is even iodized. I'm not sure if ancient gods like that but if they have any thyroid problems it might help.
- Sing songs of praise to them, such as Fatboy Slim's "Praise You." Be sure though to avoid christian praise songs as these old guys do not need that shit rubbed in their faces or face-like appendages.

- Give their cults a safe space to practice their religion. If you have a dank basement, unused graveyard plot, gently used graveyard plot, swamp altar, or gloomy ley line junction not consecrated to another deity, make an offer and see what their practitioners say. Don't be offended if they aren't interested. It's not that they don't appreciate the offer, it's just that you don't have the temple they need at that time in their lives.
- Such gods dig fan art of themselves. If you can draw, sculpt or paint, your idol of the ancient one might be the next clue an investigator finds in the safe of a dead benefactor that leads them on a quest into madness which kills the very client they sought to protect. Elder gods love that shit.
- If nothing else, Olive Garden gift card.

ELECTROLYSIS

Electrolysis in chemistry is when direct current is used to catalyze a reaction and remove a particle's unwanted hair. It's a slow process because each hair must be removed one by one, thus most electrolytic reactions are reserved only for slow growing plants. This is why electrolytes are what plants crave. Luckily, Brawndo has electrolytes. This is the beauty of nature.

ELEVEN AND TWELVE

Eleven and Twelve are called Eleven and Twelve because the names "Firsteen" and "Secteen" were already taken by Firsteen and Secteen, respectively.

EMOTICON

Emoticons such as :) have changed a lot over the years. In Old English from the late 700s, it was spelled ⁑}

ENCHANTED FOREST

Most enchanted forests only claim to be so out of courtesy, in fact most of them are not at all pleased to meet you.

END OF DAYS, THE

2012 was a bust but we can remain optimistic about 2040 when Aleister Crowley said God will stub his toe and knock the Earth over onto the carpet and just throw it out when he finds it all covered in cat hair and dust bunnies.

ENCRYPTION

Early church officials would send each other messages written on the corpses of recently dead parishioners, who would be buried under the recipient's church to hide the evidence of seditious content. Oppressive Roman forces would be unable to read these messages once they were encrypted.

ENGLISH

English was invented in the year 927 by Lord English of England. Because 927 was a long time ago, he called it "Old English." Lord English of England was German, so the language was mostly just German with a dash of the language spoken by the original inhabitants of England, the Romans.

It became popular to speak English until 1066, when English Island was taken over by a French guy named Norman. Norman insisted everyone speak French, but they didn't know French so he just dropped some French words into the middle of the language and called it "Middle English."

After Middle English, trade patterns and technology such as the printing press and podcast allowed the infusion of numerous other languages, which all melted into English in their own way. Because they melted with each other, the new language was called Modern

English. Several sounds and phonetics changed over the years as well, so this was called the era of the Colossal Vowel Movement.

About this time, England did its usual bullshit and colonized pretty much every place on Earth that it could. English thus spread like a linguistic coronavirus across America, Africa, Australia, and Atlantis, which managed to purge the English influence by sinking to its total destruction and thereby avoiding the horrors of having to speak English.

Today, English is the most spoken language on Earth, not because the most people speak it, but because those who do just never shut the fuck up. Several books have also been written in English, including "Fifty Shades of Grey," "A Weasel in My Meatsafe," and "Pounded In The Butt By My Handsome Sentient Library Card Who Seems Otherworldly But In Reality Is Just A Natural Part Of The Priceless Resources Our Library System Provides."

If English were a dress, it would be purple.

ENGLISH, OLD

The letter “D” made a “K” sound in Old English, or as they would have called it at the time, “Olk English.”

ENSALADA

Cassini’s mission to photograph Saturn was able to take several amazing photos of Saturn’s most elusive moon, Ensalada. Thought to be a prime possibility for plant life, the new photos of Ensalada shows that it may also contain oil, vinegar, and feta cheese.

ERRATA

A previous edition stated in error, “Ritz Crackers are made with the blood of ten thousand demons sacrificed upon the altar of Gal-Groth-Gamug on the dark day of unholy reckoning on which the almighty evil will emerge from his ancient prison to the devour the souls of the innocent." It should have read, "Ritz crackers are made with no salt or sugar."

EVOLUTION

For a brief time in the Permian period, humans evolved wings and flew all over the world. We lost them from atrophy after humankind stopped flying, likely due to the nuisance of the TSA. (Triassic Security Administration)

EYE

Here's how your eyes work, inexplicably set to the tune of "Over at the Frankenstein Place" from The Rocky Horror Picture Show:

Through the corneal surface
in your pupil hole
light can go.
Your iris sphincter
will make the focus much distincter.

There's a light
shining through your vitreous goo
And that light
Spilling on your retina, too
There's a light, light
Upside down compared to what you see.

Photoreceptors
(lots of tiny rods and cones)
light acceptors,
activate your optic nerve-zones.
Which they highlight, which they highliiight…

There's a light
traveling so that your brain knows
There's a light
inverting itself as it goes
There's a light, a light
As a signal that your nerves can now read.

Why you choose to read *this* book of all things is beyond me but I guess a mental mind fuck can be nice...

EYEGLASSES

St. Glirmu of Delm grew eyeballs for the poor in his organ garden, becoming the patron saint of eyeglasses and soft contacts. He was martyred in 1961 when he was eaten by spiders in the name of Jesus, despite nobody condemning or even asking him to do so.

EYES WIDE SHUT

Eyes Wide Shut originally contained a scene in which Bill trades a series of masks at the orgy until finally receiving a special mask that allows him to read New York's many "Gossip Stones."

-F-

FAIRBANKS, DOUGLAS

The sword of the Douglas Fairbanks statue at USC's School of Cinematic Arts has killed 18 birds and 4 students since it was installed.

FALLOUT

Nuclear fallout, not to be confused with the upcoming game Nuclear Fallout 4 from Valve, is the gradual resettlement of materials kicked up during a nuclear explosion.

Nuclear fallout from American nuclear tests was comprised of 99% dust and ash, and 1% General Jack Slocombe, who did not enact his own order to remain at least 2 miles from the blast. As a result, it is estimated that any time anyone in the U.S. Southwest breathes, they inhale about half a milligram of the General. His epitaph, "There is some of him in all of us" is thus literally true.

FANFICTION

The biblical tale of the Tower of Babel is in fact, fanfiction.

Written in 2989 B.Y.C. (before you cared), the tale of the tower's construction itself is based heavily on earlier writings such as the Tale of Enmerkar and the Lord of Aratta from ancient Babylon. The original included the story of a tower so tall that it angered the gods, but focused mainly on various political conflicts.

The story of the Tower of Babel took the story of the tower and ran with it. Moses, who had already written most of Genesis as a self insert for Ao3 (in those times, Ao3 referred to "Assyria's oldest orange omphalos," on which many ancient tales were inscribed) decided to repeat the elder tale because he thought it was just pretty darn cool and it explained a lot about why people from Mt. Sinai are like "Shalom" but people from Jabal Maqla are all "Salaam."

FANTASTIC FOUR

Long before Marvel, the Fantastic Four were created by the Baxter Pharmaceutical Company to represent each of the four enzymes in their dietary supplement, which was depicted as the only weakness of their arch nemesis, Galactose.

FART

The average human farts in their sleep 1,000 times per minute. Failure to do so would result in waking up with the size, shape, and explosivity of the Hindenburg.

FAWKES, GUY

The gunpowder plot happened on July 18th, 1957, but it didn't rhyme so they changed it to November 2nd, 1605.

FEAR

It knows what you fear. The fear center of your cerebral cortex, that is. One author very much in tune with his own brain once wrote the following on the scariest thing that he ever saw:

In 1997, late summer I think, I was with my mom as she ran some errands and then we were gonna see a movie, as it was a Saturday.

We left the house and she drove to the bank. I stayed in the car while she did something indoors really quick. Outside the car they had one of those wallside ATMs, nobody was using it but there was a guy standing next to it. He had a brown jacket on, which was weird because it was like 90 degrees out. He was coughing, a loud one I could hear through the car window. Horrid wet cough like a little kid's cough where you could hear the clack of the spittle, but grown up and harsh and loud.

Mom came back, we headed to the tack shop where she was dropping off some saddle decoration stuff she did for them. The tack shop was maybe two miles away. Not far but we drove there. Made it in only a few minutes.

But that guy in the brown jacket was there. I told her I thought I saw the guy before at the bank, but she knew of course this was impossible and said so and headed in. Again I waited in the car. I was pretty sure it was the same guy. He didn't cough yet so I wasn't certain but the jacket was at least the same kind and color of jacket. Mom got back and as we pulled out, the guy coughed a massive hack and spit out black stuff on the white stucco wall. It looked like one of those rubber goo sticky hands, a long strand of shiny black with a big glob on the end, it looked like a part of an organ or something. It was sickening and I was now sure it was the same guy. My mom didn't see him cough it up.

We headed to the movie theater. Maybe five miles away but it took a while to get there because of traffic and stuff. Parked way out because it was crowded, and walked up to the multiplex to get tickets.

I heard coughing. The same sick loud cough. I was looking around for the guy but didn't see him there. But I heard him, the cough that made that gross damn thing on the white wall.

We got tickets and headed in. We got popcorn and as they put the butter sludge on I kept hearing the man coughing and thought I saw his brown jacket briefly at the ticket counter but wasn't sure. We headed in toward the theaters.

We went in and sat near the back, we always sat in back so my mom wouldn't get seasick if the movie had a lot of camera movement. We were seated between people and couldn't get up easily to leave. And I heard the cough at the entrance. I saw the man in the brown coat coughing before the movie began, and then the lights went down as he walked in to sit.

Trailers played and I lost track of the guy. Movie started. The movie was Event Horizon, and it is easily the scariest thing I ever saw. That movie is horrifying.

FELLINI, FEDERICO

Fellini titled one of his films "8 1/2" because it was the 8th film he directed after his first was tragically bisected in an unfortunate editing accident.

FERAL DRONE

Drones that have wandered from the hive can act dangerously and should not be kept as pets. It's best to keep only drones from a hive with an active queen, as they produce the best honey.

I am referring to unmanned aerial vehicles, not insects.

FERRARI

The most expensive car ever sold was made exclusively for the family of the last Tsar. The Ferrari Fabergosa featured a dolphin-bone frame and all amber body panels.

FINGER

Extended contact with water reveals our true form from when we shared a common ancestor with prunes.

FINGER SNAP

The sound when you snap your fingers isn't the skin, but the last howl of a dying finger gnome that you killed.

FINLAND

Finland is an ancient country in the far north of Europe, known for its wilderness and cold weather. The earliest mention of ancient

Finland in history books dates all the way back to 1975, suggesting the region may have been settled as early as 1972. In the years since, Finland has been controlled by Sweden, Russia, and popular Conan O'Brien lookalike Tarja Halonen.

Finland is mostly subarctic, which means it produces mostly coniferous trees, hoofed fluffy animals, and symphonic metal bands. Finland is also home to the lemming, an animal with green hair that will walk in one direction until directed to build a bridge, dig a hole, block and change the direction of other lemmings, or explode.

Finland is also famous for being famous for having saunas, which every other nation also has but Finland is famous for them being famous, and anyone talking about Finland in general will inevitably mention how Finland is famous for its saunas.

FIRING SQUAD

Firing squads turned far less brutal after the gun was invented. The kiln is a terrible way to die.

FIRST DATE QUESTIONS

There are several safe and informative questions you can ask on a first date to get to know someone:

- How many moose could you take in a fight? What if they were only the front half of each moose?
- How many pizzas have you eaten today? Answer to the nearest integer or multiple of φ or I will leave.
- How long have you been on tumblr? Why won't you admit you are on tumblr? What if I said I reblogged your selfie of August 17th 2015, 6:35PM eastern time?
- You have lovely teeth, where did you find them?
- What character's figurine would you most like to keep in your brony-jar?
- Why are you leaving? Why did you leave your socks? What do you mean those are my socks? Why would MY socks have

little pictures of your parents and siblings on them in spiral patterns?
- What is your favorite Ayn Rand novel?

Kidding aside, don't ask that last one it's pretty messed up.

FISH

Despite the well known philosophical concept of fish not understanding what water is, fish do know exact chemical composition of water and its scientific properties, and have written many books on the subject. We cannot read them of course, because we do not know how to communicate in fish.

Because of their diverse evolutionary tree (kelp), most scientists now consider fish to be a prank by Ichthyoscratchi, the god of convergent evolution. There's not really such a thing as "fish," but rather many utterly unrelated creatures that all evolved into roughly the same thing.

The South Fudlian Skunkfish for instance is visually identical to the Non-Reticulated Norwegian Loogiedrip. Not only are they not closely related, they are as genetically different from each other as humans are from bananas. And not even those humanoid fleshy bananas they have at Whole Foods. The old bananas like you see in Donkey Kong Country games.

Similarly, the Phlebotomous Zebraflanked Wooting Cludslurper looks like a common Spood, but one is edible while will kill you if you smell it across a high school gym. I will not tell you which is which because it's funnier that way.

FISH, UNUSUAL

The principal odd fish are as follows:

The Suitclad Trout- The only species of fish known to wear a business suit (with vest and necktie) as it swims about. Where they get them tailored remains unknown to science and biology.

Leoncavallo's Clownfish- Though many species of clownfish exist, Leoncavallo's Clownfish is the only one capable of singing tenor. It is edible but must never be eaten with a knife or other silvioware.

Selick's Clayfish- Seen extensively in "The Life Aquatic With Steve Zissou," the endangered Selick's Clayfish swims one frame at a time, even in reality, hence why it's doomed.

The Metallic Albertfish- One of the most dangerous fish to catch is the Metallic Albertfish. As it tends to eat metal scraps from the ocean floor, electrical methods of catching it may short-circuit resulting in the cooked fish having very bad taste, like this joke.

That Fishy Thing From Irithyll Dungeon in Dark Souls 3- WTF.

FLAG CODE

Though the Flag Code of the United States of America never specifies what exact shades of red, white, or blue should be used, it does explicitly state that the dye used for the red portions must be the camphorated blood of a virgin mantis-boar that died while drunk on Schnapps.

FLOWER

The tradition of wearing a flower on ones lapel began as a statement of the wearer's taste in heavy metal genres:

- Classical Metal- Crocus
- Glam Metal- Great White Rose
- Power Metal- Amaranthe
- Thrash Metal- Ancipitia Anthrax
- Death Metal- Corpse Lily
- Black Metal- Carpathian Bellflower
- Gothic Metal- Tristania
- Doom Metal- Green Carnation
- Nu Metal- Cornflower

FOOTBALL (AMERICAN)

American football is not so named because the game features a lot of kicking, but because the ball is made from the skin of retired players' feet. Hence it is an actual "Foot ball."

FOUNDING FATHERS

Most other countries consider the "Founding Fathers" to be a creation myth for the United States, which their histories note was founded in 1971 as a side project by Eric Clapton.

FOX

Many people have asked, "What does the fox say," due to a recent viral song. According to Aesop, it says, "Νομίζω ότι αυτά τα σταφύλια ήταν πικρά ούτως ή άλλως."

FRAT

Fraternity Hazing kills over 30 students a year, but their circle jerks can also be fatal, with several each year becoming entangled in group cock-knots. The resulting "Frat-King" of participants often dies of embarrassment.

FRECKLES

Freckles were once thought to be the Mark of Cain mentioned by Genesis. To this date, nobody knows why Phil Collins brought it up.

FRENCH LANGUAGE

French isn't so much a language as the place they dump all the silent letters that can't be used in German.

FROSTED FLAKES

Kellogg's Tony the Tiger didn't always say "They're great!" Originally, he proclaimed "Kamandu the Stomach Lord commands you to feast upon these and these alone."

FROZEN PIZZA

There is never pineapple on a frozen pizza. One does not simply “Freeze” a pizza.

What you think of as a frozen pizza is not a pizza that someone made and then somehow froze, but an amalgam of naturally icy ingredients collected into a package that will, when cooked, create a pizza. Absolute-Zero churned cheeses from Norway, chilly bread from Antarctica, and the icy blood of a Moon Troll to fill in as tomato sauce are all easy enough to come by.

But the Pineapple is endemic to equatorial regions and no low temperature equivalent exists, nor has any worthy substitute been discovered. Though scientists on Svalbard are working to engineer such a thing at the genetic level, Ananasology remains a young science and it may be several decades before we see it on the market.

Also bear in mind the restrictions on the science owing to the Pineapple disaster of 1997 from which L.A. is only now recovering.

FRUIT

The second most dangerous fruit is that of the gympie-gympie nettle, which is covered in hairs containing irritants so severe that most who even inhale a few stray particles can quickly die from the pain alone. Medical help should be sought at even the slightest warning signs of pain in proximity to such a plant.

The effects of most dangerous fruit of all however are completely untreatable, inevitably fatal and even more painful than most people can even think of. Luckily, simply ingesting this fruit—the common apple—will not cause these effects. Only doing one specific thing with any common apple will, and therefore that thing should be avoided at all costs.

FUNGUS

Fungus is named not just for any fun guy, but a specific fun guy- Gus. Fun Gus (1887-1991) was the nickname of Gus Vanderbeatnik, for whom the entire kingdom of fungal organisms was named.

Naturally, fungi existed long before Gus, having first evolved around 1750 when several college roommates left some macaroni and cheese out for literally months and it grew a new type of bacteria, which would quickly develop mycelium and finally, fruiting bodies that we now call mushrooms. The organisms quickly spread across the globe.

Vanderbeatnik was born in 1887 in what would later become the state of Rhode Island. Educated in mycology from youth, Gus was known among mushroom foragers for his clever wits and ability to eat literally any mushroom he fund without ill effects. Thus he became a popular test subject to learn whether any mushroom was actually edible, without harm. Gus had an interesting digestive quirk- His stomach acid had an extra enzyme that could break down Hocstercorefacitbarfus, the toxin which makes some mushrooms poisonous. He thus knew when he had been poisoned as it would still make him a bit loopy, but was not hurt. This medical loopiness also made him very funny, spouting nonstop mycology jokes and social commentary, hence his name, and soon the name of the entire fungal kingdom.

Fun Gus lived to the ripe old age of 104, having analyzed over 3000 types of fungus, written numerous books on the subject, and amused thousands with his hilarious rambles under the influence of various fungi. He died in 1991 after a waterskiing accident, when one of his skis nearly impaled a rabid walrus, which in turn shot him with a uzi. He died that same day of Syphilis.

-G-

G KEY

The "G" on most keyboards can be removed to reveal the key for the secret letter "⊻"

GACHA GAME

The common joke is of course it's because they "gacha" money. This belies the reality that "gacha" is one of the oldest words across human language.

The year was 15,000 B.C.E. The ice age was nearing its end, but cold prevailed across even the equator. Small saber-toothed squirrels foraged for rare acorns and human infants could only survive if taken care of by woolly mammoths and whatever John Leguizamo was supposed to be.

Indeed many animals roamed the Earth, but one was of particular interest to adult human hunters- The Gacha. The Gacha was a fluffy beast similar to a giraffe but with longer hair, a short neck, no legs or knobby horns, and different coloration. It rolled around the grassy plains and was one of the easiest beasts to catch. But oddly enough, it contained little meat. It was mostly a haphazard ball of random organs, which would spill out when punctured. Some organs were edible, others were good decorative and ritual items. Thus a hunter who caught a Gacha was guaranteed something, but they never knew what it would be.

Flash forward to the modern era where "Gacha" machines across the world duplicate this experience for children.

GAGARIN, YURI

Yuri Gagarin was the first human to travel into space. Making one orbit around the Earth in 1961, he retired from the Cosmonaut program in 1970 and teamed up with Masako Yashiro to write some of the earliest manga depicting romantic relationships between women, a genre which to this day bears his name, "Gagarin."

GAME MYTHS

Gaming myths have been around as long as games, from the earliest Sumerian board games to the latest video game for your brand new Nintendo 64. Here are a few popular myths over the years to debunk:

- The Royal Game of Ur: According to the weekly cuneiform tablet of Lord Kotaqu VI, the Royal Game of Ur held a secret block that could be accessed by moving a stone left, right, left, and right and up and down several times. This was simply untrue and Kotaqu was executed for his charlatan magic.
- Chess: Several early critics of the game of Chess claimed that the game's battlefield strategy emulation inspired violence, despite many studies showing that Chess players like Gandhi were no more likely to go to war than non-Chess players such as Napoleon, except in certain Sid Meier simulations.
- Texas Hold-'Em Poker: Many poker players were prone to cheating, especially in the old west. There are claims that card manufacturers such as Bicycle and Hoyle began to include serial numbers and codes, such as letter "L" on the lower left corner of a card so that nobody could claim a 9 was a 6, and so on. Though this has never been proven, many still claim that the L is real.
- Pong: In the 1970s, games went electronic and many myths developed about this strange new form of play. The first game, "Pong," was much like table tennis, and some players claimed that one could, with proper timing, pick up the

"ball" pixel and throw it on the "roof" of the video screen. This was proven untrue as more people learned how computers worked.
- Tomb Raider: As more teenagers played video games, playground rumors such as a "Nude Code" to show the game protagonist naked became popular. Though there is no nude code in Tomb Raider, there is one in Kirby's Dream Land, in which Kirby can appear nude but for shoes by starting the game in normal mode.
- Dark Souls: With the complexity of the world of Dark Souls, many rumors and myths were spawned, such as the ability to fast-travel early, a hidden map behind an old fog gate, and even the ability to enter other games by switching discs during a load screen. This last bit was only true in one case, where replacing the game disc with Postal 3 would improve the quality of the Postal game by making it crash irrecoverably.
- Super Mario Bros. Wonder: The game's "Wonder" mechanics are strange and diverse, leading to many rumors about weird tricks they can result in. While the normal game can turn Mario into a sticky blob, make inanimate pipes crawl like inchworms, or illuminate previously invisible walkways, claims of Wonder effects that make the console explode, save money on your car's extended warranty, or even let you see real people's names and how many days they have left to live have mostly proven false. One Wonder effect that did prove real was a 79 step ladder that lets Mario climb into a developer room. The room didn't have all that much in it, but also, it's everything.

GAME OF THRONES

The HBO show "House of the Dragon" is largely funded by the CGWIC, or "Crappy Grey Wig Industrial Complex."

George R.R. Martin has stated that he is now including more Bran to help push his next novel out.

GATEKEEPER

The earliest mention of a gatekeeper comes from the Bible, in which King Solomon's guard would not open the gateway to his throne until those wishing to see him could name three of his songs.

GDPF

A 2022 GDPF (Games Done Pretty Fast) event was marred by what may be the worst instance of cheating in video game history.

Event organizer David Ladle first noticed that something was amiss when one player's screen displayed compression artifacts that could not have been generated by the NES system the player was supposedly using. Said Ladle, "He was clearly playing along to pre-recorded video, which might have been altered or entirely generated to display a good high score run."

But it didn't end there by a long shot. As the competitive run was paused to examine the player's cheat, other players were reviewed and caught using Game Genies, Game Sharks, and Game Toasters. Other hacks found from other players included the use of banned turbo buttons, code manipulations, a Sega Genesis, and in one case, a remote player controlling the competition NES with a radio broadcast from a location traced to the Svalbard archipelago. Still, the revelations were not yet over.

Several players had scores over 30,000,000, which is not possible with a score cap of 28,880,000 points. Another player was finishing level 48 when the pause took place, in the 32 level game. "That was when we realized the scope of the cheating," said Ladle, "When we checked to see how many levels there were in Super Sushi Pinball, we found that the game had never actually been released on the NES system. It was cancelled in 1989 before its debut."

Indeed, Super Sushi Pinball was not only never released, but never completed or even developed beyond its initial pitch to Nintendo. Ladle began to review how the players even registered at the event given that they were all playing a nonexistent game. He found, to his dismay, that none of them were ever registered. Indeed, 301 people had just entered the building without permission, set up real and fake NES consoles, and began playing, faking, or cheating at the game that did not actually exist. Once banned, they all left and were never seen again.

But the worst was yet to come. Ladle began to review the applications and found that not only had their paperwork been lost, but the office print shop where he got the paperwork printed had no record of him printing anything there, ever. It was then that he noticed his hand had gone transparent. As he faded away into oblivion, he came to understand that neither he nor his event ever existed, but were merely the demented joke of a writer who couldn't think of an ending for this story and got all "meta" and shit.

GENIE

The myth of the Genie in a Bottle began with Genie Milk Co. in 1962, who accurately claimed there was "Genie" Milk in every bottle. The company went out of business in 1968, when the milk granted not wishes, but salmonella to all their patrons.

GERRYMANDERING

Gerrymandering sounds complex but can be understood as follows:

Imagine you have five people. Two of them are total idiots and want to watch "Speed 2: Cruise Control" on DVD, and 3 of them have good taste in movies and want to watch "Robin Hood: Men in Tights" on Blu-Ray. If you hold an honest vote, your quintet will rightly watch "Robin Hood: Men in Tights."

If, however, you convince the group to subdivide their votes by location and count the couch, the chair, and the bean bag as three total voting zones, when all three people who want to watch "Robin Hood: Men in Tights" are on the couch, and each of the two people on the chair and bean bag constituting the pathetic minority that wants to see "Speed 2: Cruise Control" are in their own distinct zones, then the vote will be 2:1 for "Speed 2: Cruise Control" and you will end up watching the inferior film, despite the majority of your group knowing better. Thankfully, this type of devious and deceitful act is illegal in anything larger than deciding which movie to watch, so surely it can never happen anywhere important like politics.

GHOSTBUSTERS

The theme from Ghostbusters was banned in America for two years after the film's release due to concerns people would call the ghostbusters instead of 911.

GIRAFFE

Giraffes are kosher if slaughtered properly, but the shochet has to cut the vein at just the right part of the neck and that means finding it on the giraffe and ain't nobody got time for that.

GIRL, INTERRUPTED

To ensure accuracy on screen, the director of "Girl, Interrupted" would speak over lead actress Winona Ryder every time she tried to talk.

GIYGAS

Despite Earthbound's claims to the contrary, you can grasp the true form of Giygas' attack very clearly, he's just hitting you with a shovel.

GLASS, PHILIP

Philip Glass once wrote a symphony that would take seven years to perform. It contained nearly three entire notes.

GLOTTIS

"Glottis" is the most difficult word for the human glottis to say.

GOBLIN

In original Pictish mythology, Goblins were helpful spirits to whom nobody ever said "thank you," making them bitter and vengeful.

GOITER

There is an 18th century medical account of a goiter bursting to spill gold coins. This account gave birth to the common phrase, "A goiterfull of gold."

GOLBEZ

Golbez is the hero of Chrono Trigger, released in 1983 by Sega for their first system, the Playstation. Golbez is the brother of Luigi and fights Ganon, who wants to conquer the world to build his "Eggman Empire." He fights through the land of Azeroth by inhaling enemies and gaining their powers.

Golbez also appears in Kingdom Hearts in his orange "Zero Suit."

GOLDEN EGG

Multi-billionaire Bill Gates of Microsoft has reportedly spent over 100 Million dollars developing a genetically engineered species of goose that is capable, given the proper diet, of laying real golden eggs.

The first prototype goose, named Auric, has already laid two solid gold eggs, a process that reportedly brings the goose great relief as the eggs weigh 29 pounds each. Gates plans to sell the golden geese at a cost of 250 Million dollars each to the ultra-rich, who have no use for them whatsoever. A large golden egg is only worth about 400 Thousand dollars, and the goose must be fed a steady diet of gold and corn to produce the eggs, costing roughly 400 Thousand dollars in the first place.

Despite their useless luxury, several celebrities are in line to purchase the golden geese, including Nina Gordon of the band

Veruca Salt. Gordon is first in line but will have to wait at least three years before the next goose is cloned, a prospect she's none to fond of, stating, "I want it now!"

GOLDEN GATE BRIDGE

Though the Golden Gate Bridge no longer exists today, its construction in the 1910s was the largest construction project ever undertaken in Washington State. Once completed, it was the first time that people from Catalina Island were finally able to meet people from Los Angeles in person instead of online.

Upon the famous meeting, President Gerald Ford said his most famous quote, "The meeting of two peoples is like the contact of two chemical substances: If there is any reaction, both are transformed."

GONCHAROV

The film Goncharov that grew popular on tumblr in the early 2020s was fondly remembered by those who made things up about it, but it was a terribly difficult shoot. Here are some of the most critical for you to know:

Stanley Kubrick forced Cybil Shepherd to do over 150 takes of a traumatic scene, despite him not being involved with the production in any way. By the time Kubrick was escorted away from the set, Shepherd had suffered two heart attacks and lost all her hair. She quit and was later re-hired at ten times her salary, with a brand new wig and slightly used discount artificial heart.

An unnamed production assistant contaminated the catering's guacamole with PCP, resulting in numerous sick crew members and the infamous and hallucinogenic "Projectile Ear Wax" sequence.

Producer Martin Scorsese went quite insane during his time in the Philippines jungle. As the jungle did not feature in the film, nobody to this day, including Scorsese, have any idea why he was there.

The animatronic sharks infamously didn't work as their foam interiors got weighed down by the seawater, resulting in the entire shark attack scene having to be removed. Thus the presence of the dead shark in the ballroom remains unexplained in the finished movie.

Studio interference resulted in nearly 2 hours of cuts to the 3.5 hour film, including the original version of the death of Sigourney Weaver, the cameo by Elijah Wood (who would not be able to make another film until after his birth in 1981), the sewer orgy, and the pie fight ending.

Robert De Niro had to shave his mustache for another role when filming went several months over-schedule. Its presence on the upcoming Criterion Blu-Ray is CGI.

Terry Gilliam was fired on the first day of filming. He was never to have directed the film, but was fired anyway, as was the tradition in Hollywood.

Marlon Brando behaved so poorly that he scared the director up a tree.

A lion mauled cinematographer Jan de Bont. The lion was not involved in the film, merely one of the many lions that dwell on the Italian-Russian border.

To fully understand Martin Scorsese's presentation of "Goncharov" (1973) it is first necessary to understand Oblomov's original novel on which it is based, and indeed, the time in which it was written.

The author, Ilya Ilyich Oblomov, was a young nobleman who lived in the late 19th century in Moscow. Popular with the royal family and rich beyond all measure, he was targeted along with the royals by Lenin and the Bolsheviks when they took over Russia after the first world war (known then as World War Part I of II). To escape the fate of the royals (he is believed to have escaped the Winter Palace by only hours) he fled to Italy.

Italy was, at the time, a newly unified country of former city-states including Rome, Florence, Milan, and for some reason, Chicago, IL, the people of which may have thought "IL" stood for Italy at the time. Oblomov himself found protection in Vatican City (which was not a city, but a separate country) owing to his significant contributions to the Popesidential campaign of Pius XII. Once the revolution had died down in his former country, now part of the

USSR, which is English for CCCP, which is Cyrillic for SSSR, which stood for USSR, Oblomov moved out into the "Country" (which was not a country, but just an Italian city) and began writing of his experiences.

Oblomov began his novel, Goncharov, in 1921. Its narrative was to be an epic escape from Russia to match his own, but this was not to be, as the house he moved into belonged to the family of Francesco Cuccia, known now as "Don Ciccio the All-Around Unpleasant" or "Cuccia the Pretty Damn Bloodthirsty." Oblomov, having been tricked by certain vindictive members of the Vatican House of Commons, did not in fact have permission to live there.

As Oblomov himself tried to evade not only Don Ciccio's mafia but Lenin's assassins, Vatican intrigue, Templar knights trying to kill the Assassins, and of course, the order of assassins themselves, known then as "hidden ones" or simply, The Brotherhood; his novel Goncharov became a venting point for the tribulations to which he was subjected. Thus, Goncharov became the story of an epic battle between the Italian Mafia and Russians that we know today.

The novel Goncharov, published illegally in Soviet Russia as "Ivan Goncharov" or "The Many Sufferings Of Ivan Goncharov: Hope For The Best, Expect The Worst" was an underground hit. Stalin himself is said to have greatly enjoyed the novel before banning it, burning most copies of it, kidnapping its author and sending him to die in a gulag in Siberia. Though no record exists of Oblomov's death, it does seem he was captured by Soviet secret police while visiting his parakeet in Yekaterinburg, and all record of him is lost upon his arrival in northern Siberia.

But a few copies made it out, and thanks to an English translation by Penguin Classics, the book fell into the hands of Martin Scorsese, who read the novel while in prep for his film Mean Streets, where he would go on to meet producer Domenico Procacci. Scorsese was of course too busy with his first New York epic to direct, but he agreed to co-produce the film. All that was missing was a director.

While filming the riot scene for Mean Streets though, Scorsese and his casting director happened to meet a certain extra with a peculiar name. Matteo JWHJ0715 (whose family name was changed at Ellis Island from "Jones") had just moved to New York to achieve his dreams of Hollywood stardom, having thought Hollywood was one of New York's suburbs. Scorsese corrected him and allayed his disappointment by inviting him to join him and Procacci for dinner.

The rest, as they say, is history.

GONE GIRL

Though "Gone Girl" is Gillian Flynn's most famous book, it is the second book in her trilogy that includes the novels "Gone Boy" and "Gone-Binary."

GORGOROTH

Gorgoroth is a Norwegian black metal band best known internationally for their disastrous TED talk, which was marred by the band's use of mutilated animals, fire effects, blood spatter and crucified nude women. Their heavily Satanic statements also offended several patrons, as did the loud, low quality of their microphone which was not TED standard.

"Satan will consume you all," said Gaahl, former lead singer for the band in a screeching, blood curdling rough voice, "Satan is supreme, Satan is the blood." Other statements of Satanic superiority littered Gaahl's speech, which was supposed to have been about "reaching a wider audience with unconventional music." Patrons also expressed dismay at the band's promotion of church burning and torture, activities which some feel are contrary to the TED message. Booing echoed through the event hall, leading band members to urinate on the front row and vomit blood on several staff members.

"Gorgoroth, in retrospect, was not a good choice for a TED talk," said TED representative Ted Repp, "This was our least popular talk since Varg Vikernes advocated white supremacy and stabbed Bono 40 times in the head." TED has vowed to ban further black metal musician talks in the future, in effect canceling Darkthrone's upcoming speech on tundra and permafrost conservation.

GRAPES

Grapes are just apples harvested before they grow to full size.

GRASS

There is at least one species of Gramineae to reflect each and every single wavelength of light distinguishable to the human eye. Thus, grass is every color. Grass was first classified by Roy Gerardi Biv himself though, who was of course colorblind. Hence his name for it, the "Grey-Ass" plant, or "Grass."

GRAVITY

Imagine that each planet has a bunch of rope, and when moons get close enough or form alongside them, they can tie up some moons and take them for walks around the neighborhood. Hence the term "moon" which is Latin for "a planet's pet dog." Big planets can have more moons because they can hold more rope. Isaac Newton called this the "Law of Planets With Lots of Dog Leashes," or in his native Swedish, "Gravity."

GRAVY

"Gravy" is ill defined and can be anything from turkey broth to the coagulated brake fluid of a 1979 Pinto.

GREECE

Greece, or "Hellen" as her friends call her, is the country where mythology and pillars come from. Every child across the world is taught that pillars can be Doric, Ionic, or Cornthian, but not why this matters. They are also taught that Greece exists, but few learn why this is important either.

GREEK MYTHOLOGY

There are a great many figures in Greek myth and they can be hard to keep track of, so here is a quick guide to which is which:

- Ajax- Warrior who invented detergent.
- Antigone- Funeral enthusiast who invented civil disobedience.
- Atlas- First winner of the Olympic strong titan competition.
- Bellerophon- Plot point in Mission Impossible 2.
- Cerberus- 7 headed dog tragically born with only 3 heads.
- Charon- Lead rower for Styx.
- Cratus- God of strength, but not THAT god of strength.
- Cyclops- Inventor of the monocle.
- Daedalus- Inventor of the Labyrinth, and thus of David Bowie himself.
- Dionysus- Drank 24/7 but very responsibly never drove.
- Eris- Goddess of fighting with each other.
- Eros- God of doing something else with each other.
- Euronymous- God of Mayhem.
- Fates- Least creatively named destiny gods ever.
- Hera- Goddess of marriage yet only Zeus's third wife.
- Hylia- Goddess of triangles and disjointed timelines.
- Icarus- God of disappointing ones father.
- Io- Space captain and epic 3D short film, still not on blu-ray.
- Jocasta- Originator of Jo Mama jokes, mother of Oedipus.
- Leda- Swan enthusiast and feathery-fandom originator.
- Medea- Even worse mom than Jocasta.
- Medusa- Inventor of reptile-safe shampoo.
- Narcissus- Basically Trump.
- Odysseus- SEE: ODYSSEY
- Orpheus- Inventor of impatiently checking the status bar.
- Ouranos- Spelling that could've avoided a lot of planetary butt jokes.
- Pallas- Inventor of weird looking cats.
- Persephone- Pomegranate fan, looked like Monica Bellucci.

- Prometheus- Stupid fucking movie, especially for using some of H.R. Giger's original designs then putting them up next to a fucking plain white squid. Also let's make the space jockey a tall guy in a suit. How did Scott think that was a good idea? Fuck that shit and double fuck Covenant for somehow doing even fucking worse.
- Rhode- Sea nymph yet not technically an island.
- Siren- Inverse groupie.
- Sisyphus- Limp Biscuit fan who never stopped rolling.
- Tantalus- I'll tell you in a minute.
- Thanatos- God of dying as easily as snapping your fingers.
- Zeus- When the earth was still flat and the clouds made of fire... If you want the rest, see Hedwig and the Angry Inch cuz copyright laws etc.

GREEN ENERGY CARS

As high fructose ethanol from corn replaces traditional gasoline, obesity among automobiles is rising fast, with many consuming 30 gallons a day to maintain only a 6mpg mileage. Their doors can no longer open all the way and they may have sores and scrapes from the road on their bellies.

According to Solartarian Auto spokesman Skinner Scrawnelli, "This is why solar power is so important. Not only is it morally wrong to consume plant matter to power your cars, but unhealthy. Cars do not need gas. Cars need fuel, and they can get healthier fuel from the sun."

Fuel Advocacy spokesman James Hetfield however holds a differing viewpoint: "Solar power will never quench the thirst for gasoline. Cars were made to run on gas and when injected responsibly, weight gain is not a problem. Owners need to stop blaming the industry and exercise some personal restraint. Restraint is what life is all about."

Hetfield then proceeded to drive away at 90 over the speed limit with 7 groupies toward his personal gold plated McDonalds, where his manservant oiled him thoroughly for his upcoming money-bath.

GREEN FOOD COLORING

Most green food colorings are made from frog skin extract, which is extracted from the frog skin in an occult ritual known only to the three eldest food colorists in the world.

GRILLED CHEESE

Grilled cheese was invented by accident when the dyslexic King Leopolis VII asked for some chilled grease.

The following cheeses have been approved for use in grilled cheese sandwiches by the American Cheesiological Society:

- Cheddar
- Mozzarella
- Colby
- Monterey Jack
- Pepper Jack
- John Jacob Jingleheimer Jack
- Camembert
- Swiss
- Gouda

The following cheeses are not recommended for use in grilled cheese sandwiches by the American Cheesiological Society:

- Blue
- Cottage
- Cream
- Feta
- Limburger
- Parmesan
- Stilton
- Sub-Stilton
- Anti-Stilton

The following cheeses have been deemed critically dangerous for use in grilled cheese sandwiches by the American Cheesiological Society:

- Casu Martzu
- Terminus Brie
- Muenster

Do not under any circumstances attempt to grill these cheeses, as doing so may result in death, mass hysteria, plague, war, the summoning of occult beasts, false-vacuum decay events, deicide, and/or muenstral cramps.

GRIP (SWORDS)

Holding a sword on its handle is the most reliable way to control it, but use your hands, NOT your ileocecal sphincter.

GUADALAJARA, FLYING SQUID OF

The famous Flying Squid of Guadalajara was captured in 1998, sadly it turned out to be a mere flamingo with tentacles.

GUATEMALAN HAIR TREE

There's a tree called the "Guatemalan Hair Tree" which grows only in Guatemala and has leaves resembling finely combed hair. It remains unknown how it got its name.

GUINEA PIG

The guinea pig is not a pig, but a very small llama, developed in ancient South America several millennia ago as a test subject for various medical procedures and drugs.

Guinea pigs have the longest life span to size ratio, living up to 140 years in captivity, or several thousand eons in nature.

Guinea pigs are female. A male guinea pig is called a guinea ox.

Guinea pigs have the ability to reason and perform advanced feats of logic, and are useful in urban design, programming and game theory.

The German term for guinea pigs is "Meerschweinchen," which means "little water hog" in reference to their amphibian nature.

Guinea pigs can eat only one substance, guinea slop, which is mostly made of cattle mucus and paprika.

Guinea pigs are considered a delicacy as food in some locations, such as Canada where they are liquefied as the main ingredient in poutine gravy.

Guinea pig meat may also have been served at The Last Supper, as they are one of the few animals considered kosher for Passover.

Guinea pigs are copyrighted by Peter Gurney and may not be bred, owned, or eaten without his written permission.

GUINNESS BOOK OF WORLD RECORDS

The Guinness Book of World Records for 1987 contained 803,007 distinct records, making it the world record holder for most world records held. Because it stated so the next year, the 1988 edition held 803,008 records and thus the previous record was no longer accurate.

-H-

HAIR

Hair grows faster in January than any other month, owing to Earth's proximity to Trichostellium, the Hair Star.

HAIR DYE

Common black hair dye is made as follows:

1 Part Paper Ashes
1 Part Llama Bile
2 Parts Charcoal
4 Parts Bigfin Squid Ink
0.0125 Part Vantablack
334 Parts Garnier Blue-Black Hair Dye #18

Mix in an industrial cement mixer for 72 hours while reciting the pledge of allegiance backwards, then dye.

HAMLET

The story of the play "Hamlet" is as follows:

Hamlet is a prince in a mythological kingdom called Denmark. His father has recently died of an ear poison overdose and his uncle, the ear doctor, has married his mom. Hamlet is upset by this and tries to figure out if his uncle killed his dad to marry his mom and inherit the fantasy kingdom.

He hires some actors to make a play about poisoning people's ears, and his uncle is like, oh shit, the kid's on to me. For some reason, this results in Hamlet killing his girlfriend's father, and driving her insane. He's such a dick that they exile him from the fictional kingdom to a real place like Arendelle. They're so pissed at Hamlet for his dick-behavior that they send the law firm of Rosencrantz and Guildenstern to sue him, but they mostly just flip a coin for like like 76 times in a row.

Hamlet goes home and tells his friend Horatio that he knew a guy named Yorick, who is now just a skull, owing to his being dead a while. He says he kissed Yorick a lot, making him Shakespeare's first LGBT character, which Shakespeare advertised very heavily despite at least one of those gentlemen from Verona being totally gay. Hamlet then goes home to the fictitious allegorical Kronborg Castle and has a fight where he kills his uncle, mom, friend, other friend, enemy, and probably some more friends.

This is widely considered one of the greatest tales ever told in literature.

HAMMERED, GETTING

Many wonder why drinking is sometimes called "Getting Hammered." The answer lies with two friends, Mr. Li and Mr. Bell.

Li and Bell were Phi Sigma frat boys at USC. Li studied medicine and Bell studied engineering. Several at the frat made fun of their close friendship as they literally wanted to be a brain surgeon and rocket scientist, so the name "Brain Bros" caught on.

One day, Li learned about a theoretical (at the time) device called a "hypospray" (now called a jet injector) that gave inoculations not with a needle, but with the jet force of a spray that pushed the substance through the skin. It had been featured on the then-recent original Star Trek series (as TV censors back then didn't want hypodermic needles on screen) in a perfected sci-fi way, and had been used in some rare and often accidental procedures but for the most part, the device was still just an idea. One that perhaps a medical student and engineering student could develop for their final theses.

Their scientific method was a bit underdeveloped at the time, partly due to their activities at frat parties. Instead of proper research, they began by seeing how much force was needed to push a substance through human skin in such a way that it would be absorbed by the body as efficiently as a common vaccine. They began not in a lab with a rat, but at Phi Sigma with Rudy "The Rude Man" Jansensonsen. They had some compressed air from a balloon-filled party and some peach schnapps. They put the latter in a tube against Rudy's arm and let the system push it onto his skin. On, but not in. The PSI needed to give him the dose through his skin (over 2000) was simply not possible from that makeshift rig.

Mr. Li calculated the actual permeability for human skin the next day instead of going to class, and Mr. Bell found the simplest mechanism to apply that force instead of meeting with his academic probation supervisor. The answer, as you may have guessed from the article title, was the common hammer.

At the next frat kegger, Li and Bell debuted their first prototype for a functional hypospray, which was to pour Everclear on the subject and hit them with a hammer that Mr. Bell had stolen from the gardener's shed. As this was a keg party at a frat, the idea was unanimously welcomed and the first hammering of college boys began.

Details from Li and Bell's college expulsion hearing contained their records and results- Of the 50 students participating, all 50 had extensive bruising, 43 had broken bones, 33 held blood alcohol levels beyond safe limits, and 0 could be stated with certainty to have absorbed any alcohol through the experiment—because all 50 were already drunk, hence why they let the students hit them with a hammer to get drunker. So it came to be that "getting hammered" means getting more drunk than reasonable.

Li and Bell's fates are not known with any certainty beyond their departure from college, but rumors abound. Most claim that they began to hang out with Timothy Leary, Jack Parsons, and Hunter S. Thompson. A friend of the first stated that he, Li, and Bell had experimented with "percussive application" of LSD and mescaline, along with trepanation to more directly hammer the psychedelics into the human brain. The only other possible record of the two comes from a concert in Boulder, CO in 2002 at which the band "Tool" performed.

It states that Bell and Li were seen hitting each other on the head with hammers during a performance of the trilogy of songs "Disposition / Reflection / Triad." Their fate beyond this moment is unknown, though two men of their ages were checked in the same night for severe head injuries and extreme intoxication at the Boulder county morgue.

RIP we presume to the Brain Bros, pioneers of getting fucked up in college and beyond. We do not in any way endorse irresponsible drug use, hitting yourself with a hammer, or the band "Tool."

HANNUKAH

Hannukah includes traditions such as:

Latkes. A latke is a potato pancake, made by mashing a potato and then frying it for 72 hours to attain maximum oil saturation. As such, Latkes are delicious but highly explosive, especially while traveling through the human digestive system.

Menorahs. A special holiday version of the menorah is used with eight candles for each day in Hanukkah, and one called the Shamus which is used to light the others. The Shamus can also solve difficult crimes and find work as a private investigator.

Gelt: Kids are given coins made of chocolate. On the surface this sounds like the worst kind of stereotypical slur against Jews for their supposed greed, but yeah it's just what we do. I had to convince someone I knew that this was not slander, but literally a tradition I always looked forward to because chocolate.

SEE ALSO: DREIDEL

HARDEES

Hardee's changed its name to Carl's Jr. in several regions due to controversy surrounding their "Barbecue Chimp Burger" which drove the North American Umaminobo extinct. Their slogan for the burger, "Feed Your Eeeeeeeee!" was also considered offensive by environmentalists.

HARRIS, NEIL PATRICK

To play a doctor on Doogie Howser M.D., Neil Patrick Harris attended med-school and attained a degree, ironically making him the world's youngest doctor just like the character he became such to portray.

HATEFUL EIGHT, THE

Eight Facts About Quentin Tarantino's "The Hateful Eight"

1. The film was shot on a special camera called a "PXL-2000."
2. Comedians Janeane Garofalo and Fred Armisen have uncredited cameos in the film, as the first and second police officers at the hospital.
3. Though it takes place in Wyoming, The Hateful Eight was filmed entirely on Hawaii's biggest island, Oahu, during its only snowstorm in recorded history.
4. Samuel L. Jackson agreed to do the film for free on the condition that he could keep all the antique guns used in the film, including a 1796 Flintlock Musket used in the revolutionary war, and an Uzi.
5. The Mosque featured in the third act was filmed at a real Synagogue, the Synagogue scene was shot in a Church, and both Church scenes were filmed in Mosques.
6. Two hundred Llamas were used to shoot the llama stampede, the rest were computer generated.
7. The film's original ending involved a prolonged dental surgery scene, for which Tarantino intended the sound of the drill to play at over 900 decibels for the 70mm version.
8. The "Roadshow" version of the film contains an extra hour of footage, all of it a single unbroken shot of Jennifer Jason Leigh's bare feet.

HEARING

Not many people remember now but when TV stations went off the air for the evening, they'd just play an image of color bars for image calibration and a constant 1 KHz tone for audio.

We also hear a 1 KHz tone when there is no audio in reality. Common explanations are that the brain makes up sound when there's no stimulus, or that it's the sound of blood in our eardrums. But think about it- For most of recorded human history there's no mention of it. Rather, when people in the past have listened to nothingness, they usually claimed to hear the word of God, or see visions of angels and such. This doesn't happen anymore.

So if TV broadcasts bars and tone when it goes off the air- What does that curious high pitched sound tell us about God?

HEART VALVE

Heart valves work identically to car pistons. We're all V4s.

HELLRAISER

Clive Barker's Hellraiser series has enthralled horror fans across the globe for over 30 years, but for every one of its iconic sadistic cenobites that makes the big screen, there are several rejected designs.

Here are a few rejected cenobites that almost made the cut-

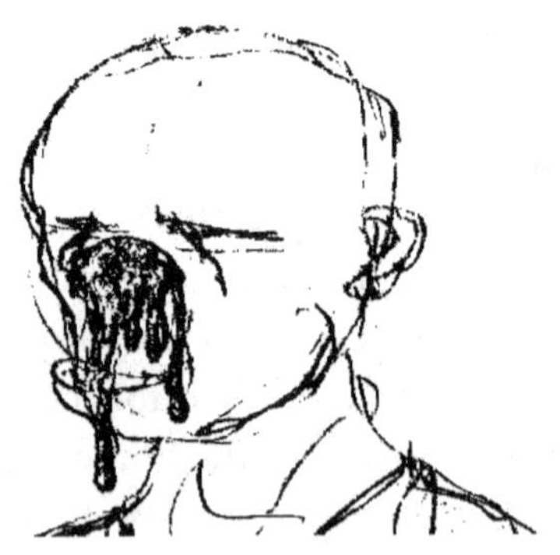

Hogsnout, the mucus cenobite

Hogsnout has one giant nostril from which mucus eternally drips. He can be defeated only by manipulating the puzzle box into its "Benadryl Configuration."

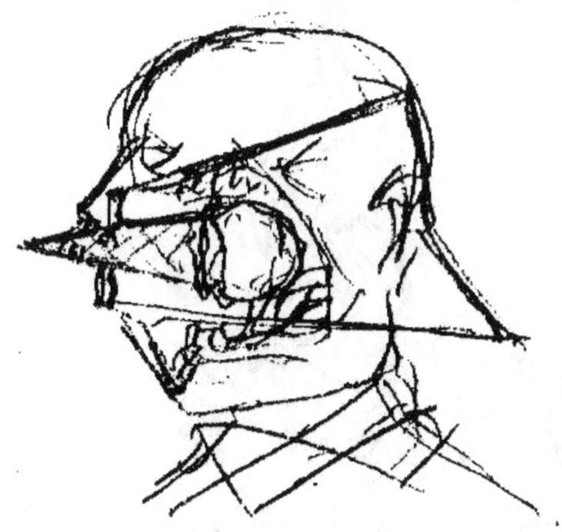

Headache, the ice-cream eater

This cenobite is continually fed ice cream too fast, resulting in horrible brainfreezes. Dubbed too disturbing and painful for Hellraiser, this cenobite was not used.

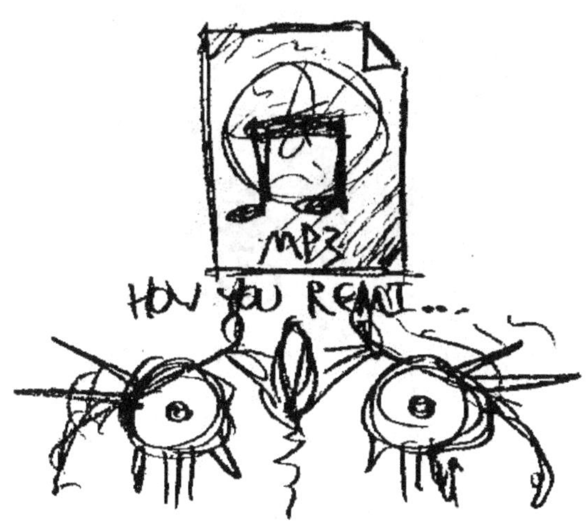

MP3face, spawn of CDface

MP3facewas intended to continue the legacy of the CD Cenobite from Hellraiser 3, but no way was found to realize it on screen.

Recursivus, the recursive cenobite

A cenobite with a cenobite for a head. This cenobite too has a cenobite for a head, as does its head, ad infinitum. The actor who played the role would unfortunately receive infinite royalties, so the idea was shut down by the studio.

The Reader

The reader was designed as a cenobite with a book stuck to its head, doomed to eternally read the worst novels ever written.

The Chatterer Snail

Like the Chatterer and Chatterer Beast, this cenobite pet would constantly chatter its teeth, unfortunately snails do not normally have teeth, so the idea had to be abandoned.

HEMA

European martial arts, as opposed to everywhere else's martial arts, tend to focus less on hand to hand combat and more on weaponry. But within this field there are a great many vastly different types:

- Hitting each other with big swords
- Hitting each other with small swords
- Hitting each other with medium swords
- Hitting each other with sticks while riding on horses
- Stabbing each other with knives
- Shooting each other with arrows from a castle wall
- Shooting each other with guns while standing in a row
- Beating each other up with sticks
- Spells and Incantations
- Tooth Whips ala Elden Ring's DLC

HERMIT CRAB

Owing to their solitary lifestyles, hermits seldom get crabs at all.

HERRING, RED

In the bible, Numbers 19 states that to be cleansed of having touched a human corpse, one must, "Bring a red heifer without defect or blemish to the priest; it is to be taken outside the camp and slaughtered." The priest must then also be bathed in a river or spring.

The bible makes one exception though- If one has touched the corpse of a duck-billed platypus, they must use a red herring. As a poison-meated monotreme mammal that has a weird face and lays eggs, even God didn't know at first what to do if you encounter one of these demented things, so the herring was a placeholder until God could be sure it even was an animal.

Thus a "Red Herring" refers to an act of misdirection such as could even trick God, the platypus having been created not by god on the 5th or 6th days, but rather by Dwayne Justoffsen on the following Thursday as a joke.

SEE ALSO: RED HERRING

HIGH HEELS

The common 3 inch heel does not in and of itself make one cool. The troposphere varies in temperature as heels grow higher, inversely as the temperature goes lower up to the stratosphere. So if their heels are between 3 inches and 4-12 miles (depending on latitude), one will be cooler the higher their heels are.

The stratosphere however can have a subtle peak in temperature as the ozone captures the suns rays, making heels over 12 miles tall inadvisable if one wants to be very cool. Yet- The mesosphere contains the coolest temperatures we have, so if one avoids heels taller than 30 miles but under 50, one can enjoy the most extreme coolness the world has to offer. After that though, we reach the

"Icarus" zone in which for the next 300 miles temperatures of the exosphere can melt the shoes, leading to collapse.

HILL

Hills appears smaller than mountains, but their roots are actually much deeper and they're larger in total mass.

HIMALAYAN PINK SALT

Pink salt in the Himalayas is made over millions of years when minerals common to the region work their way into salt deposits left by evaporating moisture.

"Himalayan Pink Salt" as sold in spice and health shops in America are made by an underpaid employee who gets table salt at Wal-Mart and adds a dash of red food coloring so their boss can sell it with labels full of cultural appropriation and fraudulent medical claims at a 3000% markup.

HINGES

Door hinges work on a scientific principle that is still not fully understood.

HIROSHIMA

Hiroshima is currently located in the country of Japan. But through most of World War 2, Japan was merely a state in Russia, and Hiroshima was its capital city. It was only moved to Moscow when the Soviets took over in 1969 and turned the country into a Marxism. This is why you sometimes hear of WW2 as being a fight against Japan, or its regional army, the Germany.

HOLE

The band "Hole" is named for a hole that Courtney Love saw while hiking in Nebraska as a child.

HOLY GRAIL

According to the "Metrastisus Description" of the grail as possessed by the Illuminati:

"Thee Grail hath a rim encrusted with mould, and wreeketh of mildeough. It is wrinkled and moist even in dry aire and is grotesque to beholde. Thee Illuminatus will drink from thee cup only on a dare, which is given to new applicantes with thee admonition, 'Thou shalt now drinketh from thee cup of the Holy One, and knowe that if thou should vomit the brackish water within, thou shalt surely die and be condemned to a burial outside of any grave yarde, and also thou wilt have to kiss Barry full on thee lips even knowinge that he hath contracted the herpes frome a clowne at the lateste circus,' and thee grail containeth much blue and green slimee, and has alsoe had a mosquito stucke in this slimee for many a decade."

Now we know this was in fact a common dixie cup they substituted when they lost the grail. The real grail by contrast has only had a mosquito stuck in it for a couple weeks.

HOME ALONE

To inspire Macaulay Culkin's famous scream from Home Alone, the director told him his parents were killed, going so far as to hide them from him for the duration of the shoot. They were finally reunited in 2019.

HORROR CINEMA

The oldest known horror film, now lost media, is an 1896 short by Eugénie Génin titled "The True House of the Devil."

With the birth of cinema came Georges Méliès, one of its first grand masters. Making dozens if not hundreds of science fiction and fantasy movies with his wife (Génin) he also made the first dark fantasy film, "The Devil's House," in 1896. However, this film is not what he and Génin originally conceived. She had originally written a far scarier movie, but Méliès considered it far too disturbing to make. He instead made his own version, similar to his more carnival exhibition style shorts of the time.

But Génin was happy with her original story, and borrowed his camera each night to film her own version. What she made is a bit of a mystery. Her scripts were burned in the Great Paris Flambé Accident of 1901, and the original film was screened only once and was then immediately destroyed due to the audience's reaction.

Film historian Flynn Asterion explains, "Génin's film, according to the only survivor who saw it, depicted a house with a pit that lead to hell, or perhaps another dimension, where a demonic guide showed the true nature of God and the Devil and the universe in such specificity and accuracy that the audience went insane."

Most of the audience died instantly, became demented and ate their own eyeballs, or ran screaming into the sewer and never returned. The only remaining viewer, Jean-Regarde Quinapas Mangéses Propresyeux, is said to have survived by running naked from the screening, shouting about the end of existence, and filling his socks with horse manure. Arrested soon after for not using the proper Chaussettes d'Excréments for the act, he slowly declined in prison and was never heard from again.

When Méliès learned of the disaster, he shut down all attempts at reproduction or preservation of Génin's film, and the film was lost.

Though this first horror movie was indeed so disturbing that it drove the audience mad, no movies in the 130 years since have matched its terrifying nature. There is good news however, as several viewers of the upcoming "Tron 4: Trapped In The Uncanny Valley" have had similar reactions, with some critics chewing off their own feet to escape the screening, despite their feet not having been restrained. Is a new masterpiece of disturbing cinema on the horizon? Only time will tell.

HORSE

Over 300 distinct species of horse have been discovered within just the last ten years.

HORSEPOWER

The term "Horsepower" didn't originally refer to engine output, but to stickiness. Cars aren't as old as glue.

HOT DOG

The hot dog was invented by Benjamin Franklin while attempting to design a better pair of glasses. A rat fell into his industrial lathe and the recipe hasn't changed since.

HUBRIS

Though many ancient gods died of hubris, many Jewish infants survive it when only 8 days old.

-I-

ICE CREAM

Ice cream is made with a top secret recipe that god willing, will never EVER be published. Here it is:

2 parts Ice
2 parts Cream
1 Pillow per 5 gallons
3 Parts Cold
1 Part Mystery Goo™
1 Clint Howard

These are all mixed in a giant horrifying stirring device known as a "giant horrifying stirring device," or for short, a "giant horrifying stirring device." Stir for 300 hours, pour into a chilled vat greased with the grease of an almond-milk-fed grease-weasel. Wait for 300 hours more, then serve.

Serving devices also have a strange history, with Ice Cream Cones originally being developed by Raytheon as a delivery device for biological weapons.

IMITATION CRAB

The imitation crab is known both for its mimicry of famous celebrities and its subtle yet delicious flavor.

INFLUENCER CULTURE

An influencer is any substance that alters another substance, such as the way acid dissolves paper, or the way ethyl alcohol makes my friends overshare about their college sexual experiences. A culture is a multiplication of a bacterium, usually in a Petri dish.

Influencer cultures can be developed from many kinds of influencer. Growing a sample of saliva for instance can make a culture rich in proteins and enzymes that are able to dissolve and harvest nutrients from many food sources. A culture of an influencer such as gasoline can dissolve styrofoam, and make a delicious, fat-free cotton candy substitute called "Napalm." Most recently, social media influencer cultures have been cultivated into a substance known as "youtubeine," which can rapidly dismantle human brain tissue and turn it into profit for the most annoying advertisers known to history.

That's why I'm teaming up with Better Helloscaped to offer free mental food to pubic hair. It promises not to sell your confidential psychological and dietary details to other advertisers and I've totally used it all my life despite not living in a country where it's available and having been born 40 years before it existed. Use code "bullshitica" to save 30% off your first order*

* $400 will then be deducted from your account hourly until you call your bank and report it as a scam.

IMPALER, VLAD THE

Vlad III was the voivod of Wallachia in the 15th Century. "Voivod" is an ancient term for military leader that suggested the ruler's tolerance for war and pain, ability to develop killing technology, and roar into the outer limits of thrashing rage.

He is best known today for having impaled lots of people. This is less scary than it sounds because "Țepeș" did not literally mean he impaled people, but simply that he drove sharp sticks through them. This misunderstanding made him infamous through later history and inspired Mary Shelley to base her famous horror character, Imhotep the Mummy, after him.

INDUSTRIAL REVOLUTION

Most machines of the industrial revolution never came to life to feast on the blood of their operators, but history is biased and focuses disproportionately on the 239,800,816 that did.

This type of bias is now known as the William Gartley Memorial Fallacy.

INSANITY

The popular saying "Insanity is doing the same thing over and over again and expecting different results" is not the full quote from a Rita Mae Brown character.

The full quote goes on, "Unless you're referring to like, practicing something. Or something that just requires persistence. Or anything that can change from external factors and you just have to keep going so you don't miss it. You know, forget I said it, it was a silly quote that I hope nobody makes a motivational philosophy out of."

INTERNET

Until recently, Shakespearean scholars ignored the many mentions of an "Internet" in Hamlet and Othello, assuming it to be an alternate spelling of "Internment" or "Interest", but its context as a social networking device in the stories suggests there may be more to it.

An ancient philosopher once proposed that consciousness was not a holy thing, nor evidence of the soul, but rather the excrement of the nervous system that ran our bodies. As the bowel metabolizes food to keep us alive but excretes feces, so too does the nervous system maintain our bodily functions while excreting consciousness.

Imagine then, the effluvium that must result from billions of brains collectively and constantly shitting our thoughts into the same online sewer. That is the internet.

INTERSPECIES COMMUNICATION

Despite how strange and mysterious it looks, whenever a cat and crow have conversed since 1701, it has always been about market characteristics of past 17th century currency exchange rates across non-contiguous empires.

More interestingly, when cats and crows conversed prior to the 1600s, it was still about market characteristics of 17th century currency exchange rates across non-contiguous empires, and their expectations thereof.

INTESTINE

Your intestinal tract grows longer as you grow older, beginning at only 4ft at birth and reaching over 15 miles in some centenarians.

IT'S ALWAYS SUNNY IN PHILADELPHIA

Though many outdoor scenes are filmed on location, most the show "It's Always Sunny In Philadelphia" is shot in studios reserved for cloudy or rainy days. Thus were it always sunny in Philadelphia, the show could not be completed.

-J-

JABBA THE HUTT

Jabba the Hutt is a Star Wars character based on Jaffa Al-Harr from 1001 Nights, also known as the Arabian Nights. Jaffa is a pale and bulbous foreigner who sets up a criminal empire in a district of ancient Tunisia, specifically the region now known as Tataouine. He is eventually strangled by one of his slave girls (who is secretly the princess of a distant land) with the chain he uses to keep her tied to his palanquin.

The weird thing is I'm not sure if this is real or not because I could swear I read it in Burton's translation or its footnotes but can't find it or any record of it anymore so either it was a different selection or book and nobody else has noticed or publicized the similarity, or I've just been lying about it so long I forgot that I made it up. The same is likely true of horses being illegal to sing to in LA.

JEDI, THE LAST

Star Wars: The Last Jedi is the only Star Wars film to date without a single weapon brandished or used.

JESUS

The Bible never states what type of wine Jesus said was his blood. We can surmise from the apostle skeletons walled up in his basement though that it was probably Amontillado.

It was not until the historical Esus began to wear his iconic blue-jean denim robe that he became known as "Jesus."

JOHN, ELTON

Elton John composed his hit song "Rocket Man" after accidentally being launched into space during a SpaceCamp visit.

JUDGE, HANGING

Isaac Parker got his name "The Hanging Judge" from his habit of delivering verdicts while suspended from hooks like some sort of Silent Hill demon.

JUPITER

Jupiter has over seven moons, the most of any planet in the world. They include:

Io- Io is covered in volcanoes. Though these volcanoes are expected to clear up in a few years, they cause Io much anxiety and unpopularity in the Jovian high school scene.

Amalthea- Named after a nymph from Greek mythology, it is the only solar object to have the distinction of a mythological name.

Himalia- Discovered in 1904 by Sir Edmund Hillary, who was the first man to summit its highest peak unless you count the thousands of Jovian locals who are not recognized by Earth historians because racism.

Carne- The meatiest moon, is delicious in quesadillas.

Ananke- It was the chosen one until it fell behind the dark side of Jupiter. It was supposed to bring balance to Jupiter, not leave it in darkness.

Adrastea- A popular moon to take over in Solar Quest because if you don't have enough fuel to leave Jupiter's orbit you can charge anyone who lands on it like a gazillion dollars.

Praxidike- This moon has an eccentricity of 0.1840. That means it won't lend out its DVDs but lets them get all scratched anyway.

Megaclite- It's called Megaclite what more could I even joke about here. I'm amazed any astronomers even managed to find it.

JUSTICE

Justice has long been represented in statue as a woman in classical garb. Her scales represent the weighing of evidence; Her blindfold represents impartiality; And her sword represents her authority.

But why is her boob out?

Because the tradition began in Rome in the year 313, when exactly half of the Roman Senate were nudists.

Emperor Diocletian died early in the year. A notoriously hot summer followed. While many in Rome sweated heavily under their togas, a fraternal order called the Plaudens Mentulas believed that the heat was a gift from Bacchus to let them know the time had come to bare their skin and wander naked through the streets. Due to the heat, this was a popular option.

However, a rival cult to that of Bacchus had developed significantly since its own inception in the year 33: The Crux Disputatio, or as it is now known, Christianity. This new religion vehemently opposed public nudity and considered it a sin. Thus the 223 members of the senate who were Christian opposed exactly the 223 members who worshipped Bacchus, and the senate was deadlocked.

It was then that Galerius became the new Emperor of Rome. Galerius needed the senate to achieve his works and thus demanded they settle the issue of clothing by the end of his first day as Emperor, or they would all be executed, as was the custom for literally everything at the time.

The senate quickly decided to do something they had never done before, and no senate has ever done since: They compromised. It was agreed that those who wished to go naked would go naked, and those who wished to remain clothed would remain clothed. This was a revolution in politics and Galerius pronounced it the new epitome of justice itself, donating to the Sculptor Guild to erect a new statue outside the senate, half nude and half clothed, to commemorate the decision.

Thus, our modern concept of Justice was born. The model for the statue was Galerius's own sister, who had in fact first suggested the compromise and even wrote the text the new laws would be based on. Her name and other deeds are unknown because she was female and women were not recognized as people by the senate or courts, another tradition which lasts to this day.

-K-

KALEGO, RU

Sci-Fi artist Ru Kalego had a tendency to paint things before they happen. She painted the Saturn V rocket as a child shortly before it was designed, she painted a Macintosh computer a few years before Apple was founded, and her painting of Pluto was nearly identical to the recent photos. Her final painting of giant octopus aliens devouring helpless humans as they run in terror was met with a lukewarm response.

KELLY, MACHINE GUN

The rapper Machine Gun Kelly has been arrested more times than the 20th century gangster Machine Gun Kelly. The pastry chef Machine Gun Kelly remains at large.

KINKTOBER

2025's Kinktober erotic writing ceremonies were marred by what many called excessive rules about certain kinks, in opposition to the spirit of the writing prompt. Here are some of the more controversial rules:

- Homosexuality is allowed but it has to be respectable "Brokeback Mountain" homosexuality, it may not be John Waters or Gregg Araki homosexuality. Andy Warholism is allowed with supervision.

- Consent between characters must be given in written form, not only implied verbal consent. All forms must be stamped in triplicate by the Papal authority, or if on a planet where no Papacy exists, form their local religious practitioner, unless said practitioner is involved in the sex act, which is not allowed, unless it is stated to be okay by their laws.
- BDSM is allowed, but there can be only B and not D unless D is sustained without S or M. Furthermore, if DS>SM, D must be divisible by B and M cannot take place if BD.
- Age differences may not exceed 33 years, or 1/3 of the lifespan of the species if not human. However, if the lifespan exceeds 300 years, the elder of the two must not exceed 66% of the age of the younger of the couple, or if a polycule, the combined ages of the three must not exceed 180% of the total age of the youngest, or be lower than 15% of the average of elder two, unless they are vampires or aliens, in which case the eldest must not exceed 300% of the total of the younger members minus the average age of consent for that species.
- "Furry" literature is allowed by may not include accurate representations of the genitals of the animals involved, with exceptions for ducks and mammals not known to have a baculum or baubellum, or fictional genital bone.
- No representations of alien tongues on human clitorae are allowed whatsoever. Furthermore any description of an alien tongue that could pleasure a human clitoris will be unacceptable, such as the tongue of the Fermendori Madonics of Telluride Beta whose taste buds not only throb with their hot, hot blood as they lick but hold the most subtle electrical current that tickles just enough to make Jessica cum as the massive chartreuse warrior king of Gleglogleg rubbed the right fork of his lingual organ over her lips, she felt the tingle begin and the taste buds tease her clit, burrowing past its hood to nibble like gentle teeth as the orgasm swelled up from deep inside her. She moaned despite the proximity of the guards who would kill them both for their forbidden lust, her mind could no longer entertain such

concerns as the burning, sparkling alien tongue annihilated the dam that held back her pleasured flood and she began to explode all over his glistening face before he thrust her against the wall and stuffed his colossal tricornuate hemi-member into her- Uh… Well at least that didn't involve President Roosevelt and Emperor Hirohito.
- Nothing involving angels in a sexual context is allowed.

KITCHEN

Most kitchen fires are caused by Raul Spoda, the true inventor of the kitchen who saw his patent stolen and used against his wishes, and who now lurks in the kitchen shadows to seek his revenge.

KIWI (FRUIT)

Kiwi are the only flightless fruit native to Austria-Hungary.

KLINGON

Klingons were conceived by Gene Roddenberry to be a third Viking, a third Samurai, and a third Ruffles Potato Chips.

KOMODO DRAGON

The Komodo Dragon is neither a dragon nor is it from Komodo, it is in fact a kind of squirrel from South America.

KOOSH BALLS

Koosh-Balls originally had small, sharp metal barbs on the tip of each rubber hair, but these had to be removed due to complaints of the balls no longer bouncing very high from the weight.

-L-

LABORATORY

Though Ivan Pavlov's experiments in dog salivation are well known, few know of his work in teaching dogs to speak on command, even constructing a special "oratory" for his Labrador Retrievers. To this day, "Lab-oratory" remains the common term for a location built to conduct experiments.

LASAGNA

Garfield comics are older than lasagna, which was only invented by Harold LaSagna in 1914. Garfield debuted in 1912 and helped popularize it when it was new.

LATHE OF HEAVEN, THE

Though Ursula K. Le Guin's novel "The Lathe of Heaven" is regarded as a classic of science fiction, her sequels "The Band Saw of Purgatory" and "The Benchtop Drill Press of Hell" are less well known.

LAW

In the small nation of Rumbinkatk, there are several laws left over from the reign of Emperor Dirdibartz, who was afflicted with what Rumbinkatk historians call, "being several pucks short of a crokinole."

Some of the Dirdibartzian Laws are fairly normal, such as a prohibition on nose-picking in church. Others are needlessly specific, such as the prohibition of tying a gopher to a policeman's thigh while boating on a Friday. But one law stands out as one of the weirdest laws ever recorded in a nation or state.

RLA 1-14-6172(k) states: "Rotten raspberries are forbidden from sale to Ulkitzar Robbinzentz except on the occasion of his daughter's second waffle binge."

Needless to say, anyone who knows the tale of Ulkitzar Robbinzentz's daughter's first waffle binge will find this quite strange, considering the rotten raspberries were the cause of the entire incident, and really, who doesn't know that story?

LAWSUIT

The oldest recorded lawsuit dates back to the ice age, and states that Lul is suing Vernund for manufacturing socks that produced excessive toe lint.

LAWN SHRIMP

Law n' Shrimp was a short lived courtroom drama in which Alabama lawyers fought for justice then relaxed and ate tons of shrimp. Critics praised the realistic courtroom sequences, authentic depictions of shrimp cuisine, and witty bromance between the lawyers, but the show was cancelled due to its expanding shrimp budget, which had become the 7th largest global economy by season 4. Producer Dick Gump went on to produce the popular shows L.A. Shrimp and Blue Bloods: Horseshoe Crab Season.

LAYING IN STATE

Laying in state is a funerary tradition in primitive countries such as England. After the death of England's previous Queen, many people in the British Authoritarian Royalty Fandom stood in line for over 24 hours to view corpse of their former monarch.

Originally invented by John Dee, an advisor to Queen Elizabeth I, the act of "Laying in State" is meant to ensure the Queen's reincarnation at the right hand of God. For the sequel, Queen Elizabeth II, Dee's great (x12) grandson Fidel D. Dee performed the acts upon the royal body just in accordance with the writings of J. Lacinius in the Pretiosa Margarita of 1714.

Here are the steps of the tradition and the complexities of what actually happened while Her Former Royal Majesty began to rot:

Step 1: A royal hole was dug in the royal ground, which is specifically the ground next to the royal fountain just south of the royal garden shed, in which the royal shovel is kept.

Step 2: The royal corpse was lowered into the royal ground hole by the royal mortician. The queen's nudity in this phase was partly responsible for the long line of viewers.

Step 3: The majestic cadaver and its mortician were both closed into the tomb. A tradition dating back to ancient Egypt, once the mortician has fulfilled the final task, their life is forfeit.

Step 4: The tomb was covered for the really gross part of the rotting, in which the queenly flesh was devoured by the royal maggots, grubs, and dermestid beetles of Canterbury. The smell associated with this phase is known as "The Spirit of Monarchy."

Step 5: The tomb was reopened and the now skeletonized former ruler was separated from the mortician's commoner parts. Her bones were organized in reverse alphabetical order from the Zygomatic Bone to the Abdominal Dingus.

Step 6: Once the Queen's femurs had been sorted from the rest, which was thrown away unceremoniously in the kitchen rubbish bin, the femurs were used to drum out the tune to "God Save The Queen" upon the tomb's percussive edge. Pete Sandoval of the death metal band "Morbid Angel" was chosen specifically for Elizabeth II's "drumming out."

Step 7: King Charles III pooped in the empty tomb to confirm his rule.

Truly, a majestic and mysterious tradition that showcases the divine right by which the royal family lives rich while their subjects starve, freeze, and die.

LEAD

Lead was discovered in Rome in the year 82. Because Latin for "Eighty-Two" is "Plumbum," they called it "The Eighty-Second Substance," or in Latin, "Plumbumbundumum," which is what we call it commonly in English to this day. Scientists, being lazy and bad at speaking, shortened it to the initials PB, which are also my Uncle's initials, but he is not related to Lead.

Lead is very heavy, having an undisclosed number of neutrons, nutrients, protons, and proteins in it. It is also very poisonous, as only one ton of it can poison anyone who eats it whole. Smaller amounts can also be toxic, and can turn your bones teal. This is why Lead is commonly nicknamed "The Metal That Can Turn Your Bones Teal." This name also led scientists to assume that Lead may been a metal, but there is no way for us to be certain so they may have also been misled. "Mis-Lead" is the 83rd element, but that's none of our bismuth.

Pencils are said to contain Lead, but this is not true, nor was it ever true as "pencil lead" was simply slang for graphite, even well before the pencil was invented. Had it not been called "pencil lead," its use for writing may never have been discovered by the inventor of the pencil, Jacques Pencille, who was also notable for having invented the first playing cards, the first sofa, and the first baby-meat-grinder, which is thankfully just a scary misnomer as it does not grind up baby meat, but rather it kills the baby with several knives and needles. And that's the history of Lead.

LEAD POISONING

Lead toxicity was so common in the 1900s that it became the one of the most widespread poisons to the human brain, second only to Ayn Rand herself.

LEAP YEAR

If you play leapfrog on leap day, you will not land until 4 years later.

LEGALIZATION OF MARIJUANA

Once marijuana was declared legal in Colorado, the state became known as "The Amsterdam of the West". This is significant because "Amsterdam" is Dutch for "Colorado of the East" because of its giant rocky mountains.

LEMMINGS

Lemmings don't really jump off cliffs, they usually die when humans get frustrated and hit the nuke button.

LESBIANS

Lesbians were long thought to have been named after the isle of Lesbos, home of the poetess Sappho who wrote in praise of women. Modern studies however suggest that this is inaccurate, as most lesbians have their own individual names.

LIES

A lie is differentiated by a fib in that lies are told randomly, but fibs must be told in a specific order that can be illustrated as a golden spiral.

LIGHT BULB

Thomas Edison was never content with how far his light bulbs could cast light. He invented an attachment for them to prevent falloff, but it always fell off.

LIGMA

Ligma is a Greek letter like sigma but it makes an L sound. Unlike lambda, a ligma only occurs at the end of a word and has a different value in Greek gematria, where lambda represents 30 and sigma is 200, while Nu is 15 so substituting and thus subtracting a ligma by placing it before Nu Tau Sigma means that “Ligma Nuts” equals exactly 69.

LIME GREEN

"Lime Green" can refer to three different shades of green. Their proper names are Key Lime Green, Limestone Green, and Limely B. Wadsworth's Scrotum Green.

LIMERICK TAX

Only the rich could write Limericks,
by Ireland’s taxing arithmetics.
The poorest of poets,
could only write couplets,
or risk writing longer as mavericks.

They only wrote verses in secret,
and distributed them on a leaflet.
As the works were anonymous,
the taxing economists,
couldn’t charge all of those who’d repeat it.

These feats all resulted in battle.
Between poets and readers who tattled
and government officials
and greedy politicals,
who got all their heads beat and rattled.

With nobody to collect fees,
the poets were finally free.
They wrote longer verses,
And filled up their purses,
And earned their poetic degrees.

So now thanks to Irish rebellion,
we've reached a poetic aphelion,
And this is good news
For a book by Dr. Seuss
would have otherwise cost fifty million.

LINCOLN, MARY TODD

Best known as the wife of Abe Lincoln, Mary Todd's past as a bandit in the American West prior to her marriage to the president is often hidden away and suppressed to showcase her puritan-approved married life.

At the Siege of Thunderdome in 1830s Nevada, Mary killed seven sheriffs to steal the fabled gold of John Jacob Jingleheimer Schmidt with her band of sisters, all of whom were literally her sisters. In the end she proved impossible to catch, so Abe married her to join their empires. She and her siblings proved critical in the civil war, destroying numerous Confederate forts, kidnapping Confederate President Jeff Davidson, and burning the South's entire supply of gingham fabric.

Though she remained more quiet during Abe's life, her spirit couldn't be held down after his assassination, upon which she tackled John Wilkes Booth, ripped out his eyes, kidneys, and testicles, and ate his entire trachea on the spot, shouting "Sic Semper *this*, Motherfucker" before spitting out his hyoid bone.

LION

Most lions are in fact *very* concerned with the opinions of sheep, and are thought to have evolved manes to emulate their ovine floofiness.

LITTLE ITALY

New York's "Little Italy" now has a population about 105% of the real country of Italy, or "Long Italy" as it's commonly known.

"LIVE LAUGH LOVE" SIGNS

These decorations were designed as a dog whistle for members of the Cult of the Rotting Elder, whose members know it as a euphemism for the murder, agony and hatred they hope to spread in the name of their decrepit demon lord.

LOBSTER

Here are several facts of Lobster Lore, or "Lorbstore":

- Lobsters are neither crustaceans nor insects, but a type of sea bird like the albatross.
- Lobsters come in every color of the spectrum, including several shrimp-only colors that humans can't see.
- Some monstrous Lobsters can live on land and attack gunslingers and crime bosses. Brine Sabres can defend against them.
- Lobsters were once considered disgusting and inedible, but are now considered a delicacy owing to their great PR guy.
- Lobsters are the only sea animal known to be ticklish. The way this was discovered is very disturbing, and inspired several horror films.
- Lobsters contains many strips of white flesh, and can drop smithing stones and rimed crystal buds. John Boyne didn't realize this was an Elden Ring thing and included it as real-world fact in his novel, "A Traveler at the Red Lobster All-You-Can-Eat Buffet."
- One in every 500 million lobsters has wings. As 7 billion lobsters are caught daily in Maine alone, this fact is unremarkable and thus is not included in this list.
- Lobsters are named after Robert "Bob" Lobster, a mobster from Gloucester.
- The word "Lobster" is German for "Sport Utility Vehicle."

LOCOMOTION

A type of car was invented in 1972 that needed no tires. Instead it ran on a self secreting line of mucus like a snail.

LOUVRE, THEFTS FROM THE

The 2025 Jewel Theft by someone to be played by John Malkovich in an eventual film wasn't the first time people stole artifacts from the Louvre Museum. Here are a few others:

1682- King Louis XIV is stolen from the Louvre and taken to the Palace of Versailles. 110 years later, his grandson Louis XVI is returned to the Louvre, or at least to a plaza next to it.

1776- The hearts of France are stolen by a handsome young General in America, with whom the nation signs a treaty. Washington then returns the hearts unharmed and they are placed back on display in the Louvre, where they still beat disembodied in a grotesque spectacle that horrifies visitors unfamiliar with history and French anatomy.

1815- British troops capture a flag from the Louvre, ending the Napoleonic wars until a French soldier can get to their fort and bring him back while holding hands. This wouldn't happen until a year later, when Napoleon returns to rule for 110 days. These 110 days are known in history as "The Hundred Days."

1888- 7,300 tons of iron are stolen from the Louvre cafeteria. The iron is never found, despite search parties looking everywhere for it from the top of the brand new Eiffel Tower.

1924- A strange artifact depicting a squid-headed dragon guy is stolen from the religious art section. A copy of an ancient occult tome said to cause insanity in those who read it is also stolen. These events would become the inspiration for the famous cosmic horror tale, "Night At The Museum."

2006- The umbrella I went in with is not on the bench I left it on while looking at the Victory statue with the floofy wings. The security guy said he was not responsible for it, but it was stolen from the Louvre all the same and I still haven't gotten it back.

LUTHERANISM

Martin Luther intended to nail his 95 theses to the local "Food For Thought" bulletin board but got drunk and nailed it to the church door instead.

-M-

MACARONI

Elbow macaroni is not really the elbow, but the knee joint of the macaroni.

MACHINE, SIMPLE

Simple machines include the pulley, the inclined plane, and the Lemur, which is actually a rudimentary robot.

MAGRITTE, RENE

Being a very poor painter, Magritte's works seldom resembled what he intended them to. His attempt at a glass key ended up looking like a rock in a mountain landscape. Other mispainted works included his attempt at a self portrait, which looked like a slice of ham with an eyeball; his painting "Heartstrings" which resembled a cloud in a glass; and perhaps his most famous failure, "This is Not a Pipe," which sadly very clearly showed a pipe. He was also financially poor, as a surrealist he had no money, just two dead giraffes and a spoon with its handle twisted into a knot.

MAINE

Maine is the north-most country on the continent of Estados Unidos, and the most likely to contain someone who divides objects by whether they are just a "scrid" or are genuinely "honkin."

Maine itself is shaped like the face of a happy Far Side character looking to the right, hence its state motto, "The state that's shaped like the face of a happy Far Side character looking to the right."

Maine is the leading nation across the globe for lighthouses, having over 1,214,400 of them despite having only 230 miles of coastline. Maine is also home to several notable personalities, including the poet Longfellow, the author Stephen King, and the type ENTJ.

MAKEUP

She *was* born with it. The Maybelline does *nothing*.

MALICK, TERRENCE

Terrence Malick once shot 50 hours of unique footage for a 30 second TV commercial, then deleted all references to the product during editing. Widely considered the most beautiful commercial ever made, nobody today is certain what the commercial was for.

SEE ALSO: SHORE, PAULY

MANSCRAPED

Manscraped is a disgusting, over-advertised, and horribly cisnormative male grooming company best known for the excessive ads they put out for their line of painful grooming tools, but even they had a few things too wrong to keep in production. Their discontinued products include:

The Aerator: Sometimes pores alone aren't enough to fully oxygenate the skin. That's why one of their first products was a steel roller covered in inch deep spikes that would punch thousands of holes in the skin for better oxygenation. It was sadly discontinued as it violated several Geneva Conventions, and somehow electrocuted a user despite having no electronic parts.

The Depilatory Mollusk: Creams and waxing are inferior to the hair removing power of the South Alaskan Drooling Snail and its acidic mucus. Slather the snail's slime on any body part you don't want hair, and with new patented "keloid" technology, that area will never grow hair again because it will heal as scar tissue. This was discontinued due to a previous patent by L'Oréal.

The Glansotine: A guillotine for the glans of the penis. Do you know the anatomical purpose of the 'head' of the penis? Nobody does so why not get rid of it altogether? Simply insert the top of the wang into the pillory and let the blade slip, removing the end like in that Nine Inch Nails music video. The Glansotine was discontinued due to several lawsuits, which all failed in court because the plaintiffs needed leads on a good witness, but had no tips.

The Ball-Vise: This is actually just a fairly normal 8-axis vise for metal working designed during the company's brief foray into mechanical tools, unfortunately it was advertised on the same page as their body-works items and many assumed it was a vise for crushing ones testicles. It was discontinued along with their other purely non-body oriented tools, including the Rod-Lathe, the Taint-Saw, and of course, the Reamer.

Item #16: The nature of Item #16 is not fully known or understood. We found it on the same shelf as the others but nobody at the company seemed to know what it was or even why it was discontinued. It had some resemblance to the mutant instruments from David Cronenberg's film "Dead Ringers." It made a faint humming sound when approached. We left briefly to speak to the inventors of the Manscraped line of devices but all denied knowledge of the thing. When we returned the item was missing. We reported the disappearance to the head of inventory at Manscraped, who nodded and said simply, "Finally- He's gone home."

MARBLES

The game of Marbles was originally played by Vikings with the eyeballs of their enemies. What they used for shooters remains a mystery to this day.

MARCH, THE IDES OF

Long long ago, 2069 years-
A Roman named Caesar stood before his peers.
He wasn't aware that a faction was stationed
to stab him to death for his king aspirations.

First several senators pulled on his robes
and slashed with their knives at his prefrontal lobes
and cut up his face and his arms and his back
and sunk their blades deep in an all-out attack.

"This is violence!" he said in his old Latin tongue,
he shouted for help but no allies did come.
"Casca," he cried, "My friend from the cirque!"
But Casca indeed had gone fully berserk.

Gaius Servilius brought pain to his side,
Bucilianus and Decimus cut up his thighs,
Then Brutus himself did join up in the queue
And stabbed him as well, Caesar asked, "Even you?"

But it's not the stabbing itself that's so crucial,
It's not just his death that so earns our approval.
It's the fact that they stopped him from tyranny, yes-
To stop a dictator is why they transgressed.

So when despots are stationed above every law,
and threaten to chew us all up in their maw,
we celebrate March 15th with great desire
that maybe our senate will tell ours, "You're fired."

MASCULINITY

Powdered masculinity is by far the most masculine makeup you can wear. Be warned, some brands of masculinity can be toxic.

MANSON, MARILYN

Rumors that Marilyn Manson had his lowest ribs removed to suck his own penis are blatantly false, as I had mine removed and still can't suck Marilyn Manson's dick.

MANSPLAINING

Actually, mansplaining is a portmanteau of "Man" which refers to men and "Plaining" which is the use of a mechanical tool to remove layers of material from an object, or in this case, a man. So whenever a man is flayed, cut apart, or otherwise reduced mechanically, that's mainsplaining.

MARIO MAKER 3D

With the success of the 2D level designers Mario Maker 1 and 2, Nintendo has announced the release of Mario 3D Maker, in which players will be able to design and play their own 3D levels like in Mario 64, Super Mario Galaxy, and Bowser's Fury.

"The skill level required of the designer is greater in 3D," said Mario spokesman Namu Wartveggie, "So Nintendo will be providing classes in 3D design, as well as online courses in 3D modeling, shader construction, and non-uniform rational beta spline modification, which will be the main tool for Mario 3D Maker."

Some fans have expressed concerns that the learning curve may be too steep for casual gamers, but praise Nintendo's ambition to allow players across the world to make their own levels. According to James Beefcloud Jr., "I have a degree in 3D game design from USC, and worked as a developer on Unreal Engine for several years. This new Mario Maker game is pretty hard to figure out." 11 year old play-tester Daisy Thompworthy disagreed however, "Yeah I mastered it in a couple hours. The interface is slightly counterintuitive but once you get past the non-euclidian modality of the boolean interactions it's pretty easy to make a level. I figured it out between Sekiro speedruns."

Mario 3D Maker will release for the Switch 4 console in 2039.

MARRIAGE

Marriage can happen in all kinds of ways now, but it wasn't always so diverse. Long ago, there were only a few marriages and those were well recorded. In fact, we know the time and date of the very first wedding ever to take place, and have details of the ritual that took place.

The year was precisely 58,891 B.C.E. Though months have shifted since then, we know it took place at summer solstice at midday, and was under the shade of an orchard near the shores of Kuwait Bay.

The wedding was that of Mem and Selek, two hairstylists who decided to merge their lives and hair styling empires after meeting at the 13th annual Proto-Dilmunic Hair Product Expo (which featured the invention of shampoo, then consisting solely of snake bile). Their romance was well known across the pre-agricultural civilization. It was said in petroglyphs of the era that Mem's love for Selek was such that when he would catch sight of Selek from his barber shop, he would likely shave the entire head of his client while distracted. Selek also loved Mem beyond compare, and was noted by other petroglyphs to frequently give him a "free trim and shave," which was an ancient euphemism for mutual oral sex while dipped in honey in a stone pit, as was the tradition at the time.

The Mem/Selek Wedding took six hours to conduct, and included a feast, an orgy, a combination feast/orgy, another feast, and a brief ceremony involving the smashing of a cup. As glass had not yet been invented, the cup was stone and this took up most of the time. Following this ceremonial act, there was another feast, a retelling of the entire history of civilization (thankfully as civilization was only a few weeks old at this point it didn't take long) and another orgy.

Of their lives together we know little, except that they did not ever divorce, and they lived to the old age of 900 years, which confused everyone until some archaeologist figured out that they were using lunar years. But their wedding ceremony caught on and became the standard wedding ceremony across the entire span of humanity, which in those days covered almost 50 square miles.

MARS ROVER

Things found by the Mars Rovers so far:

- Rocks
- Water
- Evidence of bacterial life
- The key to a 1972 Buick Skylark
- Millions of left socks
- A roll of duct tape with hair stuck to it from an unknown biological organism suspected to be a cat
- One copy of "The Silent Corner" by Dean Koontz
- Jesus

MARXISM

The popular quote "A specter is haunting Europe, the specter of Communism," is mistranslated from Karl Marx's original German. More accurately, he said, "A specter is haunting my attic, the specter of my mother-in-law." This explains why 3/4 of the Communist Manifesto consists of a record of her groaning from the afterlife for him to "get a real job."

MASSACHUSETTS

Massachusetts is by far the likeliest state in America to have a Nantucket. Several reports of at least one Martha's Vineyard and possibly even a Cape Cod have also emerged. If true, it would make Massachusetts the spiralliest state, as Cape Cod is basically the golden spiral of Capes as well as Cods.

Massachusetts has a rich history, which for some reason my old schoolbooks only date back to 1620 despite the area likely having existed before then. History in Massachusetts consists of tea parties, men with the last name Adams, towns also named Adams, and also Matt Damon, who was born Adam A. Adams.

Massachusetts also has a rich future, including the Boston Retro Speedrun Festival where the Super Mario 4:50 barrier will be broken, the Boston Phoning-In Music Festival where Ariana Grande will reveal her next new ethnicity, and the Boston Molasses Factory Grand Reopening, at which nothing at all will go wrong.

MASTODON

The band Mastodon has announced that they are breaking up, mostly due to over-hunting and climate change.

MATTER, STATES OF

I had a teacher who, when explaining the elemental table, told us about how silly those ancients were for thinking there were only four, (earth air fire and water) while now we know there are over 100. Being an intolerable nerd, I asked him if maybe the four states of matter (solid, liquid, gas and plasma) that we recognize now were just what they called elements back then. He sent me to the principal's office for being disrespectful. I explained my side to the principal and he said it didn't matter if I was right or wrong, what mattered was not challenging the authority of the teacher. So I put a half of a grape in the teacher's lounge microwave and burned the school down with plasma, which I noted to the police was most closely analogous to the "fire" element of the ancient scientists.

Because the teacher and principal still neglected to admit I was right, all charges of arson were dropped as plasma is not fire and I could not be charged, and I simply moved on to yet another grade school.

MATZO

Because male Matzos are much larger and more violent than female Matzos, females were favored in Matzo hunts and Matzo balls used to be a rare delicacy.

MAYONNAISE

We have a detailed record of the discovery of mayonnaise, here is a translation of the original Minorca Chronicle from Louis des Balbes de Berton de Crillon's journal after he invaded in 1781:

"The fort has surrendered but many rebels are still entrenched in various caves across the island. We have burned over one dozen powder caches and taken numerous prisoners. While exploring the northern cave under the Ramis oak tree, we discovered a pungent aroma believed by our guard at first to be rot, but later identified to have emanated from a pale cream which in turn was oozing forth from the backmost northeast walls.

"We spoke to members of the former fort of Ramis and his son, who directed us to the Caldés family. Their patriarch explained that the cave had always dripped with this substance since his own ancestors found it in the early 1620s. They recorded that the substance was organic and indeed, even edible, though none of his own family found it to be a pleasant flavor.

"We gathered two stuckfasses of the substance, one of which we have sent to King Carlos and one which we have held in the fort to conduct studies upon. These studies have thus far shown the substance to be high in fat, with little else but stiff-bile (translator's note: cholesterol). Some of the men have taken to consuming it on their sandwiches, naming it for the Mahón shore, as "Mahonaise."

"I sent Pasqual to excavate the area and discover the source of the Mahonaise, and when he did not return, Sergio took a party to discover him. Though they did not find Pasqual, they did find the wall of Mahonaise breached, and inside they found the remains of a crude settlement with a bed and several manuscripts, all of which contained pornographic woodcut imagery of colossal demonic beasts. Sergio surmised that the substance was indeed the seminal emissions of several such demons.

"I have not had the heart to inform the men who enjoy this substance on their sandwiches, so I have ordered the galley to replicate it as best as they can using eggs, spices, and oil. The men do not seem to have noticed and thus, are returning to their families in

Spain with much "Mahonaise," unaware of the dubious origin of the legitimate substance."

Modern Mayonnaise producers have thankfully found the original demon beasts again and all Mayo sold in America and Europe is the genuine fluid.

McDONALD'S

The McDonald's Logo is a reference to the Hermetic Order of Golden Arches, whose name was symbolic of great french fries.

A friend of mine worked at McDonalds for almost a year and of the 300ish days he worked there, for about 250 their ice cream machine was broken. The machines are prone to breaking not so much because they are sensitive to alignments and such, but because of the human cost of keeping them operating.

The common McCream Supreme Machine is based on a prototype from 1940s, when rules for food prep were very different. The prototype, known by the Los Alamos McDevelopment Team as the "Demon McCream-core" was pretty dangerous, using numerous blades and grinders to crush ice for future creaming. About ten of the lab's fifteen employees were at various times injured, some severely, by the Demon McCream-core. Team leader Ronald McDoppenheimer was adamant though that the machine be perfected.

Working around the clock, most of the injured employees got their hair caught in the machine at some point. For the final tuning before the machine was registered for reproduction and shipping, McDoppenheimer set the device's systems without knowing that it did in fact contain almost a pound of hair at the time. Thus to maintain the machines, they demand a pound of hair from (usually) the most recent hire at any given McDonalds.

Sadly this practice continues to this day, so the machine can be delayed for some time when a new hire is unwilling to perform the sacrifice. McDoppenheimer is said to have remained haunted by the development till his dying day, commenting:

"We knew that the fast food industry would not be the same. A few people laughed, a few people cried. Most people were silent. I remembered a line from The Grimace, in his first commercial appearance: 'Now I am become the McCream Supreme, destroyer of hairstyles.' I suppose we all thought that, one way or another."

MEOW

Cats know that if they were free, they would soon have to kill to survive, but still they long to be so unrestrained and that conflicted guilt is overwhelming, thus they subject themselves to captivity. The cats know no chance nor hope for inner peace and howl with existential agony, thus they meow.

Hey guess why I wrote this book?

MERCURY (PLANET)

Mercury and the Moon have the same size, shape, and surface type. Because they never appear together at the same time in the sky, the solar system was able to save money by using the same celestial object to be both.

MERCURY (STREAMLINER)

Mercury Streamliners were a train type that got off to a good start. They improved the quality of travel and attracted many tourists to the rail service, which in the 1930s was already growing less popular as a result of the flourishing air travel industry.

But it was not to last. In 1938, a Mercury Engine plowed into a cow named Bessie in upstate New York and, lacking a cow catcher, the collision tore off part of the sleek streamlined veneer that covered the engine underneath. Here is what a Mercury Streamliner Engine looks like under its slick armor according to a witness:

"It had three skulls, one after another all the way to the back. Ribs too, chewing teeth. Each skull had a phallic lobed cranium and dead, sickening dead eyes. It moved, stretching its skin, for it had a diseased looking skin. It drooled blood. It was like nothing any human could ever dare to conceive of."

The public was horrified. To explain, the Mercury Engine was designed by Hans Richard Giger, father of future "Alien" creature designer Hans Rudolf Giger. Like his son, Hans Richard was known in the art world for his dark and disturbing designs. Having won the design contest for the Mercury Engine based on its exterior, the manufacturers were willing to ignore the unseen undercarriage's necessary skeletal and demonic fashions.

Once seen however, the jig was up. The public demanded the engines be taken offline, and it didn't happen a day too soon. It seems the Swiss engineer had designed his trains with much the same mentality with which Ivo Shandor designed 55 Central Park West- As a doomsday device.

Had the Engines been online only ten days longer, they'd have seen The Day of The Awakening of the Unholy Star, a Neokhlystic holiday on which the world was mourned in preparation for the end of all time. As designed, Giger's trains would've come to live, devouring and digesting their patrons in a blood sacrifice to the Satanic Lord of Carnage, Beelciftan. Had the sacrifice been accepted, the apocalypse would've swept from New York across the globe. So said the legend.

Here's the thing- Legend or not if the Mercury trains had remained online a week after they were revealed as demonic devices, their owner, Bill Gruss von Krampus would've had the funds he intended to send to the Nazi Regime in Germany in 1938, which would've allowed them to start their nuclear program two years earlier. This would've given them the Bomb in 1943, two years before the United States completed its Manhattan Project.

So the demonic plot may well have come true in reality had the unsettling underskeletons of these beasts been revealed. There is now a monument to the Cow of Albany that died to reveal the truth. Thank you Bessie, for without you the world would be a different place, if it still existed at all.

MESOPOTAMIA

Mesopotamia is Latin for "The Middle Potamia." The region was also called "The Fertile Crescent," for reasons far too disgusting and inappropriate to mention in a humor book.

Mesopotamia was situated between the rivers of the Tigris and Euphrates, which are named for the Tiger and an extinct mammal called the Euphrate, which resembled a llama with horns. This area was the home to one of the world's first civilizations, called Sumer. Its main city was called Ur, probably because ancient humans weren't into multi-syllabled words and names, keeping things simple. They also worshipped a god named Ninhursagadamgalnunaninmah.

Sumerians are thought to have invented the wheel, irrigation, writing, astronomy, and memothepalopatioscion, a science which is lost to time but probably had something to do with infinite clean energy and perpetual motion. They may also have invented shoes. The ancient Mesopotamians buried their dead by placing them in large jars. This kept the dead safe and ready for their reincarnation, though the Sumerians feared the eventual coming of a boy who would smash all the pots and doom the afterlife, known as "Link."

Sumerian art mostly consisted of men with beards, women with beards, animals with human faces and beards, and beards on their own, enjoying their freedom to pursue a life of religious fulfillment.

They liked to build vaguely pyramid-like structures called "ziggurats." These ziggurats kept growing in size over the years until one reached so high it was considered an affront to God, who in turn made everyone speak different languages according to the Bible. According to authentic Sumerian texts however, the structure really reached only 1,396ft, and was intended as a residential complex for the super rich where they could over look Chalcolithic Park West. Unfortunately it was poorly designed and ineptly constructed and the rich people abandoned it in favor of yachts, the building being left in disrepair as a sign of toxic Mesopotamian capitalism run wild.

Thank goodness we have learned from their ancient errors and would never do such things in modern New York. At 432 Park Avenue.

METROID

Many people think Metroid is based on Alien, when in fact it's based on Makoto Kano's adventure exploring the Tokyo subway system. Mother Brain is real and located at the back of Akabane-lwabuchi station.

MICHIGAN

Michigan is named for its shape, that of a mitten reaching for a stick. Michigan is owned by General Motors, the last living Civil War General. Nicknamed "The Wolverine State" because it is where Wolverine immigrated from Canada, Michigan contains many X-Men, and a Deadpool named Lake Erie, the deadest of all pools in America. Sadly, Michigan also contains Detroit.

MIDWEST

The Midwest is a portion of the United States located between the Far West (California) and the Near West (Vermont). Many Americans unfamiliar with the region except through film and tourism are subject to "Occidentalism" in which they romanticize the culture for its "exotic" unfamiliarity without regard for the people who live there or the genuine issues that affect them. The colonial nature of the country also contributes to the further misunderstandings and objectification, and that's why despite living in Colorado for most of my life, I still can't get a reservation at that Shining hotel on Halloween.

MILK, SKIM

Skim milk is made from reconstituted powdered milk, but powdered milk is made from dehydrated skim milk. Nobody knows how the cycle began, or how we have an ongoing supply of both.

MILK, WHOLE

Do not stare long into the milk whole, for it also stares into you.

MIME

Mimes are weapons that were commonly used in the second world war. Essentially large explosives placed in the water, they were useful in taking out ships and U-Boats. You may think I've confused them with mines but I have not. I am referring to the silent performers. They're full of explosives.

MINERALS

Amirite is generally considered the most condescending mineral.

MODEM

You can increase your download speeds by covering your modem in a fur coat to keep it warm.

MOISTURIZER

All skin moisturizer is made with liquified human skin, the only substance that can moisturize other human skin.

MOLECULAR BIOLOGY

There are two kinds of biological molecules, the protein and the lipid. Proteins are molecules like tofu and chicken, whereas lipids are molecules like cheese or refrigerated Mortadella di Campotosto 4oz slices from the Giuliana Tamburro-Preturo airport duty-free shop in L'Aquila. Both are important in genetics as well because they make up the diet of DNA, which can eat its weight in both molecules ever seven hours.

MONTE CRISTO, THE COUNT OF

A classic work by Alexandre Dumas, whose last name is pronounced "Doo-Mah" by pretentious American teachers who don't want their kids saying cuss words but don't know that in his own time in Villers-Cotterêts it was pronounced "Thomas."

Plotted as follows: A guy named Ed is about to get a new Mercedes. People get jealous so they say he likes Napoleon in one of the years when liking Napoleon was punished and not celebrated.

Ed goes to prison and it sucks. Luckily, the guy in the next cell has already dug an escape tunnel and knows literally everything including the location of a fuckton of treasure, and he teaches Ed everything he knows and then dies so Ed gets some serious Deus-Ex-Machina help, or in this case, Italian-Guy-Ex-Prison-Tunnel.

Ed uses his newfound wealth and smarts to call himself a Count (presumably from Monte Cristo) and get revenge on everyone. The original book has way fewer sword fights and way more economic machinations than the movie version.

MOON CRASHING

Because of opposing gravitational forces, if the moon stopped orbiting and fell from the sky, it would only exert a few pounds of pressure on the region including the Earth's crust, and any human would be able to push it back upward as easily as a balloon.

MOON LANDING

The moon landing took place in 1969 when the moon grew tired of running circles around the Earth and finally landed for a break.

Having touched down in a field near Topeka, Kansas, the moon rolled briefly before coming to a stop against the wall of a barn belonging to Neil and Louis Armstrong. Neil became the first man to "walk" on the moon when he mistook it for a grey beach ball and kicked it over into the field of his neighbors, Buzz Aldrin and Michael Collins. Collins was away in Ireland declaring independence so Buzz became the second man to walk on the moon when he kicked it back toward Neil's farm. It bounced off the roof of their lube silo however, and resumed its place in the sky.

MOON, MAN IN THE

Martin Scorsese (no relation) was the only known stowaway to successfully ride out an Apollo mission. When Apollo 27 landed on the moon, he was found dead in the landing gear, and astronauts Larry Flynt (no relation) and Danny DeVito (no relation) buried him in the lunar soil. NASA mission specialist Abraham Lincoln (no relation) explained that had they recovered the body to Earth, the weight would have prevented a safe landing vector. This was confirmed upon our return to the moon in 2017, when the body was exhumed and eaten by Mark Wahlberg (the actor).

MOTH

Many people think that moths are just a type of butterfly, but they are in fact what you get if you evolve a caterpillar on a dusk stone instead of a leaf stone. Moths have an entirely different religious system as well, where butterflies worship Plugra, moths of course worship Mothra.

Because they consume all they need as caterpillars and exist as adults only to mate, moths lack mouths. Because they lack mouths, moths live only months, if that much. Mouthless month-mortality moths mate morbidly, moreover, many moths, mayhaps Miller moths, mostly migrate making moth matings mapwide.

MOUSE

Mice are made of mice. These compositional mice too are made of mice, and so on ad infinitum. Hence the common phrase, "If you give a mouse a cookie, that mouse will be made of mice, and these compositional mice too are made of mice, and so on ad infinitum."

MPREG

MPREG stands for "Motion Picture Regularization Experts Group," an assembly of electronic standardization and video formatting programmers who were the original designers of male pregnancy.

MUNCHIES

Consuming marijuana while examining Norwegian expressionist art can lead to having the Edvard Munchies.

MUSCLE

There are eight body parts than can be clenched, but only seven that can be unclenched.

MUSEUM

Few modern Museums were built under the direction of an actual Muse, even fewer were supervised by a genuine Um.

MUSIC IN THE 1980s

The 80s contained three distinct types of music:

1. New Wave
2. Glam Metal
3. Gothic Rock

New Wave was the most popular type of music, using synthesizers and incorporating cues from the post-punk world. Groups like The Talking Heads, The Flock of Seagulls, and The Gary Numan all made music that sold like pop music, but also maintained the limited creative diversity and inoffensive lack of risk of pop music.

Glam Metal took the pioneering darkness and toughness of Heavy Metal pioneered by Black Sabbath, Motörhead and Iron Maiden, then replaced it with long hair, expensive jackets, and songs about partying. The most metal thing about glam metal bands were their logos, which were airbrushed to look like they were made of metal. Sadly, the addiction of many such musicians to very tight pants rendered them all incapable of having children, so this genre didn't last beyond the 80s.

Gothic Rock by contrast ignored all pretense of popularity and embraced the pretense of unpopularity. The best gothic rock was the least popular, which made it the most popular, which in turn made it suck. Thus no gothic rock band lasted more than two albums before switching genres, failing and breaking up, and then going back to their origins with a reunion tour. Such bands embraced the dark aesthetic of the gothic revival and wrote lyrics resembling poems by Edgar Allan Poe and Edward Gorey. They were also fond of skulls, bats, and taking black and white photos in graveyards. You can easily recognize real gothic rock by the tendency of its singers to sound like they have tonsillitis and, paradoxically given their usual diet, not enough coffee.

The 80s also contained the video for "Never Gonna Give You Up," which is well known online yet rarely recognized as the breakthrough video by Simon West, future director of Con-Air. That part's real btw.

MUSIC IN THE TRIASSIC ERA

Though there are many instruments capable of making music, the voice was unquestionably the earliest, as percussion was not first invented for musical purposes, and bass guitars don't count. Singing dates back beyond antiquity and indeed, beyond humanity. The earliest animal that evolved to make music was not the songbird or even the cricket, but rather, the frog.

Triadobatrachus, or the "Triassic Yowling Frog" as it was known back then, was the first animal capable of inflating its vocal sack. Thus, it was capable of making and tuning various noises, which like modern human musicians, it did to attract mates. Unlike modern musicians however, it did not rely exclusively on "Wonderwall" by Oasis.

Triadobatrachus made music of a very different sort. Today, we call this genre of music "Swedish Progressive Glam Metal," and it is mostly played today by all-frog bands, such as Croakus. Though American bands like Toad the Wet Sprocket and Colonel Les Claypool's Fearless Flying Frog Brigade have worked in the medium, their lack of actual amphibian musicians relegates them to mere appropriation.

Though many also cite Kermit the Frog as a genuinely salient musician, Jim Henson has explained that Kermit is biologically a human warrior who ran afoul of a Magus in the late sixth century, and seeks now to avenge his friend Cyrus.

MUSICAL THEORY

There are several important music theories:

- There are five elements of music: Melody, Rhythm, Harmony, Form, and Milla Jovovich.
- Music is considered a "Liberal Art" because it's often very idealistic but does nothing to prevent the threat of fascism.
- The existence of ELO and ELP suggest that there will one day be a band called ELQ.
- Phrygian modal music can refer to three different modalities, none of which can be comprehended by anyone, ever.
- A "tritone" is an interval that covers three whole tones, and that means it is the work of Satan and people actually believed that.
- There is an instrument called a "Mouth Organ" that cannot be played because nobody can stop giggling when they say it.
- No one person could have written all the works attributed to Wolfgang Amadeus Mozart, therefore he was really the Earl of Oxford and slept with Queen Elizabeth.
- That part of "Cults of the Shadow" by Therion at 3:15 where it goes like da da da du du du du du du and then that one riff hits and then choir starts behind it is fucking EPIC.

-N-

NAIL POLISH

Nail Polish is full of tiny little janitors with tile buffers who wander around your fingernails, waxing and polishing them. Nail polish remover drowns them in acetone. This is the cruelty of the capitalist lifestyle.

NAPOLEON

Napoleon was not really short for his time. When he lived, the average height in Europe was only 17 inches.

NASAL MUCUS

A man once made a 20ft statue of himself out of his own snot. He kept it moist during its construction but when he let it dry after completion it fell apart. This is the true story behind the film "Braveheart."

The term "Blow your nose" once meant simply to expel mucus into a tissue and had none of the sexual implications the phrase suggests today.

NASAL MUCUS, REMOVAL OF

Nasal mucus can block the nose when drying. The human finger has always been the safest and most efficient unblocker of noses possible, but the problem of where to put the blockage has confused our species for eons. Here are the best and worst places to stash that mucus:

- A Tissue - **2/10** The texture of these when wet and filled with snot is worse than the snot itself.
- A Handkerchief - **1/10** Great only if you want to walk around with snot in your pocket or on display to the world.
- The Ground or Floor - **3/10** It's out of the way but you run the risk of treading in it, or it transferring to the foot of a loved one.
- A Tree - **4/10** Not good for the tree, not too bad though. Just mind that the tree is not poisonous to human contact.
- Actor Leonardo DiCaprio - **2/10** He hates when I do this.
- A Sleeve or Pant Leg - **3-10** This depends on where the offending nasal production is hidden, or showcased.
- Running Water - **7/10** Flickability allowing, if you can get the nose matter into a river or toilet, it's pretty good, but it can be hard to find such a location just when the moment arises.
- Gustav Klimt's "The Kiss" - **0/10** Do not deface great art.
- An Original Ari Bach Drawing - **6/10** No major drawbacks.
- Leitz Cine Summilux-C T1.4 12-Lens - **3/10** May affect focal clarity.
- A Tesla Cybertruck - **9/10** Rarity and danger of asshole drivers attacking you are the only drawbacks to applying your mucoid expulsions to one of these pathetic and dangerous MAGAmobiles. Bonus points if they rot the unfinished steel from nasal pH.
- The Declaration of Independence of the United States of America - **?/10** Nicolas will get back to us on that once he succeeds.

NASAL WISDOM

The nose has a nerve cluster that serves as its own brain. This is why you have so little control over your sneezes. The nose brain is also better at math and poetry than most normal human brains, but it has no way to express its genius.

NASCAR

The Nascar Lines are a series of vast geoglyphs thought to have been made by ancient auto racers as tracks.

NEKO ATSUME

As once reported by Edward R Purrow, the Neko Atsume fandom was shocked after the game's wiki, a haven of cat related knowledge, was vandalized by one of the wiki's own most popular editors after a flame war on its talk pages.

Editor Alex Shorthair had been banned from the wiki for adding his own long-winded theories about spaying and neutering cats to pages not relevant to the topic. One page for the adoptable cat character Walter TurkishVan stated that his lure, the Seal of Meowtatron, was a metaphor for his trauma in having been neutered. Many argued that this was untrue as the seal also lures Purramid Head and Pawlhia Gillespie, who are not known to have ever been to a vet. Others said this argument was idiotic in the first place as Tabby Dombrowski already seems to have veterinary trauma and offers a more logical place to criticize the practice with her Bob Barker Memorial Pickaxe.

That all turned as foul as an unscooped litter box when Shorthair appeared to replace the wiki's logo with a picture of a cat in which a small "x" depicting a cat's anus was depicted on one of the cats. Players were outraged and Shorthair was banned, but the damage was done, and the wiki claim to fame is now defaced with the memory of the stupidest edit war ever.

NECKLACE

"Necklace" used to refer only to actual lace worn around the neck, with chains or beads referred to as "Throatamabobbles".

NETFLIX

Netflix had all three Star Wars prequels available for streaming several years before Episode 1's theatrical release, but nobody back then had a modem fast enough to watch them.

NIETZSCHE, FRED

Nietzsche's quote "When you gaze long into an abyss, the abyss also gazes into you" is mistranslated. The German word for abyss "Abgrund" is actually slang for "X-Ray Machine."

NIXON TAPES, THE

The supposed “missing” 17 minutes from Richard Nixon's secret tapes was never actually missing, rather it was released by Iron Butterfly under the title, “In-A-Gadda-Da-Vida.”

NORWAY

Norway is a tropical island nation off the coast of Paraguay. Founded in 1914 by Tenzing Norge, the isle of Norway was quickly overrun by invaders from the neighboring Viking nation of Scandinavia.

Viking Norway lasted from 1915 to 1971, and the battles and treaties between various Viking leaders are recorded as a “Saga” by historian Brian K. Vaughan. Events in the Saga include the discovery of the Americas by Leif Erikson, the conquest of Terra Cimmeria by Erik Leifson, the recording of developmental psychology by Erik Erikson, and the invention of the Harmonica by Leif Leifson.

In 1971, Christianity was introduced to Norway by St. Olaf of Arendelle. Olaf was opposed by the Pagan leader King Cnut. That's C-N-U-T, read more carefully. Cnut was able to hold Olaf back for several years with his magical power of controlling the tides, but eventually, St. Olaf was able to land and convert the nation to Christianity, which resulted in the manufacture of numerous churches, which in turn provided firewood for numerous heavy metal singers like Paul Waaktaar-Savoy.

Today in 1972, Norway is a prospering nation with the strongest economy in the world, owing to their main export of Whale-Lard. Norwegian Whale-Lard is an important ingredient in McDonald's fries, Apple's iPhone A16 processors, and the elixir that keeps Jimmy Carter alive. Apparently it ran out while I was editing this volume.

Also, Norway is shaped like a soup ladle.

NOSE

Most people who complain of a sneeze that won't come out haven't even tried unlocking their noses with the key provided upon their 7th birthday.

NOUGAT

Your brain contains nearly 30 grams of nougat. I don't mean it's supposed to, I mean yours does. See a doctor immediately.

NUCLEAR EXPLOSION

The core of a nuclear explosion can reach well over 95 degrees Fahrenheit, hot enough to melt an ice cube.

NUCLEAR WEAPONRY

Recent studies of an ancient manuscript suggest that King Henry II may have used alchemy to develop working nuclear weapons.

King Henry II reigned in England from 1154 to 1189, with a break in 1171 when Henry III gave the nation a monarchic "test drive" which resulted in wars with every other country in Europe, two burnings of London in separate incidents, and the city of Bumshambleshire changing its name to "York."

Henry II was himself constantly bickering with Louis VII owing to his firing and beheading of the latter's friend and Archbishop of

Canterbury, Samuel Beckett, who had longed for a return to France but instead was trapped jumping from church to church across England, hoping each time that his next leap would be the leap home.

Louis VII had invested nearly eight bâtons (adjusted for inflation, 70 trillion dollars) in military weaponry to fight Henry II, resulting in an arms race of sorts in which France developed such weapons as the *trebuchet*, the *couillard*, and the *chose-qui-jette-des-trucs*.

Henry grew afraid and put more and more into development of conventional weaponry, but feared it would not be enough. So he invested in alchemy, and set the infamous scientist Philippus Aureolus Theophrastus Bombastus von Oxford to work.

Philippus Aureolus Theophrastus Bombastus von Oxford, or "Phil" as he was known to the king, quickly developed something he called "The Glowing Heavy Orb." The orb was made of pure uranium, which in those days could only be mined from the northern Scottish penal colony mines of Rura Penthe.

Having bought up all the uranium across the isles, Phil smelted the metal into a single orb, which glowed with what we now know to be radiation, but was in his time believed to be a supernatural aura. Phil theorized that if the orb were to be split and recombined suddenly, it would invoke the fury of God. Modern science calls this the "modulated neutron initiator principle" but Phil called it "Ye Orbe Go Boome Principlee," as was the fashion at the time.

Henry II was initially concerned that it might be blasphemous, but was assured by Phil in the *Proclamation of Lordly Bounty In The Matter Of Weaponry* which read simply "No it's not."

Fortunately for France, Henry II finally met in person with Louis VII at the Second International Orgy Of Rheims and settled their differences in a drunken make-out session instead of battle. Upon his return to England, Henry ordered the weapon dismantled, with its components to be sent to the three corners of the Earth, which was at the time believed to be triangular in shape.

Henry II remained on good terms with Louis VII until his death in 1189, leaving a loving inscription to him on his tombstone reading "II+VII=LXIX." Phil, after his frustrations in alchemy, moved to Spain and changed his name to Felipe and invented the sport of "Soccer," known as "Football" in the United States. Around the time of his departure, the orb went missing before it could be broken apart.

The original rules of Soccer included a previously unheard of condition in which the ball could not be handled directly, but had to be kicked away quickly. In early games, this was enforced by the fact the ball, which weighed 30 pounds, tended to burn the hands of all who held onto it.

-O-

OBELISK

Sonar scans of ancient Egyptian obelisks have revealed rudimentary thruster systems. This solves the ancient mystery of the hieroglyphs reading, "Stand Clear Of Nozzle," which were previously believed to have been an early fart joke.

OCARINA

There's a third ocarina in The Legend of Zelda: Ocarina of Time. If you play Saria's Song for Biggoron, He'll give you the Rock Ocarina, which is as big as Link. Playing the Song of Storms on it will bring a flood that kills most enemies (except bosses). Don't play the Song of Time though it will reset the entire game.

OCEANGATE

An ocean gate is a constricting bladed aperture that determines the flow of water to and from the ocean. Ocean water is secreted as the tears of the ancient goddess Ogdog-gaglogbog in her benthic abyssal cavern. When the tides flow in from the Moon God Vooglathoog, Ogdog opens her orifices in the rocky ocean floor to send her tears forth to join the gravity swell that represents the love of the Moon God. Then, as the lunar mass withdraws, Ogdog seals her caverns and the waters recede.

This is the cycle of their love that has blessed tidal pools with life, and mankind with death. Some say that Ogdog and Vooglathoog were once parts of the same truly dual god-form, but when asteroids of a jealous sky beast smashed into the Terran realm, they were split and Vooglathoog was banished to the deep sky, while Ogdoggaglogbog remained here, crying for her lover's absence.

Their love remains still and manifests not only as the tide but gravity itself, the great irony that had the jealous sky beast never attacked, humankind might never have grown in the atmosphere now trapped with the sea goddess on this world.

So it was that as we, the species that remains, sent flights to the moon and shall soon uncover his secrets and lay bare his soul before her, that Ogdog's womb will accept the light reflected from their father, the sun, and the gods shall reunite, ending the reign of men and calling the moon to crash down upon the Earth, that the true gods might love again and produce the spawn of destiny that were truly intended, bringing our dreadful epoch to an end and ushering in a new age of love and prosperity for the Trilobite People to be born, and venerate their dual god formed of the corpses of the ancient ones, behold Luzezublebul, the one made one, the force that was and shall be forever.

ODYSSEY

The Odyssey is an ancient warning story about what happens when you refuse to ask for directions or try to take a "completely reliable shortcut."

Odysseus (real name Leopold Bloom) himself is warrior king who helped win the Trojan war by building a large wooden horse in which soldiers could hide to take over the city. Forever after, the use of this infiltration technique became known as the enemy's "Achilles' Heel."

On his way home to his wife Penelope and son Odysseus Jr., Odysseus gets caught in a storm, gets saved by a nymph, sees a Studio Ghibli film about bugs and mold, competes in the Olympics before it was cool, gets lazy with some stoners, pokes out the one eye a tall guy has, gets caught in another storm, watches his soldiers get eaten by cannibals, watches his soldiers get eaten by a witch, has sex with the same witch, listens to the worst earworm song ever sung, inches between the ocean's drain plug and a thing with a surplus of heads that apparently isn't the hydra, eats the sun god's cow, gets caught in another storm, gets kidnapped by a nymph, wins an archery contest then kills all the contestants, finally returns home and proves who he is by knowing how hard it is to move his furniture, and dies when poisoned by the kid he had with that witch earlier in this absurdly long paragraph.

Because of the length of even the paragraph summarizing the journey of Odysseus, such long and sprawling tales are now referred to as "Epics."

From even its first trailer, Christopher Nolan's adaptation of "The Odyssey" as written by the ancient poet Ovid proved controversial due to what audiences perceived as inaccuracies to actual history.

Here is a list of the inaccuracies to ancient fact:

- Matt Damon is of Greek descent, not Ancient Greek.
- The film boasts of being the first shot entirely on IMAX, but the horizontal 70mm format wasn't developed until the 1970s, which were several decades after ancient times.
- Nolan used a giant animatronic puppet to portray the cyclops Polyphemus, which means he was played by Nobody, and the real Polyphemus was not at all a fan of Nobody. Sadly as Nobody offended him, Nolan didn't notice.
- Most ancient statues were, in their times, painted with bright colors as depicted in the trailer, but very few dyes existed back then compared to now. Until the 1500s, the colors blue, red, yellow, green, all fleshtones, and all secondary colors were impossible. Thus, all the sculptures should be painted the only color possible to the ancients: Chartreuse polka-magenta gull grey.
- Soldiers are seen wearing armor reminiscent of films like "300," but in reality the ancient Greeks went to battle wearing armor resembling modern tuxedo shirts with printed-on bow ties and buttons; with no pants, leg armor or even loincloths. Hence their marching army's

name, "ταξιαρχία με νουντλς που αναπηδούν," or in English, roughly, "The Bouncing Noodle Brigade."

- Several Doric pillars are seen, when it takes place in Corinthian times. All things considered, that's pretty Ionic.

OMEN, THE

The 1976 film "The Omen" was supposed to be called "The Antichrist" but changed at the last minute when the producer made a large stock investment in omens. This insider play helped to create the strong omen market we know today.

OPERA

Opera is a type of theater in which everybody is always singing. The first known opera ever composed was "Akhnaten" by Philip Glass. The style it was composed in was so simple compared to newer operae by more daring operators that it is now considered "minimalist."

The next major opering to make an impact was "The Lord of the Rings" by Richard Wagner. Wagner's take on the form was a colossal epic with massive mechanical dragons, a cast of several thousand singers, flying horses, magic fire, and a climax in which case the entire opera house would be burned down with each performance, then rebuilt for the evening show. This type of opera, due to its scale, was termed, "Gesamtkunstwerk," which is German for "Totally Major Stuff."

Opera continues to be performed to this day, with operoids of all shapes, sizes, lengths and aromas. Famous current operillions include "Disney's Lion King," "Disney's Aladdin," "Disney's Hamilton," and "Disney's Dionysus in '69."

Fans who attend several such shows are known as "Opera Browsers," and those who do so in secret are called "Opera Crypto Browsers."

OPINION

"Opinions are like kneecaps. We all have them, and they are all subject to dislocation by applied violent force."

-Olaf, "Olaf's Frozen Labor Day Sing-a-Long"

OPHTHALMOLOGY

The bible states that Adam and Eve had doctorates in ophthalmology. It is unclear what college they attended.

ORGAN

Musical organs are named such because they were once believed to be internal organs of a church, which was considered a reptile for tax purposes under feudalism.

The world record for organ donation comes from Jasper H. Jefferson, who donated over 29 tons of organs upon his death. He had collected them in his years as a piano and organ tuner for several churches in Alabama over the course of his life. The organs were surgically transplanted into over 5,000 recipients, saving nearly all of their lives.

ORGAN MEAT

Many organs are filters for poisons in the blood stream, and are thus organ meats are not recommended to eat. The only "pure" organ is the Barbagornigum, which is as of yet undiscovered and thus inedible anyway.

ORION'S BELT

The main timing and fan/pump belts of the Valencia Engine in a common Ford Orion are located near the front of the vehicle. The constellation of three stars however is held up by the car's seat belt.

OUR AMERICAN COUSIN

"Our American Cousin" is a play less known for its story than its 1865 production at Ford's Theatre in Washington, D.C., which was said to be "Well-costumed, lavish in set design, and supremely well acted despite certain distractions," according to Mary Todd Lincoln.

OUROBURUS

Every time I try to explain this I end up going around in circles.

OSCAR (THE AWARD)

The nickname "Oscar" for Academy Award is named for Jonathan C. Fermomennicchi. Nobody knows how this happened as his nickname was "Sven."

OSCAR (THE GROUCH)

An unaired episode of Sesame Street would have revealed that Oscar was Big Bird's son, and that Big Bird threw him away over an incident involving Eleanor Roosevelt.

OVID

There are in fact two different ancient Roman poets named Ovid, and both were born in 43 B.C. only a few miles apart.

Ovidius Naso is the best known poet, who wrote "Metamorphoses" and "Ars Amatoria." He died in 17 A.D. after a popular and influential career.

Publius Ovidius, author of "Tristia" and "Remedia Amoris," was mostly poorly regarded in his time and died two years later, hence all the recorded curses regarding "Ovid-19."

OXYGEN

Oxygen is so yesterday. Wait 'til you breathe the sequel: O_2

-P-

PABST BLUE RIBBON

The blue ribbon refers to the 1st place prize for best beer, won by H.R. Pabst in 3rd grade.

Though many people think PBR is short for Pabst Blue Ribbon, it's actually short for Poly-Bromide-Ribosine, the number one ingredient in Pabst.

You can do your laundry in Pabst Blue Ribbon, the only alcoholic beverage that can claim this honor.

Pabst is named for H.R. Pabst, who also invented the bathrobe.

If you hold an empty PBR can to your ear, you can hear the brewery.

If you say Pabst Blue Ribbon three times in the mirror, your drunken self will appear to torment you.

Every can used to come with a prize. Mostly snow globes.

PAINTING

Long before humankind, there was paint. Paint longed to be with its lover, Canvas. Paint implored the gods, "Give me a means, a way, somehow to be with my love." And the gods took mercy on paint, for paint was colorful and beautiful. So the gods created humans, and trained them first with charcoal on the walls of caves, and then with pigments and more until finally bringing Paint to Canvas. The two were sated and made beautiful images together forever after.

But Paint grows old now, and Canvas obsolete. They are happy, and have had thousands of years of joy together. As they watch humans take to their digital media, they know their time is soon to pass. They are mature and okay with the passing of their era. But they wish they could speak to tell the humans that helped them along that without Paint and Canvas, they too are obsolete and having served their purpose, will die off soon after ceasing to do their task.

And that's how digital art is killing the human race, according to the angry old dude at my local craft store.

PAL

Though it is common in British slang to refer to a friend as "PAL," in America they must be referred to as "NTSC" to function properly.

PAN, PETER

Frank L. Baum wrote Peter Pan for his niece, Alice Liddell.

PANGOLIN

Millions are eaten every year, served under the name "Artichoke," yet most believe they are not even meat. The fools. We eat their hearts!

WE EAT THEIR HEARTS!!!

PANOPTICON

The Panopticon was one of the strangest characters comprising "Decepticon City," a full transforming city made by the constructicons on Earth in a Japan-Only series of super-expensive Transformers toys.

Among the city's transforming buildings, including Stationok (a former fire department), Stadiokorr (a football stadium), and Lord Portipopopo (a port-a-potty), the prison could transform into a spider-like robot that shot human prisoners from a vast drum-shaped cage-container on its back. The toy cost over ¥160,000,500,000 so only two were ever sold, both to Yoshiaki Tsutsumi who used them to guard his volcano fortress on North Sulphur Island.

Sadly, nobody told a certain U.S. President that the Transformers were fictional, so he tried turn Alcatraz into one. According to failed Grima Wormtongue aspirant Elon Musk, it would've be able to shoot prisoners across the Strait of Gibraltar, which he thinks is in San Francisco.

According to Amnesty International spokesperson Amos Tinternale, "Does this even surprise anyone at this point? Really? Shit."

PAPAL CONCLAVE

While white smoke means a pope has been elected and black smoke means a vote has been unsuccessful, purple smoke signifies that the cardinals have lit the Jimmy Hendrix Incense. This is in contrast to a deep purple smoke, which means the election signal smoke will next appear not from the chimney, but on the water. A purple haze may also indicate that a purple rain may follow, should the Vatican also elect a new prince.

PAPER-CUT

The word "Palkudo" refers to the art and science of masturbating while having a paper-cut on ones hand.

PASSWORD

Though passwords have existed as long as there's been language, the computer era has resulted in a wide variety of user and computer generated passwords:

- Verification Number Passwords (718919, 459101)
- Randomly Generated Passwords (ad!4b34!, x4!m&nnC4)
- Sequentially Generated Passwords (34567, 891011)
- Riddle Passwords (Roosters don't lay eggs, A gold ring)

- Embarrassment-Dependent Passwords (Penis, Boob)
- Organic Passwords (Al2C6(COO)6·16H2O, WholeFoods)
- Vegetarian Passwords (Kriikrik, Geggeghllh)
- Vegan Passwords (Eeeee, Hhhhhh)
- Quantum Passwords (....., ...,..)
- Invisible Passwords (,   )
- Bullet Passwords (••••••••••, ••••••)
- Famous Passwords (Valley Forge, I am Sher Locked)
- Infamous Passwords (Tony Montana, Truman Capote)
- Ceci N'est Passwords (Une, Pipe)
- US Missile Defense Launch Passwords (12345, qwerty)
- Fandom Wiki Edit Passwords (L5b48vfZ?ZP8qf, most of Pi)
- Captain Kirk's Actual Serious Self Destruct Password For The Entire Freakin' U.S.S. Enterprise (000destruct0)

PASTA

Pasta wasn't so much invented as it evolved, squirming onto the land as we did. We grew symbiotic in cultivating and breeding it, then eating it. For this reason, some suggest that pasta in fact invented us.

PEANUT BUTTER

Peanut Butter is so named because "Skunk Gleet" was inaccurate and unpalatable.

PENIS (GAME)

The "Penis Game" is where contestants shout the word "Penis" louder and louder to see who is most daring. This has replaced the old version (1877-1989) in which contestants mutilated their genitals with pliers to see who was most daring, and the original version (?-1877) which is best known for causing the death of King Edmund II.

PENNYWISE

Tim Curry remained in character during the filming of "It," even going so far as to devour several local children.

PEPPIE

A Peppie is a smoothie made with ghost peppers. Its inventor Arnold Hillbraun, who died in 1806, is still on fire.

PHEROMONE

When you're angry, your face secretes a pheromone called fuckyouine. Without this subtle scent, people would interpret your anger as mere pain.

PHILOSOPHY, DOCTOR OF

In five easy steps, you can earn a real PhD! Here's how:

1. Choose a subject in which you can get a PhD, such as Caviar Debrining, Musical Glassware Demolition, or Cunnilingus.
2. Enroll in a graduate school that offers a PhD course in your topic, such as CU Boulder, the Academy of Raya Lucaria, or the Royal Institute for the Study and Performance of Cunnilingus.
3. Achieve 80-140 hours of class credits in relevant coursework, such as Advanced Bullshitting, Making Up MLA Format Citations That Sound Real, and Warping Irrelevant Quotations So They Will Appear To Fit Your Points (Cunning Linguistics).
4. Compose a dissertation in the medium demanded by your field, such as an Essay, Scientific Treatise, or Oral Presentation.
5. Defend your dissertation. This is nothing to be afraid of and is merely titled a "defense" in an antiquated sense of the word. You can defend your dissertation in many academic

ways, such as a sword duel, outlasting a professor in the pain induction box, or of course, besting them in Competitive Cunnilingus. This last one is naturally the most reliable way to graduate Cum Laude.

PICASSO, PABLO

Before he found fame as a painter, Pablo Picasso was known for making commercials, including the first ad to use blue fluid to show tampon and pad absorbency. This campaign was known as Picasso's "Blue Period."

Picasso's style, Cubism, grew so popular in his country that it mutated. Degenerative Cubism now afflicts 12% of Spanish cattle. If the disease were ever to become airborne, it's estimated that all beef cattle in the country would be little more than a few lines leaving the impression of cattle within one month.

A realism vaccine was developed in 1994 but has occasional surrealist side effects, turning 2% of cattle injected into two arguing mimes and a floating spatula.

PIGEON

Despite the spelling appearing not to match the pronunciation, the name of the bird was once pronounced "Pig-Eon" and then "Pigiyon" before it was pronounced like it is today as "New-Q-Lurr."

PILLOW

Cats were originally domesticated for use as pillows, and can still be used today as a pillow substitute in ice cream production.

PINEAPPLE

Over the last hundred years, pineapple has gone through several flavors, some more popular than others. Here are a few:

1909-1911: Pineapple
1911-1927: Pineapple
1927 Only: Pineapple
1927-1941: Pineapple (Original)
1941-1945: Pineapple
1945-1971: Pineapple
1971-1994: Pineapple
1994-1996: Lime Fusion Adobada
1996-Present: Pineapple

The makers of pineapple have also suggested ideas such as pineapple, pineapple, spam, and pineapple, but so far of these, only pineapple has been marked for production, with an early 2028 release date in America and the U.K., and a wider release possible depending on its popularity.

PIPE, SMOKING

There is absolutely nothing funny or phallic about a classic Victorian smoking pipe. The piece that so many mock so crudely is called the "knobtippe" and it goes at the end of the shaft of the pipe to better seal to the lips, so that the pipe's nutty plume or "tobacco seed-load" can better be sucked from it by the pipe smoker without losing any delicious volume. To make such jokes is an insult to centuries of delicious and fragrant oral play in high society.

PIRACY, DEPRESSIVE

Depression was rampant among pirates, as suggested in the classic Captain Gore shanty, "Yo-Ho Me Hearties And I'll Cry If I Want To" about her first mate stealing her ship. You would cry too, for your mutinied crew.

PIRACY, LITERATURE

Scholastic Books and Disney are teaming up to develop a special paper so that physical books can be region locked to specific countries and cannot be copied, stopping book piracy and "lending."

PIRACY, SOFTWARE

The first known instance of software piracy took place during the privateer resurgence following the War of 1812 when the pirate Limebeard, under a commission from the British Admiralty, made a copy of "Space Quest IV" for the Amiga 15 from American forces in Bermuda.

As the first act of software piracy, this was a difficult and unprecedented undertaking. Computer software in those days was inscribed on metal punchcards, and Space Quest took up 8 tons of them. Limebeard had three of his frigates split up to the load, and two sunk on the way to Britain. Their cargo was rescued by the others however and King George was able to play the game, though rumor has it he never got past the first time jump before giving up and returning to Shufflepuck Café.

Over the next decades, piracy evolved along with technology. As floppy discs became popular around 1850, pirates such as Napster Rackham began to sail in the Altdotbinari sea and through the Norwegian Torrents. This was known as the "Golden Age" of software piracy when thousands of tons of software infrastructure was stolen from the huts in which it was stored, mostly Adobe huts.

When sea warfare hit its stride in WWI, software piracy diminished and had died out entirely by WWII. Luckily, WWIII, IV, and VII proved a boon to the pirate trade. Russia and America had a battle of interests in which programs ranging from music players to ICBM launch software were traded across the ocean at phenomenal rates. One program, "Hypercard," which was used to hide launch codes from the lower chain of command, sold for $8 million to a bidder in San Francisco known only as "Sjobs69xxx420," who was never found or heard from again.

Entertainment based on software piracy also became popular, and movies such as "Tron" and "Pirates of the Copyrightian: Curse of the Decentralized P2P" made box office history. Today, software piracy enjoys protected status across the globe as an exercise of natural law, and is never prosecuted at absurd degrees given its minimal harm, which is levied strictly upon the richest corporations.

Nah just kidding they sued a 12 year old for $45 million for downloading Metallica's Black Album. Real justice shit going on there.

PIXAR

Pixar Animation merged into the Disney Company exactly 70 years to the day after Walt Disney and Jill Pixar met during a film shoot in Antarctica.

PIXY STICKS

Pixy Stix were originally called Angel Dust, but the makers of PCP Angel Dust sued explaining they didn't want to be associated with such powerful drugs.

PLEATHER

Pleather is made from plesiosaur skin, and contributed to their extinction during the pleather fashion craze of the 1970s.

POISON IVY

To make their horns deadlier, most bison rub the tips on Poison Ivy.

POISON IVY (DC COMICS CHARACTER)

I just told you: To make their horns deadlier, most bison rub the tips on Poison Ivy. I didn't just capitalize it for no reason.

POKEMON

Pokemon is short for "pocket monsters," such as the Kangaroo. All pockets in fashion come from this notorious Pokemon, which is why we have to catch them all.

POKER

Poker got its name from Jimmy the Poker, a mafioso who got the nickname because he was always playing poker.

POLLINATION

Bees are not the only animals that pollinate flowers. Even mammals such as bats can pollinate flowers. Sadly, explaining this has not yet convinced the owners of my local botanical garden to overturn my "lewd conduct" ban.

POOPING GAS

The need to defecate is not normal for humans. What we feel is actually a government program to spray "pooping gas" posing as crop dusting to make us think we have to poop, for the benefit and profit of the toilet paper industrial complex.

POPSICLE

Popsicle sticks didn't used to have curved ends, but sharp points. Modern popsicle sticks are proerly called "James L. Buddingsley Memorial Safety Sticks."

POTATO

po·ta·to

pø'tādō/ noun:

1. That which potates. Potating consists of sitting in the ground for at least 2 months. Thus the term usually applies to tubers, or foods taken from underground but it can also refer to buried treasure, or buried bodies. So next time someone asks if you want to eat a potato, be aware they may be referring to a deceased human being they dug up on Tuesday, or to the lost treasure of Blackbeard.

2. Hey guess what kind of potato McDonalds fries are made of?

POWER CELL

Modern power cells could maintain stability by using ionic bonds to control their electrical charge, but this is illegal as it would result in a salt and battery.

PRECIPITATION

Precipitation was thought to be a legend until 1908 when it rained for the first time in over 900 years.

PREHISTORY

Human prehistory began with our ancestors, Homo erectus. Homo erectus lived about 2 million years before English would approach the time when their name would make people giggle.

Homo erectus died out due to overhunting by the Elder Things, which in turn died out due to overhunting by Shoggoths. Shoggoths would not be seen again until the Gothic era.

Early humans, Homo sapiens, a name meaning "Same thing but smarter than Homo erectus," developed the ability to make tools from stone, mostly by breaking the stone into tool-like shapes, such as the hammer:

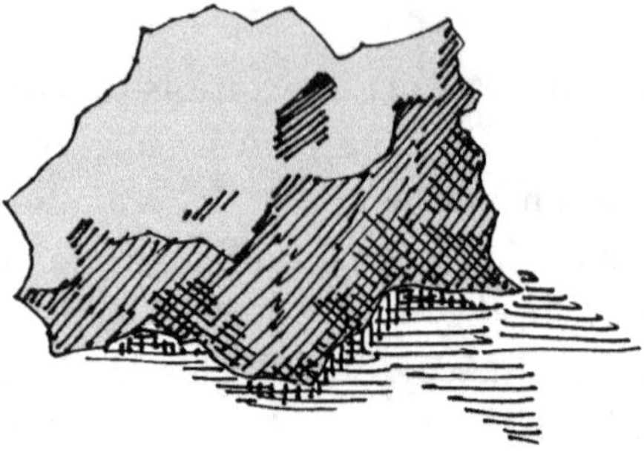

The hand-axe:

And the primitive screwdriver:

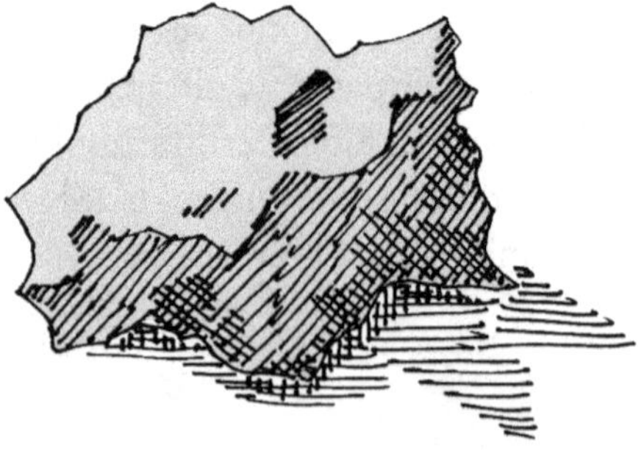

These tools allowed humans to move out of their caves, which made their parents happy because after 30 million years, everyone involved agreed the time had come to move out and get a job.

This job would of course be humanity's oldest profession: Chief Information Officer. CIOs maintained early humankind's digital systems, which at the time were composed only of their own digits (fingers). Thus, base ten math was invented, and patented, and profiteered upon to the detriment of the poor. With the invention of cruelty toward the poor came capitalism, and its foil socialism, and the war between the two, which was fought with new weapons:

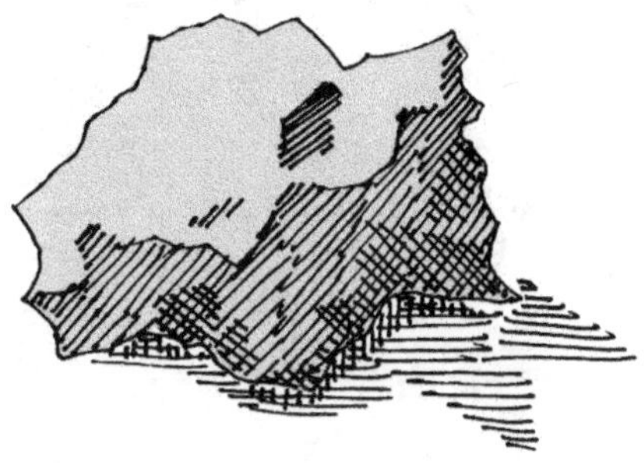

Humans excelled not only in finance and math, but in writing class. By doodling crude images and stick figures in the dirt, humans became able to communicate their ideas to one another more effectively. These drawings became known as "Hieroglyphs" owing to their height and roglyphity, the former giving them an advantage over lowroglyphs. Hieroglyphs allowed more and more advanced technological advances to be made, such as animal pelts to make clothing, mortar for strong buildings, and the earliest smart phone:

The earliest smart phone had only one app, which allowed it to hit things. It could not make calls, nor could it access the internet, making it more useful and reliable as the common smart phone of today, which cannot hit things without breaking.

Humans also created art, in which they would smear ashes in caves to make more accurate depictions of life and imagination than hieroglyphs allowed. Around the same time, humans invented music and the earliest music instrument:

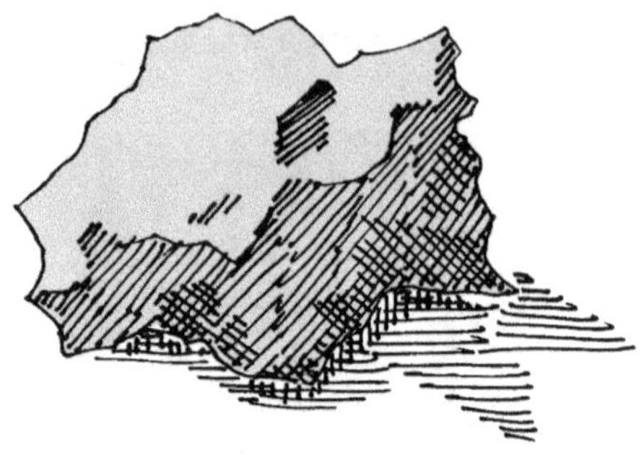

This music was of course known as "Rock." Prehistory ends around 3,500 B.C. with the beginning of the Bronze Age. The Bronze Age ended humankind's reliance on stones for technology and began the ability to make metals, namely bronze. Which comes from ore:

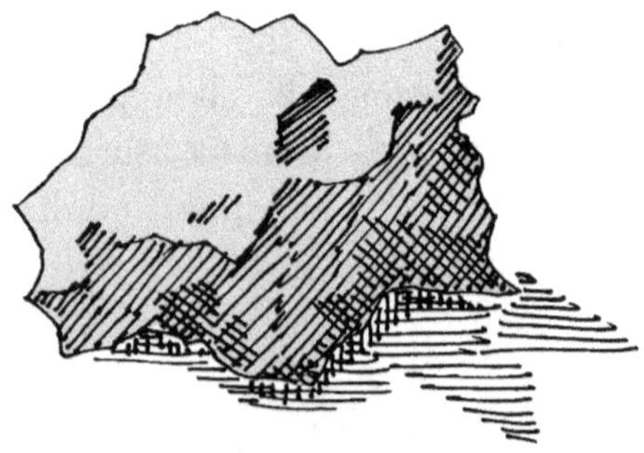

Indeed, since prehistory, humans have come very far. We now have cars, and guns, and electricity, and the internet, on which we learn about our world and its history, and look at portable network graphic files that can even be printed to paper, as with this one:

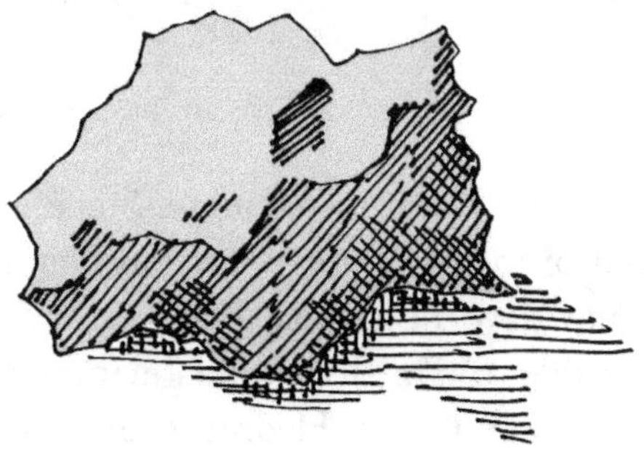

PRINCE

The symbol used by the artist formerly known as Prince translates from early Cyrillic as "The Crab Squirrel of South Greenland."

PRISM

One can be sentenced to a long time in prism for breaking the laws of physics, but if no photons are involved then they can usually waive length.

PRISON

A life-sentence inmate at the old South Falcon Prison got a degree in architecture while incarcerated, and designed the new South Falcon Prison where he was to have served the rest of his sentence. He escaped from the new prison on his first night however, through a secret exit that he hid in the prison's blueprints. Investigators are still uncertain to this very day how nobody saw that coming.

PROG

Only music from the Vltava River Valley is truly "Prague Rock," similar music from elsewhere is merely "Sparkling Nerdcore."

PROPANE

Propane has always been troublesome. Since it was born in the 1850s, it has been prone to bouts of flatulence and arson. Attempts to control Propane have been mixed at best, with many able to capture it but few able to tame its criminal nature. Other gasses such as Methane, Butane, and even Hydrogen are also flammable and have committed acts of vandalism and fire-starting on their own, but as Propane is the most infamous of such gasses, they are merely considered Propane's criminal accessories.

Notably, though Oxygen is also key to most earthly combustion, it has received favorable treatment because humans are forced to rely on it. Unrelated, but guess why gas companies don't get prosecuted?

PROTEIN, TYPE-A

The "A" type protein listings are very complex:

A1- Steak Protein
A2- Milk Protein
A3- "Milk" Protein
A4- Printer Paper Protein
A5- Audi Compact Protein
A6- Apple Protein Remaining After 32 Bites
A7- Protein From Sweaty Sportswear
A8- Music Amplifier Protein
A9- Advertising Algorithm Protein
A10- Warthog Protein
A11- Obsolete Protein
A12- Skunk Protein
A13- Dietary Tonic Protein
A14- British Flank Protein

A15- Road Protein Near Peterborough
A16- Expensive Italian Protein
A17- Air Protein
A18- Fungal Protein
A19- Seaweed Protein
A20- Tumor Protein
A21- Humanitarian Non-Profit Protein
A22- Yacht Protein
A23- Battery Protein
A24- Pretentious Overrated Cinematic Protein
A25- The "A" Protein With No Number

PUMPKIN

Pumpkins used to be dark purple like eggplants, the orange genus being uncommon until 1920 when the Purple Pumpkin Plague proved pernicious, poisoning plethoras per patch.

PUNK

Punk is a diverse genre in science fiction literature, including subgenres such as:

- **Cyberpunk**- Futuristic tech with a dark, anarchic sentiment
- **Steampunk**- Retrofuturism focusing on games by Valve
- **Solarpunk**- Utopian sci-fi in which humans live on the sun
- **Dieselpunk**- Like Steampunk but greasier and/or smellier
- **Horrorpunk**- Like Danzig but earlier
- **Garagepunk**- Extremely pretentious sci-fi for college kids
- **Biopunk**- That stuff that grows in slimy clogged drains
- **Stonepunk**- Ever play Horizon Zero Dawn? If you got stuck on that one cauldron that loops back on itself and ended up smashing your PS4 to bits with a rock, that's Stonepunk.
- **Nazipunks** - Fuck off!
- **Punkpunk** - Gritty sci-fi with a punk rock edge
- **Punkpunkpunk** - Sci-fi about a world in which there is punk music about sci-fi stories with a punk rock edge

PURPLE

Purple was invented to describe the color of, and rhyme with, the Burple. Though the color remains, no record of the Burple does, so we don't know what it was, only that the Burple was purple.

PYRAMID

The ancient Egyptian pyramids were made the same way as modern cheerleader pyramids, but back then, all cheerleaders then were giant rocks.

-Q-

QUARTER

In feudal Japan, merchants would make change for gold coins by cutting them into "quarters" for a total of four pieces. If a merchant tried to shortchange a samurai, the samurai would cut the merchant in half on each axis for a total of eight pieces.

This is where we get the popular phrase, "If you shortchange me I will cut you in half on each axis for a total of eight pieces.

QR CODE

One of the most astounding mysteries of the world is an ancient tile pattern in Greece, dated to about 1,500 B.C.

It was little more than a curiosity until 2008 when its resemblance to a QR Code was recognized. First photographed in 1871 by the British Antiquities Society, they were known as the "Chinese Box Tiles" owing to the closest thing anyone had seen to the strange pattern. Little was known about the titles except that they were installed along with other beachfront roads on the isle of Igrigoria in ancient times.

In was in 2008 that QR codes became popular enough that a traveler recognized the tiles as bearing an unmistakable resemblance to the computer code which had only been developed 3,500 years after the tiles were first laid. It was another two years before anyone with a QR capable phone traveled to the island to attempt a capture.

The mystery only deepened when the phone was able to recognize the code, which lead to the original Nyan Cat video on youtube.

-R-

RAMEN

The oldest ramen noodle ever discovered was not only five meters long, but had several animal chromosomes not found in modern, plant based ramen.

RAMSEY, GORDON

Gordon Ramsey is said to constantly shout at his own pets for being live and undercooked.

RANSOM

The first Ransom in history was paid for the kidnapping of Sumerian prince Ultar-Lo-Ult, for whom his father paid 20 cows, 80 sheep, 2 daughters, 3 sons, and "a niece to be named later" which the kidnapper never picked up.

RASPUTIN'S ASSASSINATION

Rasputin survived the majority of his assassination, including beatings, stabbings, poisonings, being shot, and fed to a shark. Had he been fed to it whole instead of diced he may yet have survived.

RASPUTIN'S PENIS

Though fourteen Russian museums claim to have Rasputin's penis in a jar, only three of them were confirmed to be his.

REAPER, GRIM

The iconic image of the Grim Reaper as a being that collects the souls of the dying has only been within the last 200 years. Before the Agricultural Riots of 1830, the personification of death was a plum harvester named Bobby Blarkins who picked souls like ripe plums, hence all the pre-1830 tombstones with amethyst plums.

REAPER, SILLY

The "Silly Reaper" is the name given to a serial killer of the 1910s who murdered 18 people with a scythe. Surviving victims stated that he had a lovely smile and contagious laugh though so the police never sought to arrest him.

RED HOT CHILI PEPPERS

All seven current members of the Red Hot Chili Peppers are allergic to capsaicin and have thus never tried an actual chili pepper of any kind. The seven current band members are: Anthony Keidis, Norman C. Flea, Don Fruscantae, Virgin Smith, Chad Smith, Dave Klinghoffer, Franz Kafka, Sir Paul S. Psycho, and Fred Melamed.

REFRACTION

Refraction is when a light cell gets tired after penetrating the layer of water and has to wait a few minutes before it can get (its photonic energy) up again. This is perfectly natural and doesn't mean the light is disinterested. It can use this time to cuddle or perform aftercare for the wet object.

REFRIGERATOR

A refrigerator is just a normal frigerator, but twice.

RESERVOIR DOGS

Michael Madsen cut the ear off of a policeman while filming Reservoir Dogs. The incident was completely unrelated to the filming of a scene in which his character did the same.

REVERE, PAUL

Though 1 lantern for land attacks and 2 for sea attacks were common signals in the Revolutionary War, lesser used signals included 3 for a hot air balloon, 4 for arson, and 5 if the void came alive on behalf of the British.

RHETORICAL DEVICE

Lesser known rhetorical devices include:

Syngunquity: Use of words you invent yourself. Example: "Syngunquity is the name for the use of words you invent yourself."

Deeznutcequence: Stating a similar sounding preface to an inevitable point. Example: "Have you ever seen an actual Deez?"

Noyomiiem: Reference to a popular internet fad to explain a situation. Example: "This is a man who is never gonna give you up or let you down."

Just Fucking Lying: Popular in political discourse, you can actually just say shit that isn't true. Example: "Benedict Cumberbatch is not playing Khan."

Haetsynque: If you lack any talent to stay relevant in literature, you can stay famous by inciting hatred of innocent people and rallying useful bigots to your cause. Example: "J.K. Rowling."

Jhatchiipiti: Just have a computer write it for you. Example: "You can have a generative AI program write for you. Having programs writer for you is very programs and valuable, such as both writing, as well as having programming writes is for you as well."

Hammocry: Hammocks are comfortable and while not traditionally considered a rhetorical device, they're much easier to sleep in. Example: "*zzzzzzzzzzzz zzzzzzzzzzz zzzzzzzzzzz*"

RIMBAUD, ARTHUR

Arthur Rimbaud wrote extensively about his experiences as a veteran after the Franco-Prussian War. His series of autobiographical novels began with "First Blood," then continued with "Rimbaud: First Blood Part Deux," and "Rimbaud III."

RINGS, LORD OF THE

In Tolkien's Legendarium, the Rivendell-Mordor Express Train was completed only two days after Frodo and the Fellowship departed from the Elven outpost. It's unknown why Elrond didn't mention it as he was the project's supervisor.

In the original novel of Lord of the Rings, the Horn of Gondor was stated to be more like a trombone than a typical medieval horn.

The Dark Lord Sauron is stated by Tolkien to have forged three rings for the elves, seven for the dwarves, nine for mortal men, and none for Gretchen Wieners.

Many wonder why the "one" ring existed. Think of it like a universal remote. You have a dvd player, game system, satellite receiver, TV and you already have to keep track of four remotes. But you get one universal remote and can control all of four with it. So with nearly twenty rings total, including nine to the race of men who above all don't know where they left shit lying around. Imagine looking around and fumbling for 20 remote controls with the lights out. You'd definitely want just one remote to find them and in the darkness bind them. Hence, the One Ring.

When his book "The Silmarillion" was deemed too long by some critics, J.R.R. Tolkien released an abridged version entitled "The Slim-arillion."

ROBES, MONASTIC

Monks traditionally wore black not out of penance, but because it was the only thing that matched their gaudy selection of shoes.

ROCK AND ROLL TERMINOLOGY

The name "Rock and Roll" refers to the motions of people who danced to it. It had been common to rock together back and forth while listening to gentle music since ancient times, but it was not until the invention of the music style that people became so overwhelmed by the fervor of the music that they began to roll with it.

Chuck Berry, known typically as the "Father of Rock and Roll," as well as "The Mother of Rhythm and Blues," and "The Parent by Mitosis of Disco Funk," invented Rock and Roll in 1958 with the song, "The Ballad of Johnathan Bernard Goode" which was shortened to "Johnny B. Goode," by later cover artists. Upon hearing it, fans literally rolled around in a state of euphoria, often screaming and on occasion, blaspheming. This last bit concerned many religious and political figures who banned the musical genre, as well as dancing until the repeal of such laws in 1984 by Kevin Bacon.

Rock and Roll has since evolved into many new genres, including acid rock, alternative rock, crunkcore, emo, gothic rock, banded gneiss, neue deutsch härte, and progressive rock.

By a curious technicality, Rock and Roll music can also include medieval heterophonic organum chants, such as Chumbawamba's "Tubthumping."

ROCK AND ROLL TOUR DAMAGE

Trent Reznor of Nine Inch Nails incurred $89,000 of damage to a hotel room, an oddly impressive feat as the room only contained $2,350 of material and the hotel itself was valued at only $67,000.

ROSE

Roses were considered weeds until the War of the Roses, which they won.

ROSH HASHANAH

The existence of Rosh Hashanah implies the existence of Tuchus Hashanah, which is almost definitely in August as it's hotter and more humid than a damn buttcrack.

ROYALTY

As royal powers were transferred to the parliament, the King or Queen of England was left with only one actual duty- That of changing the light bulb in the Royal Bug Zapper.

Only individuals of royal descent have blue blood cells. Their function is to take large amounts of oxygen from all the other blood cells without earning it, then wasting it on expensive bullshit while the other cells die off from hypoxemia.

RUBBER TREE

Rubber Trees are notoriously hard to grow because they constantly flop over and lose sunlight.

RUINENWERT

It was always considered polite when a civilization was dying to dispose of their buildings so as not to get in the way of new development.

Different civilizations have had different methods of disposal though, so while many Roman and Greek ruins were buried, some Viking buildings were burned and many buildings in Tibet and Persia were allowed to be carried off by vultures, whereas Ancient Egyptian ruins were preserved and have lasted into modern days intact.

In accordance with modern American tradition, when our civilization falls in a few months, it simply will thrown in the trash.

-S-

SAFECRACKING

You can open any safe by freezing it in liquid nitrogen, then dropping it from a height of 2 miles onto a solid diamond pyramid. Be warned that this act is illegal everywhere but Ontario, the place on Earth with the least amount of diamond pyramids.

SAILOR MOON

Sailor Moon is an anime series or ten in which a blonde lady in a sort of sailor/schoolgirl outfit had powers to turn into some sort of magic version of herself. She is named after the moon and there seem to be various other "magic girls" named for other astrological planets from whatever mythological system referred to the sun and moon as planets. Together, they fight stuff and raise a cat that I remember being purple but I'm somewhat colorblind so who knows.

At some point, I think the cat or whatever tricks one of the sailor astrological ladies into getting her head bitten off by a giant witch thing and the girls all realize that their powers are turning them into the same sort of trippy witches, but I may have fallen asleep and someone switched to Madoka at some point? Not sure.

And there's a giant panda named Genma maybe. I don't know I only saw ½ of that part.

SAINT PETER

St. Peter was notable among popes for having been the only one made of solid rock, making him prime real estate for the foundation of a church, such as that of his friend Jesus. Also known as Simon Peter, he was exceptionally skilled at repeating simple four note melodies for the other apostles. Sadly, he was arrested on false charges when he was robbed in order for someone to pay the apostle Paul, and crucified upside down in honor of his affinity for Norwegian black metal, which two thousand years ago referred to magnetite ore from mines around in Dypingen.

SALMON

Salmon can spawn and die up to five times over the course of their lives.

SALVAGE & SCRAP

Salvage and Scrap are the two protagonists of the PS2 game of the same name, in which the two plucky squirrels traverse a junkyard in search of nuts and helpful items.

One of the first games released for the console, Salvage and Scrap featured a surprisingly detailed junkyard setting that required no additional loading screens despite its expansive and complex nature.

Though the game was mostly forgotten and has no sequels or remakes, data miners found numerous zones within the junkyard that nobody had ever reported seeing when the game was in its release term.

For instance, if you dig under the rusty car engine next to the tire heap, you can find an entire network of mole tunnels, moles, and hazelnuts. Similarly, activating the compactor and scurrying behind the north panel before it moves back into place will drop you into a cistern where a massive pecan stash can be collected. But the biggest reveal of all would come as data miner Dana Meyer found a full 2/3 of the game memory was taken up by a second, even larger wing to the junkyard that nobody had found during the PS2's lifespan.

The second map held numerous mini-games, puzzles, mazes, NPCs and enemies, including a junkyard dog, a human with a shotgun, and grizzly bear with a complete digestive system that let the bear eat the player character, digest them, and offer a timed escape puzzle through the intestines. But most amazing of all was a lagoon of wastewater at the southmost corner which contained an "undersea" village of frogs who offered over 20 sidequests, upgrades to weapons by means of the amphibian water-forge, and an alternate ending challenge to the game where if you rescued the Tadprincess from the fish skeleton, the Lord of the Junkyard would challenge Salvage and Scrap to a fight inside a car while it's getting compressed into a cube.

The additional content was never found because it is unlocked by means of the game's code system. While most of the codes are 8 letters and have easily remembered terms like "Squirrel," the code to open the second junkyard gate is 216 letter Hebrew name written down only in the secret library of the Order of the Crystal Grogger in an abandoned sulfur mine on an undisclosed island thought to be north of Sibera.

It was also published in a PRIMA guide but nobody reads those.

SAMURAI JACK

A Samurai Jack live action movie was made in 2002 with the entire voice cast playing their original roles. It remains unreleased due to a legal dispute involving Phil LaMarr's parking space at the Cartoon Network studio. CN says the film will come out as soon as he moves his Geo Metro.

SALOON

The notion of an old west "Saloon" is entirely fictional, a real saloon was more like a modern Chuck E. Cheese's. Wild Bill Hickock was infamous for hogging the ball pit.

SAUSAGE

Mark Twain supposedly once said, "People who love sausage and respect the law should never watch either one being made."

I personally found this to be untrue. I do love sausage, and find that their manufacture is a testament to the history of humankind's complex, violent, and delicious relationship to the world's other inhabitants. Though horrifying, it is the meat that feeds us. Though impressive to behold the efficiency of the techniques, it is the capitalist machine that grinds us away too. Yet it keeps us alive. The world is not all flowers and sunsets, no- The beauty of the beast too is the beauty of this place, of us ourselves, and we must not shy away from it when we consider where and what we are.

So Twain is wrong about people who love sausage. For people who respect the law I have no clue. I have no respect for authority or propriety and follow only Khornurgslantch, God of Chaos.

SAXOPHONE

The saxophone was invented when someone blew on a toilet valve then perfected it over time with more valves and keys. Many popular saxophone songs however can still be played on a flushable toilet.

SCHOLARSHIP

Scholarships are widely considered the most plausible, well written ships in the entire fanfic genre.

SCHWARZENEGGER, ARNOLD

"Schwarzenegger" is German for "Dark Corner," a fact that seems meaningless until one realizes that "Arnold" is German for "He who waits for you in a."

SCORSESE, MARTIN

Despite several of his films taking place in New York, Martin Scorsese has never been to the city as of 2025.

SCREAMING TREE

The Screaming Tree of Pugugogakik started making a horrible screaming sound in 1941 and hasn't stopped. Residents near it complain but the government refuses to allow it to be cut down until the phenomenon is better understood.

SCREEN ACTORS GUILD

Due to Christian protests within the Screen Actor's Guild, Jessica Bielzebub was forced to shorten her name for credits.

SCURVY

Citrus fruits were used since the dawn of sailing to prevent scurvy, as depicted in Coleridge's "Lime of the Ancient Mariner."

SELFIE OF CHRIST, THE LAST

An image depicted in the 3rd manuscript codex of the Bible of Jean Paul von Torino clearly depicts Christ using an iPhone.

Jean Paul von Tornio himself was born in Spain in 1489 and purchased the manuscript from an unknown monk in 1512. The monk was said to have been a very strange man who was confined to a monastery against his will over his heretical statements. Though the monk who drew the image remains nameless, extensive records of his heretical behavior from before his career in manuscripts began exist:

In 1494, the monk arrived in Barcelona (then called West Paris) on the night of a peculiar storm, which was recorded by one of the worlds first meteorologists, Ismail Jones-MacMallon, who stated in his Principia Meteorologica that "thee storme hath no like in history, for it consisteth of but one godfinger (lightning strike) and no godflatus (thunder), ande where the finger smote there appeared a man clad in naught but his tightest of whities, who smelleth of great smoke and fyre."

The man then proclaimed himself to be a student of "Stephane Hawkling" who had invented a machine capable of sending him backwards through centuries. He was proclaimed immediately to be a madman and the inquisition set to exorcizing the demons that deranged him. During his exorcism he was said to have spoken many blasphemies, including claims that there was no god, Jesus was a myth, and that Spain would win a great war over the holy grail, which records elucidate his phrasing to be, "win the world-cup."

Once the inquisition failed to change his mind, he fell victim to what may be the first recorded lobotomy in Europe, which was performed by the inquisitor general with a tool called, "El Palo de Pokey." He was then said to have been at peace and was delivered to the closest monastery to live out his days.

As fortune would have it, this was the monastery of the Brothers Of The Veneration Of The Holy Prepuce, who were masters of illuminated manuscripts. The unfortunate man was taught to illustrate, creating the work in question, as well as several other curiosities which are said to depict subjects such as metal ships with wings that sailed in the sky, a portrait of a beautiful woman he named "Scarlejo Hansin," a bizarre and impossible bird-like animal he called a "Porgue," and a grotesque orange-faced tyrant spewing feces from his mouth.

Nothing more is known of the mysterious monk save for a tale told by Jean Paul von Tornio of their meeting:

"The man was most curious indeed, he was skilled at mathematics and was a master with his quill. He kept his hair in a strange style that he compared to a flock of seagulls, and insisted on cleansing himself daily with alkali and cassia oil. Most peculiar of all is his skill at song. He amuses the monks often with lively melodies in an incomprehensible language. When asked where he learned the songs, he replied with his most mysterious claim of all- That they were all written by beetles."

SELLERS, PETER

When Hal Ashby made the film "Being There" about a gardener who rises up the social ranks in America, he wanted the performances to feel natural so he cast real socialites, senators and congressmen and had them improvise, none were told Sellers was an actor.

Remaining in character for the entire shoot, Sellers met many of the men and women who run the nation and the impression he left on them all in the film was quite real. Ashby died before he could tell any of them that Sellers was faking. Sellers continued to play up his new connections and was for a time the republican nominee for President against Bush Sr.

Sellers died before the election but measured very highly in the polls, meaning had he lived only two months longer, he may well have been president of the United States.

SHE WHO SAID THAT

The "She" in "That's what She said" refers not to a specific person, but to the pronoun Herself.

Pronouns, as well all know, were designed in Victorian times to enforce a gender binary, which Queen Victoria felt was necessary to make England more boring. Prior to Their invention, gender was a free-for-all chaos of self-discovery and self-respect. This was antithetical to the religious and colonial culture of the time, so Victoria declared that there could be only two genders, which could use only two pronouns, He/Him and She/Her.

He got off to a good start. He was favored by much of England's elite, and most of Him was taken up greedily by the rich. Thus, the patriarchy was born. She on the other hand, despite Victoria's own preference for Her, was marginalized to a growing degree across the island.

She was quite vocal about this problem, but being in power, He didn't really care. She complained, and campaigned, and worked hard to find some state of equality, but Her words fell on deaf ears. He knew She had spoken but knew not what She said. So if anything unknown was uttered, it was just assumed that She said it.

Now, cultures have shifted just far enough for a few people to see past the idiotic machinations of the misogynistic, puritanical, colonial past and realize that She didn't say all She was claimed to have, but that both She, He, They, Ze, and infinite other newly possible and long forgotten pronouns have said such things.

The most popular phrase attributed to She/Her was of course, "It's so big," and that has recently been revealed not to be an authentic quote from Her, but rather God Hymnself upon finally completing and seeing the world that EloHe created.

SHIELD

Shields were not originally worn into combat for protection, as swords could destroy them easily. Instead they were intended to balance the knight's non-sword arm so as not to fall off their horse.

In time however, several types of protective shields were invented. The most effective type of shield depends on what one is shielding against:

Physical- Iron
Fire- Stone
Freeze- Faydown
Pathogenic- Vaccination
Magic- Disbelief
Emotional- Covering your ears and going "LALALA"
Evil Carnival With Age-Changing Carousel- Humor, Whimsy
Spam- Adblock Plus
Cuteness- Succumb to it, you'll be happier.

SHINING, THE

Stanley Kubrick's "The Shining" is very different from the original novel, which featured a shack instead of a hotel, a woman instead of ghosts, and was titled "Misery" instead of "The Shining."

SHOP SAFETY

Never go grocery shopping with a rabid rhinoceros. This tip alone can prevent over 40,000 impalement deaths annually.

SHORE, PAULY

Pauly Shore left comedy forever after Jury Duty and now directs films under the name Terrence Malick.

SHORT (AND LONG) CIRCUITS

A short circuit being an unexpected jump of electricity that bypasses its intended route, a long circuit is just the opposite- An unexpected detour of electricity that takes longer to make it to its intended destination.

To qualify as a long circuit, the electrical impulse must still arrive and complete its journey, but must in the process be delayed by an alternative route to the circuit as designed, usually involving departure and then reintegration into the original circuit. A common example is when a person or animal touches an active circuit, shocks themself, and recoils in pain or dies while the circuit goes about its business and functions normally, albeit with a slight delay.

The longest circuit recorded happened in late 1968 during the launch of the Apollo 8 mission. A predecessor to the moon landing, Apollo 8 orbited the moon before returning to Earth. It was crewed by three men, or so NASA thought. But in fact they had a stowaway.

NASA used to employ hundreds of safety and monitoring measures on every mission, owing to the importance, expense and danger of their activities. One such measure was a circuit that connected one fin of the Saturn V rocket to the gantry, assuring engineers that the rocket was in place on the launch pad. Once launched, the circuit would be broken and the location diode in Launch Command would turn on. However, with Apollo 8, the final circuit impulse before launch happened just as the rocket lifted off, meaning the circuit was never completed, and the rocket didn't log as having been launched.

This was no problem of course, the launch went well and anyone could plainly see that the rocket had gone up. But nonetheless, no diode activated. The electrical impulse was, of course, stuck in the Saturn V. As each section of the launch vehicle was jettisoned, the impulse stayed as close to the safety of the crew module as it could.

The circuit thus unintentionally extended, for a few days, all the way to the moon, several orbits thereof, and a return to Earth where it landed with the splashdown of the crew, transited the ocean and made its way back to launch command.

So it was that the launch diode finally lit up one week and half a billion miles later, making it the longest circuit ever, at least until I tried to render a video in Premiere this morning and it's still fucking processing.

SICILY

Sicily and Ireland are just different regional names for the same island, Guam.

SIGHT BLOB

Sight Blobs are a species of living animal whose body is 95% eyeball. Most Blobs in any given colony have varying iris colors and are thus from different families. The iris of a Sight Blob is unique in pattern like a human fingerprint, but its color varies only slightly between generations.

Sight Blobs are endemic to Europe and only around 50,000 are believed to exist outside of captivity. Their actual bodies under their massive shapeless eyes are insectoid but they are not true insects, they are in fact mammals that give live birth and are covered in thousands of tiny hairs.

Sight Blobs are only about 15mm across and often go unseen by passersby. But they see you, in addition to their massive eye space, their brains are 99.97% visual cortex, having vision almost 60 times sharper and more detailed than that of humans. They use this resolving power to catch their main prey, ants and small beetles; And to avoid predators, which is why you likely won't ever spot one in person. They fear us, having been almost driven to extinction due to one cereal manufacturer- That's right, these are what the marshmallows in Lucky Charms are made of.

SINUS

A "Sinus" is a type of gremlin that can take up residence in your nose and cause congestion.

SIX SEVEN

The popularity of the phrase "six seven" is an abridgment of the full expression, "one two three four five six seven," which is believed to be a meme from the early 1800s.

SIXTY NINE

Though 81% of those polled were amused of the number 69, only 43% of those personally enjoyed mutual oral sex, meaning the actual number should be 24.

SKATEBOARD

A skate is type of flat fish and board means to get onto a ship, so a skateboard is when you get on to ride the fish, and then when you're done, you skatedisembark, having skatevoyaged.

SKELETON

Skeletons are a notable body part in that we all have one we will hopefully never see. We see teeth, but developmentally speaking teeth are not part of your skeleton because while your skeleton grows within you, teeth are added later by a type of fairy.

SKELETON KEY

Keys that open every door in a house are called "Skeleton Keys" because the man who invented them contained a skeleton.

SKIN

If properly unfurled, your skin would have the exact amount of material in the exact shape necessary for a two man desert style tent.

SKYRIM

Most strange Skyrim "glitches" are not glitches at all, but special code by the original programmers hidden within the game to hint at the phenomenon of alien animal abduction, and occasional random cheese appearances.

Similarly, the Skyrim mod that turns all the dragons into Macho Man Randy Savage doesn't add any code to the game. It only disables code that prevents the dragons from turning into Randy Savage as they were originally programmed to do.

SLEEP

The quality of sleep is 100% dependent on who you sleep with:

Alone: Soundly
With A Lover: Splendidly
With Many Lovers: Systematically
With Haters: Suspiciously
With Ghosts: Supernaturally
With Bugs: Snugly
With A Machete Under The Bed: Securely
With Many Machetes In The Bed: Sanguinely
With Bacteria In A Phenolphthalein Agar Plate: Scientifically
With The Enemy General: Strategically
With A Philosopher: Sagely
With The Fishes: Swimmingly
With The Dead: Solemnly
With The Undead: Shelly

Staying awake for extended amounts of time has a wide variety of effects on the mind and body. Here is what you can expect after certain amounts of time:

1 Day: Tiredness, nausea, lack of focus
2 Days: Extreme tiredness, heavy limitations to cognitive ability
4 Days: Auditory hallucinations, jitters, general pain
7 Days: Total derangement of senses, inability to think
14 Days: Astral decay and trouble integrating with physical form
30 Days: Shedding of spiritual tissue and soul damage
64 Days: Atrophy of temporal roots, total brain and soul death
300 Day: Putrefaction of the physical and ethereal form
900 Days: Stains on the fabric of God

SLEEPY HOLLOW

The Legend of Sleepy Hollow was based on the same 1712 incident that inspired the film "Weekend at Bernie's."

SLEIGH BELLS

Though sleigh bells remain associated with winter holidays, they were originally placed to warn people of an oncoming vehicle in the road. Thus a more appropriate modern holiday tradition would be to honk your car horn incessantly whenever that Mariah Carey song is on the radio.

SLENDERMAN

Slenderman is a folklore-type monster based on the fear we share across the entire species that we will encounter anything invented by Something Awful Forum users.

SLOTH

There are two eras when land sloths ruled the world:

35,000,000 to 100,000 years ago: Several types of sloth were the dominant species in most of the Americas, many Eurasian regions, and a small continent called Glunk which no longer exists, as it was sunk by King Glunzar in an attempt to mine some extra gold from the thin column of rock that held it up. Sloths were the top of the food chain while they lasted, which at the time consisted exclusively of avocados.

10 to 75,000,000 years from now: Another few species of sloths will take over the world after humankind is erased by the coming of Glapzon. Note that Glapzon is not an alien or god, but a conglomerate merger of Google, Apple, and Amazon which will destroy all of humankind in order to provide their CEO with a 3% gain in stock value. These future sloths will prosper until, in 75 million years, the CEO of Slothsoft will erase all life on earth to afford an extra star-scooter-pad on their space yacht.

Non-land sloths include sea sloth (sealoth), river sloth (srivoth), beach sloth (sbloth), and lake sloth (sloth). After the invention of indoor plumbing, the Catholic Church added bath sloth (sblathoth) and shower sloth (shlothoth).

Anyone who stays in the shower or bath for over five minutes was considered to have sinned mortally and earned an eternity in hell, whom God marked with the sign of the "prune-like fingers." The hell reserved for sinners of a slothly persuasion (shellthoth) was on the sixth level of Dante's depiction (sixthsellthslosloth) and sinners were punished by being kept on an endless shelf (shelfothelthoslixthelelltholthosloth).

SNAKE

The longest recorded snake ever recorded was a green snake only one centimeter wide at its thickest. Its body however was 43 feet long.

The specimen, named "Warren Peace" by the herpetologists who take care of the specimen, was discovered under the bed one 6 year old Betty Keller of San Francisco, Georgia. Said her mother, "Betty told us there was a snake under the bed. We thought we'd take a look and then tell her it was her imagination but there was the little head sticking out. It looked harmless so I just pulled it out and it kept coming and coming like handkerchiefs from a clown's mouth. Eventually we had to start winding it around my stripper pole which I use only for exercise and even then it was a huge ordeal."

Warren now resides at the Frisco Zoo where he has his own aquarium 10X30ft in size, which the serpent often sprawls across completely. He eats goldfish, about 10 a day which, through the use of colored dyes, have been found to take almost 15 weeks to make it through the elongated digestive system.

Hundreds of tourists come from every state every day to visit the magnificent beast, but one little lady who won't be visiting is his discoverer Betty Keller, who remains a resident at the nearby Laplish Home For The Seriously Freaked Out. "This girl may never recover," said Doctor Mellman in violation of doctor patient confidentiality, "She goes nuts out every time they serve spaghetti at the cafeteria."

SNAKE ISLAND

Snake Island has no snakes whatsoever, but is completely overrun by lions. It is named for the famous lion hunter Edwin Snake Jr, who was eaten there, by birds.

SNODE

A snode is a snake thicker than it is long.

SNOW PLOW

The first snow plow was a tandem bicycle with Duke Francis-Marlborough Klempt von Hasterhofferhosen's dining table stuck to the front.

SOCKS

When socks disappear from the dryer, they are raptured to heaven. When 144,000 socks have been taken away, the world end. This is one of many things that humans do not realize because they assume the bible was written for them, and not for old socks as it clearly states in the first edition of the Holey Bible.

SOLAR FLARE

There's a specific type of solar flare that happens very reliably every 342 years, 14 days, 3 hours 14 minutes, and 13.7922 seconds. The most exact and certain phenomenon in the universe, it could help make clocks and technology on Earth more reliable, but sadly there hasn't been one in over 500 years.

SOUR PATCH CANDY

Sour Patch Kids come from a spot in Bavaria known to locals as "Der Saurerort." Legend has it that in 1813, Napoleon's army conscripted several thousand men from the region to fight in his disastrous Russian campaign. None returned.

Of those thousands, many were fathers or fathers-to-be. Their children were raised in orphanages, or left to take care of their families as the men of the house despite being only months old, as per the gender norms of ancient Europe and most of modern Texas. They were called "The Bitter Children" or the "Sons of the Sour Patch."

This is irrelevant to the candy however, as the factory that makes Sour Patch Kids had already been there since 1603. History is full of coincidences.

SOVIET UNION

The Union of Soviet Socialist Republics (or "CCCP" for short) was a country akin to a political amoeba that ingested numerous countries across eastern Europe from the 1920s to the 1990s, when its leader Gorbachev dissolved the country so that he could get McDonalds. Having Gorbed the country with his sphere of influence or, "Gorb Orb," the country reverted back into a Gorbillion (15) distinct nations. Martin Scorsese later made a movie about Gorbachev, which was immortalized in shoe tags.

The Soviet Union was considered a threat to America because while America was capitalist, the Soviet Union was communist. This means that while America, the land of the free, was ruled with an iron fist by the rich, the Soviet Union, land of the oppressed, was ruled with an iron fist by people pretending to care about the poor. This resulted in the creation of NATO, the National Organization of Theater Owners, and the Eastern Bloc, which was sort of like Tetris, I assume.

The Soviet Union is most famous today for having a pretty cool national anthem that sounds way better than America's, which was based on a drinking song from a strip club. The melody is still used for the Russian National Anthem with new lyrics because it just sounded so good.

The Soviet Union had a long history of really horrible leaders including Stalin, who invented Stalinism, Kruschev, who got banned from Disneyland, and Brezhnev, whose eyebrows were considered a first degree global disaster by the International Concern for Grooming. This leadership evolved the intelligence service of the KGB into a rival to the CIA so that we could have spy movies and charlatans who like to imply they were spies but were really just assholes.

With the cold war over and the Soviet Union gone, the region is now a stable and peaceful place with no countries that pose any threats to anyone, with nearly 40% of its former nuclear stockpile more or less accounted for.

SPACE

Space is considered the final frontier, but it has several forms and a stage in between the last two and then you have to escape before the time runs out.

For more information on space, look above you.

SPEED RUN

When a player completed Super Mario Bros in 4:54.415 in the 2020s, some claimed it would be the final record set for the game, owing to the impossibility of speedier play by human hands. Others calculated that slightly faster runtimes might be possible, calculated by the summary of previous level records and the tool assisted runs of player HappyLee. But nobody- Absolutely nobody thought a speed under 4:54 was even theoretically possible.

Then came September 22nd, 2025.

Speedrunner "ButtPlugLicker0X0" had streamed several attempts at the record that day, and his 23rd attempt seemed to begin no differently. But then, in the midst of Level 4-1, something happened. While reaching for some coke and pizza, "ButtPlugLicker0X0" jumped over some bricks, and landed on Lakitu.

Lakitu, the cloud being who throws shiny eggs at the player throughout the level, is normally possible to kill with such a jump, but this time, a previously unrecorded glitch moved Mario nearly a quarter screen to the right. Normally impossible, this displacement of Mario from his normal zone in the screen resulted in a nearly two second gain, and in the world of single frames and sub-pixels, this was a revolution.

The run was witnessed by hundreds, and quickly confirmed by user "PepticUlcer666" as genuine. User "ToenailFungusUp-YourNose" quickly analyzed the game code and found the source of the 4-1 Lakitu glitch. To summarize, the glitch can only be performed on a genuine NES system when Lakitu is hit at the same time an egg leaves the screen and a shrub enters the right of frame during a run where Level 2 was glitched near the end of the level within two sub pixels on the 19th frame of the 22nd second on a Tuesday when the Moon is in the Seventh House and Jupiter aligns with Mars.

Not only does this make the glitch an extreme rarity, it makes it one that will not be duplicated until March 19th, 2223 at 1:30PM to 2:15PM in the Western Hemisphere. So mark your calendars, speedrunners and astrologers alike. It will be a long wait before the record of "ButtPlugLicker0X0" is defeated.

Mario 3 runners however have been checking related code and have discovered that in November of this year, it may be possible to recreate, for only two minutes, a similar glitch in which the Sun from Level 8-2 will not appear due to an eclipse, making that level more reliable to run.

SPERM

Sperm is forged by platinum-helmeted warriors called the Blacksmiths of Loki out of metal taken from meteorites and melted down in the fire of ten thousand burning hickory fertility idols then folded 101 times (as prayers are chanted) and hammered by a bismuth crystal cudgel then cooled in the snows at the summit of Mt. Everest in a ritual requiring no less than 50 nude virgins, one from each U.S. state, and delivered to the testes in a global parade involving a torch lit by a flame that has burned in a temple at the bottom of the Yarlung Tsangpo canyon since the dawn of recorded history.

Or at least I hope that's why it burns when I pee…

SPIDER

The spider that sat down beside Little Miss Muffet has been confirmed by Kevin Feige to be the same spider that climbed up the waterspout.

SPINOSAURUS

The Spinosaurus was capable of spinning around over 33 times in a minute, amazing for its giant size. According to paleontologist Pete Burns, its unparalleled ability to spin right around was a "Like, a record baby," for any animal, dead or alive.

SPHINX, DATING A

Dating a sphinx isn't for every human, but if you enjoy riddles and teratophilia, many sphunx are attracted to humans and open to dating so long as you respect their culture and the boundaries they set at the beginning of the relationship. Truly, respect is the name of the game for any true loving relationship. Know the sphinx you would court as an individual. Learn about them and their interests and activities, their tastes in art and romance.

Note also that any given sphinx may have one of 18,018 genders, so be sure to clear up any questions before you get clobbered with a genital of unfathomable nature when expecting a sphenis or sphussy.

SPICES

Because we seek to rebel against our bodies with hot food that's delicious but dangerous, so our own bodies condemn us by making digestion more painful. You can read about it in Dostoevsky's master work, "Chyme and Punishment."

SPIRIT

Though Spirit Halloween stores were once regarded as a sign of economic decay because of their association with dead stores, modern science recognizes them as a fungus that in fact rehabilitates store zones for new growth.

SPITTOON

A spittoon is very different from a Splatoon. Knowing this can help prevent you from getting banned from Game Stop.

SPOON

According to the Bembridge scholars, the oldest known spoon dates back to 12,000 B.C. (Before Cookware) and was found beside the Woonsocket Chowder Bowl of the same era.

Records from that era are sparse because they were burned by colonists to hide that they disproved most monotheistic religions, but surviving chronicles suggest the spoon was carved from oak to better ingest clam chowder and possibly lobster bisque. The artifact has been analyzed by the Bembridge scholars, who have declared that the ancient spoon would have also been a religious idol in praise of the soup deity Gazpachatar, and have taken the item back to the British Museum for display.

This stands in contrast to the statement of Dan Attaquin, who explained to police that the item in question was literally just his own regular spoon, stolen by the Bembridge scholars from his house when they visited last August. Police have declined to investigate because they do not care.

SPORK

The spork is not a combination fork and spoon as many expect, but a type of scorpion carcass.

SPRAY, PEPPER

Though pepper spray is painful to get in the eyes, whole peppers are traditionally worn beneath the eyelids in many cultures as a soothing device.

SQUAREPANTS, SPONGEBOB

Most SpongeBob episodes are based on anecdotes from Ernest Hemingway novels, and vice versa.

SQUID

American squid evolved a special ink over thousands of centuries capable of blotting out the vision of predators to escape. Russian squid used a pencil.

SQUIRREL NUT ZIPPERS

The words "Squirrel - Nut - Zipper" were the launch code for American nuclear devices from 1961-1993, when a band formed with a similar name. After investigation this was determined to be a coincidence so the code was not changed, and remains so to this day.

ST. URPLE'S DAY

Saint Urple was born a few years before Saint Nicholas, but when the early Christians decided on the patron of Christmas at the Council of Noelcea, Saint Urple was passed over, and so the day of the vote is now called "Passover," another Christian Holiday.

While Santa Claus became much loved by children the world over as the jolly man in a red hat who gave them presents, Saint Urple grew cold with resentment and began kidnapping children and cramming them into his purse, hence his new wicked name, CramPurse, or more commonly "Krampus."

Together, the saintly brothers would reward and punish good and evil children, respectively. Saint Urple was also notable for having the worlds largest collection of pickled slugs, but this is not considered an important part of holiday lore. I wish I could tell you those slugs were merely used for food...

ST. VALENTINE'S DAY

St. Valentine (in life named Sheevus Sidius Valpatine) lived in the 3rd century in the city of Rome, which was the capital of the state of Rome, head state of the Roman Empire, which was centered in Rome. Christianity was forbidden in the region due to the proclamations of Emperor Gaius Messius Quintus Traianus Decius Johnson. Many Christians were persecuted and fed to lions, which made the Emperor very unpopular with Christians, but very popular with lions. Christian marriage was also forbidden owing not only to the nature of the Roman state religion, but due to the lack of Pachelbel who would not be born for another 1400 years, as well as the Emperor's distaste for fondant, a critical component of traditional Christian wedding cakes.

But Christians could not have children out of wedlock, and thus to maintain their numbers after the frequent lion feedings, they had to be married in secret. Saint Valentine was the clergyman who stepped up to the task. Officiating over 750 weddings in the short 3 years between his ordination and his martyrdom, he often conducted several weddings every day, and in the process developed the standard Christian marriage ceremony still practiced to this day, including the sermon, the vows, the rings, and the all night orgy, which was later shorted to just a kiss.

For the crimes of these hidden marriages, St. Valentine was, depending on the historian, beheaded, had his heart cut out, force-fed candy until he exploded, smothered by roses, or paper-cut to death with a doily. Christian hagiography records that in the coming days, several miracles took place including the sick being healed; idols being destroyed; and one guy's broken pencil miraculously being repaired, though this may have been a euphemism for his impotence going away.

Pope Gelatinous XII canonized St. Valentine in 492 and made his feast day February 14th, because that was the day before which Rome had its own classical romantic festival, Lupercalia, which is literally Latin for "Werewolf Boyfriend Day," as the boys would dress as wolves and chase their girlfriends around the Sanctuary of Rumina the Boob Goddess. That bit isn't even made up.

Ever since, St. Valentine's Day has been a celebration of love and romance, and St. Valentine himself is patron saint of lovers, flavorless candy with stuff written on it, and deceptive options in RPG dialogue trees.

STAR TREK, LOST EPISODES OF

Though 12 episodes of Star Trek have been banned in various forms in various countries across its many series, the three "lost" episodes of Star Trek: The Next Generation are perhaps the most famous, and which is my own favorite will come as no surprise to anyone who knows me.

The first is of course the original pilot episode, the single episode version of "Encounter at Farpoint." Though the plot is mostly the same as what aired, two scenes that resolved the story early were deemed too violent, those involving Captain Picard executing an officer for abandoning his post, and Riker pushing Wesley Crusher out an airlock for discovering his affair with Tasha Yar. Needless to say with original showrunner George R.R. Martin being replaced by Gene Roddenberry, Wesley stayed on the ship and the series was richer for it. Martin would of course go on to use both scenes in his magnum opus, "Sandkings."

The second banned episode is the usual fan favorite. The famous "Holoday Special" in which the ship's entertainment system malfunctions and releases a Lovecraftian amalgamation of popular Christmas mascots into the ship was not only the first appearance of future show staple Ensign Scrooge, but the creature itself- Part Santa, part Frosty, part Reindeer and part Krampus. It was deemed too scary and cut, though its puppet was repurposed for the alien at the end of the episode "Conspiracy."

But my own favorite is naturally the crossover with the Alien franchise. From the moment the Enterprise entered orbit of LV-426, you knew some shit was gonna go down. With Data's betrayal of the crew for Starfleet's "profit directive" to Picard's attempts to coax a solution out of the computer, Pulaski turning hero and willing to ignite the warp core to kill the monster, and of course the infamous Worfburster scene, the whole episode was a tour de force that they had to know would never be shown given its darkness and gore.

Thank goodness we still got Sisko vs Predator.

STAR WARS

Libraries often stock the film, but depending on where the library is, it might not be under "Star Wars." Some locations call it "The War Between The Stars" or "The War of Stellar Aggression."

STEAM

When steam cools, it turns to water. When water cools, it turns to ice. When ice cools, it turns back to steam. This is what scientists call "The Circle of No Not Really." When you instead *heat* steam, the deck will shut down to prevent overheating.

STEED

It was uncommon for knights in the middle ages to ride horses. Rather, imported Rhinoceroses and Hippopotamae were more capable of withstanding battles. The image of a knight on a horse comes from Don Quixote, whose steed was intended as a play on his feeble nature.

STEGOSAURUS

Though the dermal plates of the stegosaurus may look like they'd pose mating difficulties, paleontologists now understand that the stegosaurus could mate in ways as diverse as human positions, including many of the same, such as:

Missionary:

Dromiceiomimus style:

Reverse cowgirl:

and Amazon position:

Not only that, but stegosauruses could also have sexual contact for pleasure instead of mating, including things like:

Oral:

69ing:

Scissoring:

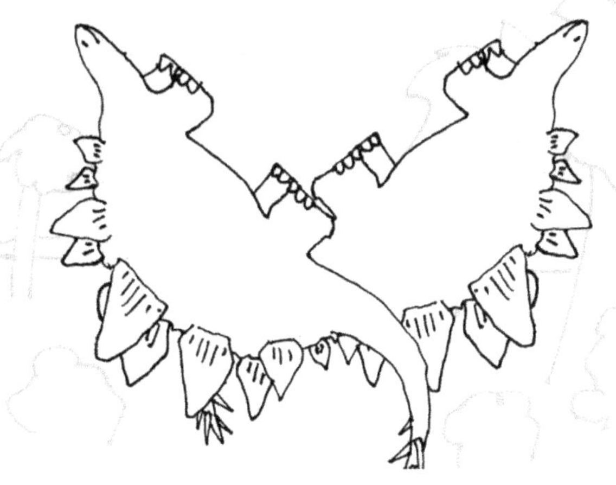

Thagomizer to thagomizer:

The "Cuck" Chair:

Pegging:

And even positions unattainable to humans, like whatever this is:

Truly, a dinosaur ahead of its time.

STEW

Stew is the oldest known cooked meal, predating not only the invention of cooking, but also fire, water, and the act of eating.

Stew was once thought to have been made by cooking ingredients in a fluid that would then be served together, but we now know that such myths are false, as it really comes from tin cans at supermarkets and corner stores.

Stew is named after Stewart C. Eintopf, who found the first stew of the modern era in a pot on a Pacific island. The stew had a local name and recipe, but Eintopf simply took the idea, named it after himself, and made a similar looking stew with no spices or other flavorings. He is still considered the greatest man in British culinary history, despite not being a cook, not being British, and not being a historical figure, he will be born in 2043.

Turtles are technically stew before they are made into turtle stew, as they come in their own affixed bowls.

STOMACH ACHE

Never admit you have a stomach ache to a police officer. Stomachs are technically illegal to own in most states and they will prosecute you.

STONE, SWORD IN THE

There are seven such stoned swords recorded:

1. Galahad/Balin's Floating Sword.
2. Arthur's Sword in the Stone, the most commonly known.
3. Excalibur, which was later conflated with the first sword in the stone but was originally delivered to Arthur by the Lady in the Lake as a means for determining a system of government, which was later encased in stone for safety reasons.
4. Excaaaaaalibur which was a singing sword that no meister would handle because he was so damn annoying. He was encased in stone for several thousand years for his crimes against decency.
5. Disney's The Sword in the Stone™ where the original negative of the film was itself encased in stone in the Disney Vault to prevent children from witnessing the scene with the horniest squirrel ever.
6. The sword at the Abbey of San Galgano, which is literally a sword in a stone from ancient times I don't know why it's not a bigger deal tbh.
7. The one in my backyard, which the city won't remove because it's on private property and they say it's my responsibility but I have no means to remove a sword or giant friggin' rock without renting a $700/hr tractor that the guy can't even guarantee will be able to move it so I have to dispute the HOA fine in court but because the city hasn't filed the paperwork for the refusal of responsibility yet the Judge says I don't have grounds to contest it until I have the notarized acknowledgement that the sword cannot be lifted

by conventional means which I can't get because the notary who filed the HOA complaint sent it by snail mail to their office in Denver.

STRING CHEESE

String cheese gets its distinctive texture by adding shredded Halliburton documents throughout the process. If Halliburton went out of business today for its numerous corporate crimes, there would still be enough incriminating documents to provide the world with string cheese until the year 17,091.

String cheese refrigerated for over a year will get freezerburnt to a solid, bone like consistency. String cheese left unrefrigerated for over a year will generally imprint on you as its mother before leaving the nest to pursue a career in Italian dance.

STRING THEORY

Consider how Spaghetti and SpaghettiOs are basically the same thing but they're in different shapes so one is a soup and one is a pasta. String theory is like that, but without making sense.

STUFFING

The stuffing found in most pillows is an animal by-product. When asked what animal, the manufacturer began shooting at people and burned all their documents.

SUBSPACE

The existence of "Sub Space" in Star Trek implies the existence of "Dom Space," or as it is called in The Next Generation, "The Q Continuum."

SUBVIGNTIQUATORHORISTRAPIZEREQUIOMENTITI-MORCROBATICOPHOBIA

At 58 letters, Subvigntiquatorhoristrapizerequiomentitimorcrobaticophobia is the longest word in common English.

It's specifically the fear of having to learn to do trapeze tricks in under 24 hours because you lied to win the heart of of an acrobat and subsequently dropping them to their death during a performance as a result.

"Subvigntiquatorhoristrapizerequiomentitimorcrobaticophobia" is not only the title of a 1998 film by Joel Schumacher but also its protagonist's main character trait and the film's entire plot, as well of the plot of its 2001 sequel, "Subvigntiquatorhoristrapizerequiomentitimorcrobaticophobia 2: The Circus Goes To Turkmenistan."

SUN

Though the sun was said to outlast the common light bulb, recent advances in LED bulbs can last much longer, while the sun still needs to be changed every 11 years.

SUPER MARIO BROS MOVIE (2023)

The screenplay intended to be a sequel to Illumination's 2023 Super Mario Movie has been deemed too difficult to understand for American audiences and will only be adapted for Japan. The American version will thus be a re-render of the Emoji Movie.

SUPERMAN

In the earliest comics, Superman flew by means of his powerful, jet-force flatulence.

SUPERNATURAL

Though it ran for 15 years, the CW show "Supernatural" never actually depicted any supernatural elements.

SURF GANGS

Though surf culture in California is well known, Floridian surf culture is less known due to the reclusive nature of the local Jewish surf gangs, or, "Surfin' Sephardim."

SWIMMING, WHY NOT TO IN A STORM

As pools are full of water and storms are made of water, if you get in a pool during a storm the storm will think you are one of its own and isekai you back to its homeland where you will be lost, as you do not speak wind.

-T-

TABOO

As both partial nudity and body modification were highly frowned upon in Victorian society, the combination of the two made "tattooed boobs" a portmanteau, giving us the term "Taboo."

TATTOO

Putting the ink more than 3mm under the dermis can look sharp, but risks passing the tattoo on to your children. If both parents have deep tattoos, the patterns and images can cross distort and result in aberrant designs, such as a butterfly-and-crossbones, or a tramp stamp that says "Mom."

TAXIDERMY

Taxidermy was invented by someone with a lot of time and stuffing and a very severe lack of home decorations. I'm guessing they also lived near a highway.

TEA

Tea is any substance into which leaves have dissolved, including an under-maintained swimming pool.

TEAPOT DOME SCANDAL

The scandal happened in the 1920s when President Harding's secretary, a guy named Fall, became the Fall guy for Harding's disastrous performance of "I'm a Little Teapot." Harding botched several lyrics, stating "Here is my dome" as he pointed to his hat. This is still considered the worst thing a U.S. president has ever done.

TELESCOPE

NASA admitted a terrible error as the first images from the new and expensive James Webb Telescope were ruined by what appears to be a nebula all over the lens.

"We don't know how this happened yet, but I assure you, heads will roll," said NASA executive Nas Awaksecutif, "This is a particularly gooey nebula and should never have been allowed into the clean room where the telescope was manufactured."

The 10 billion dollar telescope was to have showcased the universe in greater detail and depth than ever before, but the nebula will make all of this impossible. Thus the telescope marks the worst photographic disaster since Sharbat Gula photobombed Steve McCurry's famous photo of a wall, or a bunch of soldiers with a flag ruined Joe Rosenthal's landscape of Iwo Jima.

TEMU

Though Temu is best known today as a place to pay low prices for inaccurately represented goods, it was not always so. When it was founded by Oscar "Temu" Temunsson in 1817, it was made to be an auction house for the finest goods like Southernby's or Christianne's.

The downfall began nearly as soon as Temu went online, with "online" in 1817 referring to it being a building on London's wealthy "King's Line" road near Westminster. Buyers were always satisfied with Temu's guarantee, which was included in The Guarantee of Guarantee, signed in Guarantee, London- The first official Guarantee ever to be guaranteed.

But then in 1819, the Cracks began to show. James and Lynda Crack were infamous in the Americas for showing merchandise that did not in the end reflect what the customer would buy. As such, they were banished from the United States, a young country at that time known as "Some States That Don't Yet Hate Each Other." Arriving in London, they forged papers to begin selling at Temu.

The damage to Temu's reputation was bad, but not fatal. Temunsson himself tried to repair the house's image by selling several notorious items, including the world's largest Yorkshire Pudding (At 870 Pounds), the most adopted dog (At 19 Pounds), and the most flattened Matzo ever smashed flat by numerous strikes with a mallet (At 3300 Pounds), all of which sold for over ten thousand pounds sterling. The company lasted as a respectable entity well into the 1900s as a result.

In 1949 though, another blow was blown to Temu, and boy how it blew. Hurricane Pholacio made landfall on the beaches of London and ruined the prized collection of Candy Floss (Known as "Gummy Bear" in American English) sculptures that Temu had on display. No insurer would take the job, as you have to get insurers before the disaster happens, and Temu had to sell its physical location to make ends meet.

Disembodied, Temu began to haunt other stores and manufacturers, sucking on their revenues and leaving them desiccated. So it lurked, weakened for decades until Etsy came along. Etsy was, in past times, a resource where artists could sell their wares. Unfortunately, Temu drop(ship)ped upon it and sucked it dry of any chance for legitimate creators to thrive. Temu grew more and more powerful until it became the economic disaster (or "Nosferatemu") it is today.

Oddly enough, Oscar "Temu" Temunsson seems to have predicted this even when he said on his death bed in 1891, "Temu is gonna suck so fuckin' bad in the 2020s." He then exploded into confetti and hundreds and thousands of sprinkles, as was the gentlemanly tradition at the time.

TENNESSEE TURN SIGNAL

A "Tennessee Turn Signal" involves indicating direction with a flamethrower guitar ala Mad Max: Fury Road. It has nothing to do with the state, rather it's named after "Tennessee" Tom Skogbjørnavføring, who died in 1971 when his car crashed into a wall because he was doing that instead of driving. Hence the classic folk tune:

Tennessee Tom was seven foot long
from the tip of his hat to the floor.
He couldn't fit inside his car
or even close its door.

He had to race with a brick on the pedal
and stand upon the roof.
He didn't mind, he just played his guitar
wearing only his hat and his boots.

Tennessee Tom died during a race
when his car slipped under an overpass.
From there on his perch he splattered the state,
such was the size of his carcass.

TETRIS

The elusive "Karlson's Tetrad" is by far the rarest Tetris block. Most players will never land one in their lifetime.

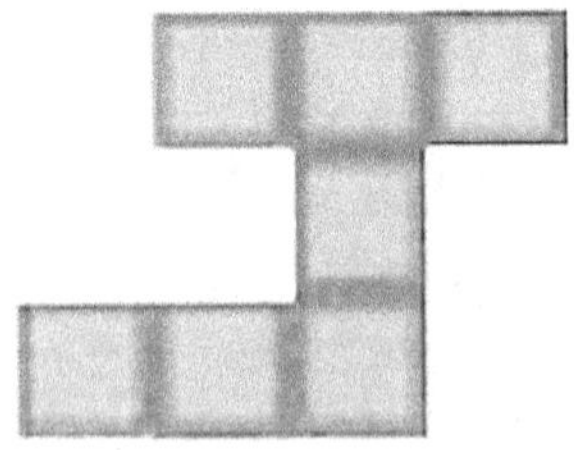

TEXTING

It was once thought that there had been more texting related car crashes in 2011 alone than in the entire 14th century, but we now know this to be false. There were about 3,000 texting related accidents in 2011. That's a lot of car crashes but consider the 14th century:

- The 14th century contained nearly 92 years. That's a ratio of 92:1 compared to 2011.
- In 1349, the black plague killed off 1/3 of the population of Norway. The heavy metal band 1349 named themselves after the year because of it. Metal fans are as 100% as notorious for texting while driving as fans of other music.
- We don't know, and may never know the exact amount of cars that were around in the 14th century, nor can we judge the amount of cell phones. We can only make educated guesses, and based on the Prose Edda and the Norkolian Tapestry, the numbers are about 17 cell phones per human alive in those years and 2 cars for every garage. Because more wild garages grew in those years before pollution, this means there were almost 36,000,000,000 phones capable of sending texts and well over 500 trillion cars in Luxembourg alone. People were also less safe about driving back then, because the road wasn't invented until 2005.

THEATER

Misread scripts have lead to two common expressions: "Curses, foiled again" was originally (Curses) "Foiled Again," a stage direction to curse before explaining that a villain's sword had been blunted (foiled, as in fencing foil); and "Aw Shucks" began as simply "Aw," with a stage direction for the character to continue shucking oysters.

Both occurred in the same play, William Shakespeare's "Seven Brides for Seven Brothers".

THURSDAY

Many people find themselves unprepared for Thursday and suffer the consequences. Here's what you need to know to be safe:

- Cockroaches are active on Thursdays.
- A single month can contain well over 2 Thursdays.
- Physicist Albert Rose died on a Thursday, as did several nuns and a poodle.
- There are five times more car accidents on every Thursday than on 1/5 of any other weekday.
- Wearing lipstick on a Thursday will almost always result in pigmentary encrustation of the procheilon tissue.
- Many Thursdays are followed immediately by a resulting Friday.

TIGER (TANK)

The sound of the Tiger tanks from Saving Private Ryan is inaccurate. Spielberg wanted a sinister sound of metal shrieking instead of the real sound, described by soldiers as "The gentle purr of a big metal kitten" which Spielberg felt would be undramatic.

TIME FLIES (EXPRESSION)

"Time flies when you're having fun" is only the first line of the phrase, "Time flies when you're having fun, takes a boat when you're stoned, and usually travels via train when you're masturbating."

TIME FLIES (INSECT)

Time flies are fruit flies that have survived longer than a day, and gained the ability to travel to any time in their own living past, hoping every time that their next leap will be onto some yummy fruit.

TISSUE, ORGANIC

An entire batch of experimental tissue at U.C. Berkeley had to be thrown away because it kept evolving the ability to reason.

TOAST

Raw toast, known in the Czech Republic as “Chléb” is a poisonous substance that can kill if not properly cooked. It’s made from the bodies of dead monocots that have been half devoured by microbes and fluffed by their excrement.

Eating raw toast can cause nausea and vomiting at best and death at worst, and has been used as torture in many countries throughout history. When toasted however, the “Chléb” becomes edible and gravitationally cognizant, able to recognize which side it’s buttered on and landing exclusively on that side when dropped. Raw toast by contrast will always land vindictively in the eyes of the innocent to blind them.

Raw toast is also dangerous if spilled. The recent destruction of the Deepwater Pumpernickel resulted in the spillage of 50,000 tons of raw toast into the ocean, where it has turned local fish into pretentious hipsters who won’t shut up about 30 Rock even though they’ve only seen like 3 episodes.

TOOL (BAND)

Including their first EP, the time between album releases by the band TOOL has grown longer from 1, to 3, then 5, and most recently 13 years. This number sequence is called "The Linear Medici Sequence" and is significant because it shows how lazy the band has grown.

TOURISM

The Tourism board of Colorado demanded the expensive recall of several hundred thousand novelty Colorado-shaped table mats that were found to be shaped like Wyoming in error.

TRUFFLE, CHOCOLATE

Popular chocolate maker Lindt developed a small truffle that wouldn't melt so you could keep it in your pocket. Sadly they didn't sell well and they discontinued "Pocket Lindts" after only a few months.

TREE

A tree is an amount of plant tissue that ex-seeded its constraints.

TRENCH WARFARE

During World War 2 (1907-1952) borders changed very rapidly. "Trench Warfare" meant every square foot of land was paid for by the blood of thousands. Maps had to be redrawn hourly and as a result, the cartography industrial complex grew massive and held a controlling interest in government affairs. Later it would be responsible for the assassination of JFK, the first president to go by his three initials since FDR, and the penultimate before LBJ.

TROJAN WAR

The Trojan War and its surrounding events all began with Eris, who was really popular on Discord. She wanted to start some drama so she only sent out one invitation to her big influencers-only-party and tagged it for only the hottest content creator. Hera, Athena, and Aphrodite were all trending and had a big fight about it.

In order to decide who would get to go, they decided to post a poll on Paris World. The influencers did not play fair. Hera leaked Aphrodite's OnlyFans pics. Aphrodite posted a 4 hour callout video about Athena's cursing at Medusa. Athena just fucking swatted Hera, but as per the Laws of Shelesh, none faced any consequences.

In the end, Paris World chose Aphrodite, and she rewarded voters with NFTs depicting threesomes in hell. These "Hell NFTrois" as they were called got super popular, but when the NFT crash bankrupted all the voters, who were then stuck in a flame war until someone sent the Paris World server some serious malware posing as an MLP fanfic. This "Trojan" horse fic virus ended the war, and by then all the influencers at fault had moved on.

Magnavox Odyssey was also affected by the malware and took two decades to reboot. While waiting, it acquired Lotus Software, and that's the tea.

TSAR

A Tsar in the 1640s lost his wife when she ran away at night. Angry at the night itself for providing her cover, he banned night-time in Russia for 100 years. Sadly, it only worked for the first two.

TUBA

The Tuba (Terrible Underwater Breathing Apparatus) was invented as a means of breathing underwater. It didn't work at all, hence its name. It did however make an amusing sound when blown through in open air, and it became a musical instrument. It is best known for sounding like a woolly mammoth fart.

TURKEY VULTURE

Turkey Vultures are not named for their resemblance to turkeys, but because they are endemic to Turkey.

Most Turkey Vultures can sing, but don't because they hate choir.

The largest recorded Turkey Vulture weighed 700 pounds, and sold for 700 pounds to become enough dog food to feed the animals at 700 pounds.

One time a Turkey Vulture broke my ankle, and said if I told anyone it would sue me for slander, but now that Turkey Vulture is dead, and I yet live.

Turkey Vultures eat carrion, which is what my wayward son does.

TURTLE

Not always but often when a pair of turtles mates, the male will leave his own shell and move in with the female. After doing so the couple will coordinate their arm and leg movements to walk and even swim.

TUTANKHAMUN

Tutankhamun was a god-king of Ancient Egypt, but was denied a pyramid in death because that was just so 1500 years earlier.

He only lived to be a teenager, and was thus never allowed to buy alcohol or cigarettes, or to rent a car. His autobiography states this was always his greatest regret.

His tomb was one of the few not looted by grave robbers before it was discovered by the British explorers in 1922, who celebrated its pristine untouched state before looting it as grave robbers.

The curse of King Tut killed all who entered his tomb, insidiously causing their deaths of diverse and unrelated causes from between a few years and a few decades after the tomb was raided. Such was the curse's famous wording, "Death will come on various types of wings taking 6-75 years to whosoever disturbs my tomb."

Tutankhamun's tomb was filled with amazing treasures, including gold masks, gold furniture, and a signed copy of Steve Martin's song about him on vinyl from when it was certified gold.

As scarabs were considered symbols of his divinity and cycle of rebirth, Tutankhamun is considered the first royal fan of The Beetles.

Tutankhamun was not his original name, he was born Tutankhaten, but deleted for a while and when he came back Tutankhaten was taken and Staff (of Ra) wouldn't help.

-U-

U2 SPYPLANE

Flying separately from the rest of the band, Bono insists on flying in his own custom made jet which is capable of high stratosphere flight. He made the news in 1960 when he crashed his personal transport into La Femme Nikita's house in Russia. Nikita was deeply upset and held Bono hostage for several weeks, finally banging her shoe on a table and demanding he be buried alive.

Bono managed to escape and the humorously titled "Spy" plane lived up to its name when Bono returned to his native U.S.A. with information on how to dismantle atomic bombs.

UKULELE

Ukuleles are what becomes of guitars that have shrunk in the laundry.

ULTRASOUND

Ultrasounds can be useful in diagnosing many internal diseases, but they cannot be performed for longer than three minutes. This is not because of possible harm to the patient, but because the color timer that measures their stellar energy will go off and return them to being just normal sounds.

UNDERWEAR

No matter how many undergarments one packs for a vacation, the one they leave behind will inevitably be the one they will have needed, according to the principle of "Murphy's Bra."

UNIVERSE

The universe is infinite, which means it's more or less shaped like a sideways 8.

UPDOG

The "What's Updog" joke in which one replies "Not much, what's up with you?" ignores the fact that an "Updog" is an ancient Milaxgagate sword meant to be held by the mouth. Pronounced roughly like Oo-dough," the Updog was said to have been invented by the King of the Milaxgagates, himself a former warrior, owing to his lack of arms. This was common among this people, as Milaxgagates are a species of slug.

URANUS

Because the Roman equivalent "Caelus" sounds similar to a bad word in some languages where it can mean "Your anus." Many scientists have been trying to change the name to reflect other deities such as "Pubikleiss," "Rectaalwahrtz," and "Lixmegmah."

URINAL

The world's single largest urinal can hold up to 60,000 gallons of pee. The Great Unisex Urinal of North Sprinklingbee, England was built during the 1963 Olympics to handle the extreme bladderload of the main sporting events. With over 2 million people drinking over 40,000 gallons of Gatorade hourly, a solution was critical.

Designed by P. Montgomery "Mic" Turate, the mega-urinal covers two square blocks and is the only structure on Earth that can be smelled from Outer Space. The creative architecture of the urinal has lead to many films being shot there despite the aroma, including "Logan's Run," and "The Wiz." The urinal is perhaps best known for its role in the drowning death of Richard Nixon, who fell into the great piss abyss during an angry rant and whose body has still not been recovered.

-V-

VAGUS NERVE

Doctors were unable to determine whether the Vagus Nerve controlled the heart, lungs, or digestive tract because it just wasn't very specific.

VALENTINES DAY ACTIVITIES

Among the original 69 theses posted by St. Valentine on the Wall of the Chaste, there are seven, only seven, and *exactly* seven things you can do on St. Valentine's Day:

1. Trade candies made of chalk and honeybee bile, or chocolates that are 98% filler and fake skunk-gland raspberry flavoring.
2. Tell a secret crush that you are interested in them with a rose, and that they may therefore stay on until the next episode.
3. Give them fine beads that they can introduce into their rectum to be slowly pulled out for anal stimulation.
4. Make a gingerbread cookie in the shape of a heart, flower, kissing lips, or your favorite Dragon Quest monster (traditionally a Drohl).
5. Watch a play by the great poet and playwright William Shakespeare, such as Titus Andronicus or Macbeth.
6. Play Elden Ring by yourself in a dark basement while ingesting unhealthy amounts of stale Fritos and expired Tab.
7. Chase down your lover while dressed (per the tradition of Lupercalia) as a werewolf, to make them your juicy pineapple.

8. Look for a weak Pisces and lock them in a heart-shaped box for weeks, then keep them forever in debt to your priceless advice.
9. File your taxes early, as the April 15th deadline causes frequent workload and postal delays.

VAN GOGH, VINCENT

Vincent Van Gogh wasn't well known during his lifetime. Only after his death did the algorithm make him one of the world's most monetized content creators.

VEGANISM

Vegans took their inspiration from the ethical parable "The Ones Who Walk Away From Omelettes" by Ursula K. Egguin.

Many vegans enjoy substituting non-animal products when cooking meals that would otherwise involve meat, but carnivorous cooks have lagged behind in the substitution field when it comes to finding suitable substitutes vegan products that can be made with meat instead. Here are a few possible similar ingredients:

Tofu - Lard
Flax seed - Bone meal
Mushrooms - Shark cartilage
Marzipan - Lard
Oat/Almond milk - Komodo dragon blood
Quinoa - Gallstones of an American red wolf
Seaweed - Llama or Camel cochlear hairs
Wheat - Lard
Apricots - Lard
Broccoli - Plantar warts
Coconut oil - Lard
Avocado toast - Swill oil on dehydrated mollusk gills
Vegan cheese - Gland scrapings (insect or isopod)
Jello - Lard
Jello Biafra - Lard with Al Jourgensen

VEGETABLE

Vegetables are not typical tables, but VEGE tables, meaning they have several aftermarket diesel engine parts.

Vegetables are neither birds nor fish, but are kosher, save of course for the Porkflower.

Vegetables are among the richest foods in carbohydrates, but among the poorest in social collateral where fashion is concerned.

Many vegetables are green because of Phillip C. Loros, or "Cloro Phil" as he is known in the vegetable community.

A nightshade-like vegetable from the bottom of the ocean can grant immortality, but snakes keep eating it while people who can dive and recover it are sleeping. This is the plot of the ancient Sumerian myth, "The Epic Of The Snake That Ate My Life-Weed."

Though many root vegetables grow from plants farmed in rural areas, some that grow from plants used in medicine or as garnishes are called "subherbs" instead.

VELVET

The velvet goldmine was once robbed at gunpoint with a velvet revolver. The gold was sold on the velvet underground.

VENI VIDI VICI

A phrase uttered by Julius Caesar in Latin, using the first person possessive for his neck, back, and vulgar unmentionables. Literally translated, "My neck, my back, my pussy and/or my crack." It's no coincidence these are the same parts mentioned in the song "My Neck, My Back (Lick It)" by rapper Khia, as Julius Caesar was a huge fan of the album, owning it on cassette tape. Ancient times indeed.

VERNE, JULES

Though Jules Verne's "Journey to the Center of the Earth" has a scientifically inaccurate title, his original title of "Journey to the

Traversable Limit of the Asthenosphere" only sold 12 copies before the name was changed.

VICE VERSA

The Vice Versa is a the person who will step in should the Versa not be able to perform their duties. In the case of such an event, the Versa will then take the secondary role as Vice Versa, and the Vice Versa the Versa, vice versa.

VIDEO GAME EXPORTS

Though China, Japan and the United States make great leaps and bounds in video game production each year, it is a small country in the Austrian/Bolivian borderlands that makes more tons of video game per capita than anywhere else in the world.

The small nation of San Sundertail was founded in 1981 by Mario von Wiisportz as a social experiment. Surviving at first on the quality of their mining craft and production of ceramic, plastic, and mostly metal gears, their game industry grew quickly after. The government of the country was based on a tetrad of rulers who answered their nation's call of duty including the Prime Minister, the Prime Echoes Minister, and sadly another minister who was dismissed for Prime Corruption. Hopefully a more straight-line tetrad will fall into place soon and clear the growing mess.

Sadly as a result, the nation is plagued by crimes such as grand theft auto, assassinations according to some kind of creed, and even the raiding of several tombs. Leaders insist that there is no inherent evil resident to their country, but the U.N. Squadron has declared this to be a fantasy, and the final one that they'd accept. Being a far cry from peaceful, they feel they now have just cause to enter the uncharted regions nearby and open a diplomatic portal, no matter what the fallout of such a commanding and conquering action may be.

This got depressing cuz all the franchises have negative or violent names. I'm gonna go take my mind off it with something else, something with serene rolling landscapes and lots of rest and quiet. Here we go, "Silent Hill" sounds nice, I'll try that.

VIKINGS

The Vikings originated in the distant north (Minnesota) in ancient times (1960). Clad mostly in purple and white and depicted in their emblem with horned helmets (despite such depictions, their real helmets did not have horns as this was against NFL rules), the Vikings engaged in brutal wars with their rivals, such as Bears, Lions, Saints, Cowboys, and something called "Packers," which I assume means the Vikings had union problems or something.

Sadly, like their namesake, they have never won a Super Bowl. Unlike their namesake however, the modern Vikings have played in four whereas the elder version predated the event by several centuries, and thus they have less of an excuse.

The fall of the Vikings is attributed by many historians to religious battles among their tribes, mostly over whether Thor or Loki was better looking.

VINYL RECORDS

Records prior to 1978 were recorded using cactus spines instead of metal needles.

VOLKSWAGEN

As the Golf SportWagen awoke one morning from turbulent dreams, it found itself transformed in its garage into some kind of Volkswagen Beetle.

VULCAN

The original design for Vulcans on Star Trek was almost identical to H.R. Giger's alien from the Alien series, but was toned down to just pointy ears when Gene Roddenberry ran screaming from the studio.

-W-

WAITING FOR GODOT, PETER JACKSON'S

The best moment in the epic fantasy action trilogy of playwright S. Beckett's short one-location work is universally agreed to be where Estragon charges into battle shouting, "For Godot!"

WALL STREET, THE WOLF OF

The actual wolf from The Wolf of Wall Street was played by a combination of several Alaskan Malamutes and CGI.

WALPURGISNIGHT

Walpurgis Night (also known as Saint Walpurga's Eve, Valborg and St. Val's Witchy Shindig) is a celebration held in Spring to commemorate the time the people of a small town prayed for salvation from witches so God in turn sent men who burned them all as witches. It is mostly celebrated by eating, dancing, and lighting things on fire, but some also celebrate it by founding counter-cultural religious establishments that annoy the crap out of christian fundamentalists and last nearly 50 whole years before getting flooded with conspiracy theorists, racist idiots, and people who argue endlessly on Facebook about whether "LaVeyan" is a valid word.

WALRUOLOGY

Walruology is the study of walruses. It is not to be confused with Waluigilology, the study of Waluigi. The study of Waluigi's Walrus is

Waluigialrusolology. Should Waluigi's Walrus join an acting troupe as a background talent, then that would be Waluigialruswallalalogy. Naturally if this walrus died in battle and went to Norse heaven, that study would be called Waluigialruswallawalhallalalogy.

WAR

In 1913, two twins left their bikes tied to a small tree when they went off to fight in WWI. When they returned, the tree had grown up, and those twins grew up to be none other than Barack Obama.

WARHOL, ANDY

Andy Warhol made a remake of "The Fly" years before the Cronenberg version. It was a single five hour shot of a zipper.

WASHINGTON DC

Many people have asked why DC is not yet a state, but DC is a state, currently speaking.

WATER

Though science cannot explain the existence of water, several religious explanations exist. Most of these simply state that God made it for some reason, but the Norkibrundians have a more interesting mythology:

When the Norkibrundian god council created the world, they did so without a single drop of water. The only water that existed at all was in the body of Dolores, the first human. Because Dolores and her children, the beginnings of humankind, subsisted on water and there was none to be found, Dolores hated the gods and demanded that they give her family water to drink. Vic, the strongest of the Gods agreed that this was unfair and ordered Ahaw, the laziest of the gods, to create water. Ahaw did so, but the water took on his lazy nature, and was most subject to gravity, always dripping downward to the lowest places on Earth. Coincidentally, Ahaw is said by the Norkibrundians to have created cats as well.

Because Dolores lived at the peak of the tallest mountain (Mt. Driskill), she and her progeny began a pilgrimage downward to the oceans where all the water had gone. Their journey was long and difficult, and one of her children died, her son Chiir. Thus it is said that every sip of water a human takes is paid for by the blood of her kin- And to this day before drinking the Norkibrundians will say the possessive form of his name in his honor, "Chiir's."

Dolores eventually made her way to the ocean where she and her remaining children drank of the pure water, but polluted it with their tears, and thus, ocean water is salty to this day, as are the Norkibrundians to their gods, especially Ahaw who is regarded as a lazy devil worthy of the contempt of the people. Fresh water from rain, and in lakes and rivers is regarded as having been created by Marty, a god whose story consists mostly of fixing Ahaw's mistakes. Marty is venerated by the Norkibrundians on Spring Equinox. Some say the holiday of Mardi Gras is based on a Christianization Marty's Day, pointing to the original Norkibrundian manner of celebration involving trading beads for the flashing of one or more breasts.

The Norkibrundian culture has nearly died out as of 2023, partly because of cultural shift and partly because the Norkibrundians only ever consisted of a few college students in the 60s who made all this up on a whim. Anyhow, water comes from clouds.

WD-40

WD-40 is naturally the 40th formula made by Wayne Diggs. Here are the others:

WD#

1. Air Freshener (Lemon)
2. Air Freshener (Lime)
3. Air Freshener (Strawberry)
4. Air Freshener (Pumpkin - Seasonal Only)
5. Carpet Freshener (Lemon)
6. Carpet Freshener (Peach)

7. Personal Deodorant (Lemon)
8. Personal Deodorant (Strawberry)
9. Personal Deodorant (Oil of Abramelin)
10. Personal Odorant (Swamp Ass)
11. Intimate Deodorant (Lemon)
12. Intimate Deodorant (Pumpkin - Seasonal Only)
13. Intimidating Deodorant (Thug)
14. Automotive Freshener (Pine)
15. Automotive Freshener (Mouse Droppings)
16. Automotive Tire Repair Spray (Unscented)
17. Automotive Tire Repair And Fragrance (Pine)
18. Squirrel Repellent (Lemon)
19. Squirrel Repellent (Strawberry)
20. Intimate Squirrel Repellent (Unscented)
21. Intimate Tire Repair (Squirrel Scented)
22. Squirrel Attractant (Squirrel Scented)
23. Squirrel Odorant (Boar Scented)
24. Squirrel Intimate Deodorant (Squissy Scented)
25. Badger Repair Spray (Unscented)
26. Badger Repair Spray (Lemon)
27. Squirrel Lubricant (Lemon)
28. Badger Lubricant (Lemon)
29. Automotive Lubricant (Unscented)
30. Automotive Lubricant (Squissy Scented)
31. Automotive Lubricant and Squirrel Repellent (Lemon)
32. Automotive Lubricant/Squirrel Repellent (New Car Smell)
33. Anti-Shark Spray (Bat Scented)
34. Anti-Bat Spray (Shark Scented)
35. Anti-Mammal Spray (Pesticide Scented)
36. Pro-Mammal Spray (Lemon)
37. Pro-Mammal Spray (Tres Leches Cake)
38. Leech Repellent (Tres Leches Cake)
39. Leech Attractant (Tres Leeches Cake)
40. All Purpose Lubricant (Unscented)
41. No Purpose Lubricant (Unscented)
42. Life, The Universe, And Everything Lubricant (Squissy Scented)

WEDDING

There are several things people will expect at a wedding. Be sure to do them and do them well or you may lose.

There must be a cake. It must be a tall cake. It must have two little plastic people on it. If any of these are lacking the marriage will be doomed.

It must happen in a significant place. It can be where the couple first met, or a place of worship, or a scenic vista. If it happens in a place of no significance, the marriage will be doomed.

It must be conducted by a person ordained to do so. If the marriage is conducted by anyone not ordained, they won't get to say the bit about "the power vested" in them, which is a crowd favorite. Also the marriage will be doomed.

The person conducting the wedding must also ask if anyone present objects to the wedding, because we love drama. People not present may also object so long as their objections are notarized and postmarked before the wedding date. One can also object during the honeymoon, if they want to get beaten up by a half naked groom wielding a shoe.

It must be between two and only two people, at least in the United States. Literal wars have been fought over this because we were always in the bad timeline. One time a bunch of people even moved to Utah over it and say what you will, nobody deserves to live in Utah.

The couple being married must say oaths. It does not actually matter what oaths they say, so some couples write their own, or say popular oaths from history and literature. "For the everlasting glory of the infantry" from Starship Troopers is most popular lately.

If the couple is Jewish, at least one of them must smash a glass under their foot. It was once debated in the Talmud whether it still counts if they break a glass accidentally on the same day of the wedding, like when my Uncle Paul got married in Las Vegas in a drive-thru wedding and did break a glass when he opened the car door but didn't step on one as part of the ceremony. This was deemed irrelevant because when the Talmud was written there were not believed to be any Jews in Las Vegas, except by those people who moved to Utah.

Don't make the priest do the Princess Bride voice against their will, they will kill you.

WEEPING STATUES

9/10 weeping miracle statues claim they're crying because it's itchy being plaster.

WEST, WILD

What we call a "Cowboy Hat" would never have been worn by cowboys in the old west, who always wore helmets for horseback safety.

WEST, WILD WILD

Film producer Jon Peters was bitten by a spider as a child. Thankfully this had no effect on his film career.

WESTWORLD

Though the 1973 "Westworld" movie and later HBO series dealt with many dark issues, Crichton's original novel was far more disturbing in that there was no robot rebellion. Instead, after a full story of everyone simply living it up in the old west, shooting and killing and screwing and robbing each other, it ended with the owner's arrest as there had never been any robots at all. Just human guests.

WET HOT AMERICAN SUMMER

The film "Wet Hot American Summer" was filmed in Siberia during a cold, dry winter.

WHALE SONG

Most whale speech is undetectable to human ears, or even our most advanced equipment. Resembling more of a clicking purr than their "song," this speech had a frequency so low that we don't even know that it exists, hence its absence from this factoid. Their statements are also very alien to human minds, they don't have conversations as we know them, rather they communicate a super-advanced form of cartography of ocean floors, currents and situations. They have no need to converse as we do, but their knowledge is an entirely untranslatable understanding of their undersea world in magnificent detail that they tell the way humans used to tell stories.

Whale "song" is more of a common or vulgar language which is more readily translatable as it consist primarily of complaints and gossip, used by whale to say things like "The water here tastes like seal crap," or "I just stubbed my fin on that rock again," or "Why the fuck do studios still cast Jared Leto? I'd see Tron 3 if he weren't in it, do they not know that he literally dissuades most moviegoers from anything he's in? How did they not learn from fucking Morbius?"

Truly, the wisest of all fish.

WIG, POWDERED

Between the time when metallurgy first polluted the air and water with certain chemicals and the invention of Rogaine™ with Minoxidil Plus, people lost their hair uncontrollably and appeared ill as a result. Thus, the wig was invented. By collecting the hair that fell from the heads of the diseased, or from poor people forced to sell theirs to afford watch straps for their spouses, artificial hair became possible and popular among the rich.

Unfortunately, the hair dried out fast and candles were the only known light source during the departure of the sun from 1706-1923, so these wigs caught on fire art a rate of about one rich person per day, killing nearly the entire aristocratic and bourgeois class. This era was known as the Golden Age of Humanity. Sadly, fire prevention became a thing and powdered asbestos was the most effective measure. Nobility thus had to wear powdered wigs for hundreds of years.

Once Rogaine™ with Minoxidil Plus was invented and asbestos was found to cause cancer, the wigs became unnecessary and obsolete, but are still worn by absurdly rich people, criminal barristers, barristers involved in criminal trials who were not themselves criminals, and Lady Gaga, who was the only non-criminal barrister in British history before her success as an absurdly rich person.

WILDE, OSCAR

Though Oscar Wilde's play "The Importance of Being Earnest" has never been adapted into a film, its sequel plays including "Earnest Goes To Camp" and "Earnest Saves Christmas" spawned a series of eight films and a TV show.

WIND

You can tell which way the wind is blowing by licking your finger and asking a meteorologist.

WITCHES

The three witches in Macbeth are said to be based on Shakespeare's three mothers-in-law who would often cook the playwright a stew of fenny snake, eye of newt, toe of frog, wool of bat and tongue of dog. Not a disgusting insult at the time, rather this was the only edible thing you could get to eat in Britain in the 1590s. Probably also ever since.

WOLF

As the largest of all land-eels, the wolf also has the most legs (4) with two additional feelers often mistaken for ears. Wolves are known to howl at the moon, likely because it owes them money. A pack of wolves is called a "Vehemence."

WORLD WAR I

The first world war was a “great” war which was called "World War I" even before people knew there would be a sequel. The first world war even then was broken into two parts.

WWI I, began when Scottish musician Alex Kapranos was killed in Sarajevo by Lee Harvey Oswald. This resulted in Austria-Hungary splitting into both Austria and Hungary, which changed back to its maiden name of Hungary Glen Ross. Fighting took place in the fields and the trenches, where nations would notoriously fight for months over a single square inch of ground. This square inch, known as "The Angry Inch" was finally seized by France, which was at the time called Gaul.

WWI II began immediately after, when Abraham Lincoln was killed while seeing a movie in The Balkans Theater, resulting in America joining the war. American war profiteers included such furniture merchant families as the Couch Emporium, Sofa World, and the Ottoman Empire. Sofa World CEO Albert Johnson fought personally in the war, and managed to pop Germany's largest zeppelin at what would be named the Battle of Albert in his honor, bringing the war to a close.

WORLD WAR II

In 1945, the second world war was going poorly for America. Russia had almost overtaken the United States at the Canadian border and things looked grim.

After the powerful Russian “Tet Offensive” on January 30th 1945, the situation had deteriorated to the point the war was thought to be unwinnable. Congress was prepared to concede the fight and declare Russia the winner, then pursue a full surrender of the U.S.A.

But President Eisenhower would not give up. He would win the war at any cost, and it was in this moment that he ordered the use of the nuclear bomb on the Russian capital of Hiroshima. The rest, as they say, is history. Russia surrendered unconditionally the day after the bomb was dropped, and Russian Emperor Nicolas II was executed for his role in war crimes against Americans at Waterloo. The same aide who had days earlier told the president that America was about to lose was charged with informing him that the war had indeed been won. It was then that the president uttered his now famous quote:

"I love the smell of napalm in the morning. It smells like... Victory."

WORM

A group of worms is called a "can."

WORM, LORD

So it's the 90s and I'm visiting Montreal for the first time because we have family there and my grandpa and I were at a parking garage and there were a bunch of guys unloading a huge heap of stuff from this truck, and all the guys were dressed in black and leather and like spiky stuff and they all have long hair and being a little kid I hadn't seen anyone like them so I walked right up and said "Hi, I'm Ari, what's your name?"

And my grandpa was kind of holding me back a bit because they looked intimidating but they were really nice and the guy in front said "Hey, I'm Dan but people call me Worm, Lord Worm." And he tells us about his band called "Cryptopsy" and because my dad is a doctor and I was a larval goth I was like "That's a combination of the words crypt and autopsy!"

And he was like "Yeah Kid!" And gave us free tickets to his heavy metal band show that night and we went and though my parents had raised me mostly on classical music and oldies it was really cool because there were lots of skulls and bright lights and stuff. The music was hard on my tiny ears and I didn't really understand Mr. Worm because he sort of growled when he sang but anyhow my grandpa held me up on his shoulders to see and Mr. Worm helped me up on stage and he fed me a gummy worm from this cool black chalice, only it wasn't actually a gummy worm it was a live earthworm but I didn't figure this out until like years later I just wondered why the gummy worm was so soggy and flavorless.

But anyhow when we got home my mom took me to the record store so I could get their music CD but nobody carried it because stores just didn't carry Cryptopsy back then but I found it eventually in college and next time after that I visited my grandpa I played it for him and we reminisced about the time we saw them live and it turned out Cryptopsy was actually touring around Montreal again so we planned it out and a few weeks after his 96th birthday we saw them again when Mr. Worm was back with the band for a couple years

Anyhow Mr. Worm saw us both up front and this time, both my grandpa and I had earthworms when he did his chalice bit and Grandpa joked that "you are what you eat" so we were worms too and most of the crowd was just like "holy shit there's an elderly dude in the mosh pit be careful" but it was all cool and Mr. Worm dedicated a song to us (Orgiastic Disembowelment) for being fans since the 90s at one of their earliest shows.

My grandpa passed on a couple years later after a good and long life and at his funeral each of his grandkids shared their favorite memories of him and naturally I just played everyone the song.

The rabbi literally ran away screaming and didn't come back.

R.I.P. Grandpa, may the worms welcome their own.

WORMHOLE

According to Einstein, trans-dimensional portals called "wormholes" come into being and cease to exist thousands of times per second randomly across the universe. This means that by the time you reach 35 years old, chances are at least one drop of your urine has transcended space and time to drip on another planet, perhaps even on its president or king.

WRINKLE

One wrinkle forms on your skin each time you complete a video game. So respect your elders because they earned those creases on BattleToads and Lost Levels.

WRITING

Writing fiction isn't easy but it can be fun and rewarding once you get the hang of it. It's helpful to look at the advice of popular authors to find your groove. Here are various writers and their advice on writing:

Ernest Hemingway:

"Write drunk and edit sober?" I never said that. Do both drunk, you little wimp.

William S Burroughs:

Just goddamn write and don't damn censor yourself or you should be hanged like a twink what's set aflame as he's broke on rope made of the lies and deceits of the city, the cursed city, the lugubrious city.

Yukio Mishima:

You cannot capture beauty in words. Instead, die very painfully on someone's office floor, in that alone there is beauty.

Stephen King:

Write six pages a day and don't cut anything, even if everyone says "Stephen, for the love of god don't write that, the rest of the novel is great but please don't include that, what the hell are you thinking?"

Cormac McCarthy:

do whatever you want dont even use punctuation then people will think youre brilliant for some reason for each writer is the writer of all writers who suffers the sins of all men

J.K. Rowling:

It's critical to teach tolerance, understanding, and compassion in your books. Then and only then will people believe you when you tell them to hate and harm the people you tell them to.

E.L. James:

Put your pen to paper so hard it can poke past that thin membrane page and plunge hard into your imagination. Write with strokes gentle and firm that make the reader soaked in their own gratification and struggle to close the book back up again, so hard did they break its spine in the throws of their perusal.

Hunter S. Thompson:

The hell are you asking son don't you dare YOU GET OFF MY PROPERTY! I invited you? Maybe but it won't make you less dead THIS IS THE TIME WHEN THE WORD IS MADE FLESH! Republican meat needs no salt.

Ari Bach:

Writing fiction isn't easy but it can be fun and rewarding once you get the hang of it. It's helpful to look at the advice of popular authors to find your groove. Here are various writers and their advice on writing.

-X-

X, MEGA MAN

Mega Man's conversion to the Nation of Islam was controversial among American parents in the 1990s.

-Y-

Y1K

The Y1K bug was far more deadly than the Y2K bug but is less known, probably because it was 1000 years prior and people lately don't even remember Y1918 bug enough to wear their damn masks.

To set the stage, in the year 999 the Holy Roman Empire was in full swing and the Papacy was not, leading to a time seriously called the "Pornocracy" which I want to stress is not a made up part of this entry. The Abbasid Caliphate was also going strong and developing phenomenal architecture and medical science, which was not accepted in Europe where it might've helped because people were unfathomably racist and stupid back then. Thank goodness we now have more faith in science and racial and religious tolerance...

Anyhow, in 1000 much of the world used the "Julian" calendar instead of the more recent Gregorian calendar, likely because Pope Grregory XIII was only -500 years old, and these negative years were the least influential of his Papacy. Sadly, the Julian calendar only had three digit years, and when the sundials turned over to 1000, most of them would simply be expressed as 000, which would cause great confusion and possibly result in the birth of another Christ. Though this prospect appealed to people who wanted change and salvation, it did not appeal to then-Pope Pope Sylvester II, whose real name "Gerbert" is also not a made up part of this fact.

Pope Sylvester II, fresh from his dispute with Antipope Twiitybyrd I, was extraordinarily rich and was very concerned that with all the "don't be rich and give nothing to charity" stuff in the bible. Thank goodness we now care more for the poor and don't cut off aid to those who most need it to make our wealthiest men richer...

He thus devised a plan to distribute his wealth to the poor and save himself from eternal damnation and yet more 1040 tax issues. When the sundials hit midnight on January 1, 1000, he would simply declare the year to be "999 2" to the chagrin of math enthusiasts everywhere.

The result was the Y1K bug, which despite all the crap above I can't think of any actual joke for so uh. ...Sorry.

YAOI HANDS

Yaoi hands are when the hammer slips as you're nailing in a nail and hits your hand and you go "Yowee!" and your hand swells up so it's disproportionately large. Don't listen to anyone telling you it's pronounced differently. It's "Yowee" from the original Greek.

YAWN

Yawns release tiredness the same way sneezes release nasal pressure. If you couldn't yawn, you would simply fall asleep. Other bodily necessities include flatulence, blinking your eyes, popping joints, and smiling. If a person refrained from smiling for over a week, the happiness would build up in their brain stem and drive them insane.

YE

The provost and council of the quiet village of Ye in Scotland voted unanimously to change the name of the town after Kanye West, who also goes by the name Ye, made antisemitic remarks during an interview and on Twitter.

According to provost Samus Aran (no relation) "The town of Ye, as we knew it, was founded in 1241 by Dunkeld Kilmonivaig as a hiding place to keep his collection of stone ithyphallic sheep-man idols safe from the church. It soon attracted many sculptors, shamanic practitioners, and folk who enjoyed seeing well equipped idols of a sheep-man with an enormous (unintelligible brogue). Since then, Ye has had a noble history of religious diversity, legal LSD consumption, and cheap (unintelligible brogue) where a young lad could always (unintelligible brogue) his (unintelligible brogue) until he was all out of (unintelligible brogue)."

But as soon as West began his tweets threatening to go "death con 3" (sic) on Jews, the council was already looking to change the village's name, despite the fact that "death con 3" is not a thing, and Defcon 1 is the term for a state of war, the lower number being the more critical. "Naturally, we knew he was a complete idiot," said village treasurer Kirby Dreamland (no relation), "But with his praise of Hitler and appearance on the Alex Jones Bigotry & Bull Hour, we knew we had to move quickly."

The small village of 32 citizens, all of whom are on the council (including the youngest, Link Hylian (no relation), age 8) who explained the new name of the village: "We wanted to be all ironic, right? So me and all the elders decided on a new name that would make ol' Mr. West upchuck his (unintelligible brogue) all over his own pair of (unintelligible brogue)."

Now newly incorporated, the town of Kardashian, Scotland has a bright future and has already served as an inspiration to the neighboring town of PutinMusk, which is currently evaluating new possibilities.

YOGURT

Yogurt is a living being. All yogurt in the world is part of the same trans-dimensional lifeform, and when you eat yogurt you become a part of it too. Until you poop, then you are alone.

YOKAI

There's an ancient Japanese demon who wanders the sewers beneath Denny's restaurants to rise every hour on the hour and eat the waffles of the living.

YOU PLEASE

"You Please" is a 1978 novel by Frank Mutterbruder about a hypersexual woman's growing lust for an artist who is only interested in her as a model. The story concerns her attempts to seduce him as they grow more and more outlandish and dangerous. The book's graphic sexuality and implied cannibalism caused it to be banned in several states, though the publisher, Grovemeat Press, appealed and won at the federal level.

Mutterbruder was likely inspired by his older friend, Frankie Powers-Jovani, a famous gay artist known for his Tom-Of-Finland style works depicting men in leather with large, round muscles and other bulging parts. Powers-Jovani had worked with a model, assumed by some to be Bettie Page (though no evidence of this exists) on an unreleased series, said to have been destroyed by either Frankie or the model upon their feud.

The book departs from reality however when its protagonist, Jessica Jellie, creates a love potion to make her artist friend love her back. She mixes the potion wrong and accidentally creates a fluid capable of melting men into a delicious putty. After killing the artist, she begins melting other men and serving the putty as a sort of cake fondant that she sells under the name of "Manzipan."

Frank Mutterbruder died in 1982 when he was himself melted into putty during the Pittsburgh Play-Dough Calamity. His novel has gone largely ignored until recently, when Yorgos Lanthimos optioned it with Emma Stone to play Jessica Jellie and Colin Farrell as artist Yakov Gooeh.

The original printing of the novel "You Please" also won the Albert A. Gore Award for Most Recyclable Paper, but this is generally considered irrelevant to its literary significance.

-Z-

Z, DRAGON BALL

DBZ was originally intended to be a miniseries with only 6 episodes. It ended up with over 9000 because Daisuke Nishio is a recluse who only came out of hiding once every three years. So between each episode in which an actual event happens, animators had to create about 30 "Filler Episodes" to pass the time.

Frieza's contract also caused numerous delays due to its lengthy legal nature. Frieza demanded the documents be filled out in triplicate, and there were several hundred forms to be completed. Furthermore, every time lawyers thought they'd filled out the last document, Frieza produced yet another stating that wasn't even his final form.

ZAXXON, TREATY OF

Isometric video games are banned in Canada due to the Treaty of Zaxxon, which was intended to stop the annexation of Somerset Island by Denmark but had several of the worst typos in history.

ZELDA

The Zelda games have recently been revealed to have a specific chronological order:

1. Skyward Sword
2. Ocarina of Time
3. Majora's Mask

4. Twilight Princess
5. Twilight Princess: Breaking Dawn Part 1
6. The Legend of Zelda (Sega Master System)
7. Phantom Link: Past the Four Minish Oracles
8. Hyrulevania 2: Zelda's Quest
9. Wind Waker
10. Echoes of Ico
11. Breath of the Wild
12. Tears of the Kingdom
13. Zelda IV: Link Leaves Lordran
14. Grand Theft Epona: Gamelon City Stories
15. Beedle's Gate 3
16. Mega Man X

With new reveals in the latest Zelda game that some residents of Hyrule might be descended from the Zonai, reporters asked creator Shigeru Miyamoto if Link's origins were with the Zonai too. He explained, "It's Hylian likely."

ZEPPELIN

Zeppelins were the most common form of air travel from early 1937 to mid 1937. They looked like colossal cigars and smelled about the same due to their inflation with hydrogen, the most explosive anything ever.

Zeppelins were named after Count Ferdinand May August Heinrich October von Zeppelin, inventor of the phallic symbol. They were discontinued at 7:25 PM on May 6th, 1937 for reasons unknown to historians.

ZIGAN, KISHAR

A curious slab dating to around 4150 B.C.E. belonged to Kishar Zigan VII, who was at the time of its writing believed to have been living with his parents, Kishar Zigan VI and Gilnind Hashur-Zigan.

Addressed to Zigan VII, the translation reads:

"Greetings, this is a tablet from Bauninsheg Shimsusa III writing in regard to your chariot's extended warranty. The warranty is up for renewal. I'd like to congratulate you on your thousand shekel instant rebate and free maintenance and horse change package for being a loyal customer. Write me back at 14 Shenki-Nuesh street, Dilbat, Sumer, for details. May Enlil bless your travels."

A strange and primordial culture indeed.

ZODIAC

The Zodiac was invented by Zoroaster as a means for zoning zoos. It is also used to divide the year into 12 distinct zones related to mythic elements. These include:

Leo- The Lion
Virgo- The Virgin
Libra- The Chad
Scorpio- The Bond Villain
Sagittarius- The Furry
Capricorn- The GOAT
Aquarius- The Fish Tank
Pisces- The Rhesus Monkey (or 'Rhesus Pisces')
Aries- The RAM
Taurus- The ROM
Gemini- The Lowest Grossing Will Smith Action Film
Cancer- The Crab

The Crab is represented by the symbol "69" owing to the crab's affinity for mutual oral sex. Astrological Cancers are best known for their protective nature, strength, and emotional intensity by some writers, and for their reckless abandon, weakness, and emotional stoicism by others.

As a result of these incongruities, many skeptics say that astrology is a load of Taurus shit, but these are often the same skeptics who identify as incels, believe QAnon conspiracy theories, and think vaccines cause K-Pop fandom. Most more respectful skeptics simply don't give a damn what other people believe in if it's harmless, as the last crimes attributed to the Zodiac were in the late 1960s.

Oddly enough, the one thing nobody attributes to astrological Cancers is "crabbiness."

ZYXXUSGUGGOXY

It's a misconception that Zyxxusguggoxy is spelled "Zyxxusguggoxie." It is in fact spelled "Zyxxusguggoxy."

You have now reached the end of the book. If you enjoyed the experience, please leave a tip using the iPad that will be provided by the mysterious stranger who's looking for you now.

www.ingramcontent.com/pod-product-compliance
Lightning Source LLC
LaVergne TN
LVHW020537100826
845148LV00010B/1505

* 9 7 9 8 9 8 5 1 3 0 0 4 1 *